Praise for *God and Love o*...

"Sometimes things happen that reveal an apparent pattern, plan, and meaning to the workings of the world. When this revelation occurs, it's as if the Universe winks at us as if to say, 'Now you're in on the secret!' The 'secret' is the realization that an infinite, unitary intelligence pervades everything—what author Stephen G. Post calls IM, for Infinite Mind. And that's why *God and Love on Route 80* is a poke in the eye of materialism, the numbing ideology that all happenings conform to the so-called blind, meaningless laws of nature. Post's 'journey west' is a coming-of-age metaphor for the discovery of ancient truths: that Consciousness is primary, that Mind was 'here first,' and that love is a kind of metaphysical glue that holds things together and provides a delightful fizz to the whole show. *God and Love on Route 80* is more than an enchanting, beautiful book; it indicates the kind of awareness that is required if we are to survive the challenges we face as a species—the awareness of our connectivity and unity with all else, the knowledge that our world is sacred, holy, and worth saving. Thank you, Stephen, for reminding us of this essential truth."

—Larry Dossey, MD
Author: *One Mind: How Our Individual Mind Is Part of a Greater Consciousness and Why It Matters*

"Stephen G. Post, in this highly readable and deeply profound book, shares his journey to that which is whole, holy, and healed in all of us. Beyond the secret passages, the dark alleys and ghost-filled attics of our individual conditioned and separate minds, there is a single infinite boundless awareness that differentiates into all observers, all modes of observation and all objects observed. We can call it Ein Sof, Brahman, Nonlocal mind, God, Allah or the Self. Transcendence to this domain is the experience of absolute love and spontaneous creativity, intuition, insight, and higher vision."

—Deepak Chopra MD
Author: *You Are the Universe: Discovering Your Cosmic Self and Why It Matters* and *Synchrodestiny: Harnessing the Infinite Power of Coincidence to Create Miracles*

"You must be ready when you open this book. It's a microburst of searching faith in a God of Love (be alert for the 'blue angel') and a spiritual and intellectual stance that everything in the universe—you, me, crickets, galaxies, microbes, stars, life, death—is connected. For the author who shares his awakening with us, the 'blue angel' offers him not only comfort but the bracing challenge to love others with a generous heart way beyond self-aggrandizement. Or, simply put, as God loves. It takes a large and open heart to take in the invitation to faith of this vocation story. I'm more alive and alert now for having read it."

—Sister Helen Prejean
Author: *Dead Man Walking* and a soon-to-be-published memoir, *River of Fire: My Spiritual Journey* (Random House August 13, 2019)

"In this fascinating and moving spiritual adventure story, which I was honored to help edit, a boy follows a dream…and it leads him on a journey of amazing encounters that reveal deep truths about the nature of the universe and the power of unlimited love. It also opens a path to a life of extraordinary creativity and achievement. Rarely has a book so vividly captured the ways in which the human mind is connected with the divine, and how through synchronicity we can be guided and supported by a presence in the universe that is greater than ourselves. Here is inspiration for anyone seeking the courage to live their dream—'because,' as Post reminds us, 'if you don't you will always wonder what you might have discovered if you had.' "

—Ann Kathleen Bradley
Writer and alumna, Harvard Divinity School and Union Theological Seminary

"A beautifully written and illustrated spiritual adventure in which readers are fondly invited to join the author on a soul-seeking, soul-reclaiming, and soul-sustaining journey. Stephen G. Post has done it again. It is good to be good to all HUMANITY!"

—Francisco Cardoso Gomes de Matos, PhD
Distinguished Brazilian professor of Peace Linguistics
Co-founder: The World Dignity University
Author: *Dignity: A Multidimensional View*

"Though very much the prodigal son, I still identify as a Quaker, believing in an 'inner light' accessible in and to each person and in all aspects of the natural world. Life is an opportunity to seek the 'inner light' in others and yourself. Stephen G. Post is someone whose light shines brightly indeed, because, to paraphrase George Fox (1656), Stephen walks cheerfully over the world answering that of God in every one. Part autobiography and part guide book of collected wisdom, Stephen witnesses in deed and word to the transformative power of love in the world. An inspirational read."

—William Grassie PhD
Founding president, The Metanexus Institute
Author: *The New Sciences of Religion: Exploring Spirituality from the Outside In and Bottom* Up and *Applied Big History: A Guide for Entrepreneurs, Investors, and Other Living Things*

"Mind, as Stephen G. Post so beautifully points out, is more than tissue, neurons and matter. Sharing his three decades of experiences with those he refers to as 'deeply forgetful people,' Stephen pulls back the veil so we can see that our souls remain whole despite the advance of deep memory loss. Underneath the chaos of deep forgetfulness dwells our profound eternal essence and nothing can separate us from it. Post has brought the message that 'Grandma's still there' in an inspiring fashion to millions of caregivers globally, reassuring them that their loved one is much more than a shell or a husk, and teaching them ways to connect with expressions of continuing self-identity. In Canada we cherish his many visits over the years to every province and city, including twice to my city of London, Ontario. He is the recipient of the Annual Award in Medical Humanities by World Literacy Canada, which he received in a packed Royal Ontario Museum."

—Cathy Chapin
Co-founder (with her husband Ross Chapin) of Highview Residences—
Excellence in Alzheimer Care, London and Kitchener Ontario, Canada

"How fortunate I was to have Dr. Stephen G. Post in my hometown of Chagrin Falls, Ohio, when I was in the planning stages for my One Million Acts of Kindness bus tour. Stephen kindly took time out of his busy schedule from Case Western Medical School to meet with me and Bogart, my Boston Terrier, to discuss the importance of having kindness as a goal in all our lives and to offer important insight as a professional in the field of the kindness of humanity. No one has contributed more to the science of kindness and giving than Stephen. On several occasions during our travels these past ten years, I was able to bounce some kindness ideas off him, and we reconnected when I drove by kindness bus to Stony Brook. He has a steady and knowledgeable mind in all things kind and is able to convey, in person and on the pages of his books, sage-like wisdom. Stephen is on loan to New York but a Clevelander at heart, and Route 80 connects the two."

—Bob Votruba
Founder: *One Million Acts of Kindness*

"After reading Stephen G. Post's personal coming-of-age story, you too will believe in 'destiny more than goals.' This compelling narrative unfolds around experiences of synchronicity that point to a subtle, benevolent source that links our apparently separate lives."

—Judy Rodgers
International Initiatives, Brahma Kumaris
Founder and president of Images and Voices of Hope (www.ivoh.org)
Co-author: *Something Beyond Greatness: Conversations with a Man of Sciences and A Woman of God*

"Of all approaches to life, I truly believe that following a spiritual path is by far the most rewarding. Out on Route 80, Stephen G. Post allowed Spirit to work at a young age with ever-expanding soul-growing experiences, increased wisdom, and a joyous contentment with the mysteries of life. He learned about the Oneness early on."

—Donna L. Johnson
President and CEO, *Unity Worldwide Ministries*
www.unityworldwideministries.org

"Over coffee at the Tick Tock Diner in Manhattan with my friend Stephen G. Post, he once remarked 'I am quite spiritual.' I corrected him, saying 'No, you are profoundly spiritual.' This book, *God and Love on Route 80*, certainly confirms my observation. Read on and you will be richly rewarded by seeing the unseen in life."

—Bill Caldwell
President: The Caldwell Group

"Few are so uniquely equipped to write about God and Love than Dr. Stephen G. Post, whose lifetime of leadership lies at the very intersection of humanity and divinity. In *God and Love on Route 80,* he traverses the physical, metaphysical and spiritual dimensions of life with personal narrative evidencing the Divine Mind that orchestrates all. On this road trip we find that Man and God are not on parallel paths, but on one and the same road. For Stephen, Route 80 is a metaphor for the Ground of Our Being traveled daily by all of us. On this road we find ourselves merging into oneness, guided by Divine Providence, and served with all manner of synchronicity."

—Jo-Ann Triner
President: Soulful Work, LLC

"Stephen G. Post offers us a fabulous spiritual journey…real, power-filled, insightful, and compelling…living into our dreams and fulfilling them along the way. Combining the finest of psychology, wisdom traditions, and theologies, Post offers us a journey into non-dualism and Unitive Consciousness. As I read *God and Love on Route 80* I kept hearing: "…God is love, and he that dwelleth in love dwelleth in God, and God in him" (1 John 4:16). TAKE THE JOURNEY. This may be the most astonishing spiritual journey book in decades. It provides a stellar road map. Dare to begin again. If any journey can help reclaim your soul, this is the one."

—Rev. Gregory L. Johnson,
President and CEO, International Center for Family Caregiving
Interfaith minister for Family Caregiving of the Marble Collegiate
Church, NYC
Senior advisor for family caregiving, EmblemHealth

"Stephen G. Post has done it again in his most recent personal and uplifting book by providing a key to unlock the experience of tasting eternity or the presence of god in everything through unlimited love. You do not need to be a mystic or prophet or philosopher but dedicated to follow your dream of helping humanity in your own special way. It is a must-read for all those to need a rudder to live a meaningful life in the wilderness of the twenty-first century. *God and Love on Route 80* is a journey worth taking."

—Ashok Malhotra
Founder of the Ninash Foundation promoting literacy for the poor in India
Emeritus SUNY distinguished teaching professor
Author: *Instant Nirvana: Americanization of Mysticism and Meditation* and
Yoga Philosophy: Health, Healing and the Stars of Connection

"Stephen G. Post was the first person to show me that it was possible to maintain a free spirit within the rigidity of academia and academic research. One would think that this realm would be full of freedom, but, in reality, this is not always the case. It can be rife with layer after layer of regulation upon regulation from an endless supply of authorities and regulators. This is hardly a place for a supposed 'free spirit.' But there we were, the two of us. I remember the day I first went to speak with Dr. Post about his newly formed graduate program. I was hooked immediately; his passion for what he did was infectious. His presentation and perspective were—although secondary to his passion—unique and commanding of undivided attention. I wanted some of that for myself. Over the years, through many office visits, I was to find a kindred artistic and creative spirit like myself, motivating me to pursue topics and experiences that would push personal, academic, and professional limits. Dr. Post validated for me that I could import elements of that creative self into my daily work, despite whatever apparent mundane environment I might be a party to at any given moment. This is also where I was to learn that listening is perhaps more important than speaking. Expressing emotion—love, caring, and empathy—is not only possible but necessary in our world, regardless of what profession you're in. Make it an art. Explore everything, for that is the path that will lead you to who you are and help you to bring something special to your chosen vocation. When you bring a true piece of yourself to your work, you transform it into something spectacular. Take Route 80 because it will allow you to become more than your goals. As Dr. Post states: 'Let destiny find you…. Look for the synchronicity.' It's certainly not going to cost you anything, but the payback to yourself and others—no value can be placed on that. Dr. Post is a teacher in the truest sense of the word, so read this book…you will learn how to *become*."

—Stacy Carey, MA, MS
Director, Office of Human Subjects Research
Florida State University

"I come from a little town in Poland named Ciechocinek. Since my early youth I felt that a Higher Love (a.k.a. 'God') had a destiny for me that I knew about deep down inside my being, but I had to respond to it. When I spoke about it to my mom (when I was five years old), she took it as a child's wild dream to travel to the US one day, to concertize there on its famous stages, to achieve great success and to meet some of the great minds of our time. But my mom and I learned years later that no one should ever underestimate a child's dreams, no matter how crazy they may seem, as all of the above came true in my life. I first encountered Stephen by reading his book *Why Good Things Happen to Good People*, which I loved and felt inspired by because generally speaking what goes around comes around, and when we are kind we cannot be bitter at the same time. Later, I was happy to actually meet Stephen in Stony Brook, where he had moved from Ohio to join the medical school faculty. We instantly connected through shared love for music and truly fascinating conversations about life's hidden purpose and synchronicities. We spoke at our friends' events or at our occasional coffee meetings in the Tick Tock Diner in Manhattan, sitting under a giant clock, where he regularly meets with the artists, spiritual leaders, and philosophers from around the globe who seek his conversation. He leaves people uplifted by his attitude, his joyous energy and his Route 80-style wisdom. I was honored when he asked if I would like to perform a meditative piece at the United Nations for the Youth Essays on Peace, Tolerance and Human Rights conference on International Youth Day 2016, as organized by Stephen and his Institute for Research on Unlimited Love. I knew immediately that this would be deeply meaningful as an action of service with my violin's music. The day of the conference, finalists and winners from all over the world read and discussed their ideas about spreading peace among all nations and religions as the only way to survive for our human kind. I met the renowned Rev. Dr. Otis Moss, Jr., with his wife Edwina, and many young inspiring writers and poets who demonstrated a new level of positive consciousness among young people. Synchronicity was alive as I decided intuitively to wear a blue dress that I had not worn in years, and later that day stood by the Chagall blue UN windows."

—Joanna Kaczorowska

Violinist, founder and artistic director of New York Chamber Musicians, Joanna has performed with Yo-Yo Ma, Itzhak Perlman, members of the Emerson String Quartet, and many others. She is director of undergraduate chamber music at Stony Brook University.

"I have known Stephen G. Post since he was fifteen; I was his house mother at boarding school at St. Paul's in New Hampshire. At that time, he was taking courses with my then-husband, Rev. Rod Welles, and talking about a dream, synchronicity, infinite Mind, and things Emersonian. Even then, he clearly marched to another drummer and had a mirthful wisdom beyond his years. It never surprised me that he went west on Route 80. I always learn something from his books, and I am reminded of how we are meant to live in faith. *God and Love on Route 80* is the book he sometimes spoke about writing when the time was right. To open this, you have to be open to surprises."

—Julia Norman
Stephen's house mother at St. Paul's

"A work of love and a gift. Stephen G. Post's spiritual journey resonates with those of us who are still looking for meaning in a world that, at times, appears increasingly meaningless. His book conveys a sense of ultimate unity that is both refreshing and inspiring in times of pessimism and divisiveness."

—Salvatore Mangione, MD
Co-Director of Medical Humanities, the Sidney Kimmel Medical College of Thomas Jefferson University, Philadelphia

"For over two decades, Stephen G. Post has been a part of Alzheimer families, care communities, and uncountable simple visits with the deeply forgetful and those who care about them. Stephen is part poet and part prophet, with a lightning fast wit and a storyteller's kind heart. All these gifts combine in this new work to teach, evoke our empathy and (gently) demand that we acknowledge the personhood and mysterious inner life of the deeply forgetful."

—Michel Splaine
Former Director of State Government Affairs in the Public Policy Division of
the Alzheimer's Association; Splaine Consulting

"Stephen G. Post explains the connectivity between mind, life, and living beautifully in *God and Love on Route 80*. His experiences of infinite Mind break through to take us beyond our small, everyday awareness to a true oneness with the Ultimate. Life on Route 80 is life at a higher level of Consciousness. What a thrilling journey!"

—Sangeetha Menon, PhD
Dean, School of Humanities
Professor & Head, NIAS Consciousness Studies Programme
National Institute of Advanced Studies
Indian Institute of Science Campus, Bangalore, INDIA 560 012

"Dr. Stephen G. Post's book *God and Love on Route 80* reminds us that we are here for a reason, we matter, there is purpose and magic to life, and that our soul and the universe conspire to support us in unfolding and achieving that purpose. When we come to truly understand this, we can embody an incredible power that rapidly expands, validates itself, and enables us to optimize every element of our life. Thank you, Stephen, for making the world a better place and for sharing your wisdom with us."

—Lawrence Ford
Shaman of Wall Street, author and CEO of Conscious Capital

God and Love on Route 80

God and Love on Route 80

The Hidden Mystery of Human Connectedness

Stephen G. Post

Mango Publishing
CORAL GABLES

For permission requests, please contact the publisher at:
Mango Publishing Group
2850 S Douglas Road, 2nd Floor
Coral Gables, FL 33134 USA
info@mango.bz

For special orders, quantity sales, course adoptions and corporate sales, please email the publisher at sales@mango.bz. For trade and wholesale sales, please contact Ingram Publisher Services at customer.service@ingramcontent.com or +1.800.509.4887.

God and Love on Route 80: The Hidden Mystery of Human Connectedness

Library of Congress Cataloging-in-Publication number: 2019905275
ISBN: (print) 978-1-64250-009-7, (ebook) 978-1-64250-010-3
BISAC category code REL062000 RELIGION / Spirituality

Printed in the United States of America

To an Age of Pure Unlimited Love

Table of Contents

Foreword

Sometimes things happen that reveal an apparent pattern, plan, and meaning to the workings of the world. When this revelation occurs, it's as if the Universe winks at us to say, "Now you're in on the secret!" The "secret" is the realization that an infinite, unitary intelligence pervades everything—what author Stephen G. Post calls infinite Mind. And that's why *God and Love on Route 80* is a poke in the eye of materialism, the numbing ideology that all happenings conform to the so-called blind, meaningless laws of nature. In contrast, Post's "journey west" is a coming-of-age metaphor for the discovery of ancient truths: that Consciousness is primary, that Mind was "here first," and that love is a kind of metaphysical glue that holds things together and provides a delightful fizz to the whole show.

There is a chorus of agreement affirming Post's view of infinite Mind, a universal One Mind that subsumes and unites all individual minds. This view is threaded from antiquity through the present. As Plato wrote, "[H]uman nature was originally One and we were a whole."[1] Hippocrates stated, "There is one common flow, one common breathing, all things are in sympathy."[2] Pico della Mirandola, the Renaissance philosopher, believed that the world is governed by a "unity whereby one creature is united with the others and all parts of the world constitute one world."[3] In the nineteenth century, the German philosopher G. W. F. Hegel called distant mental exchanges between humans "the magic tie." He believed that "the intuitive spirit oversteps the confines of time and space; it beholds things remote; things long

---

1 Plato. Quoted in: Wilber K. *Eye to Eye: The Quest for the New Paradigm*. Garden City, NY: Anchor/Doubleday; 1983: 234.

2 Hippocrates. Quoted in: Watson L. *Dreams of Dragons*. Rochester, VT: Destiny Books; 1992: 27.

3 della Mirandola P. Quoted in: Watson L. *Dreams of Dragons*. Rochester, VT: Destiny Books; 1992: 27.

past, and things to come."[4] Arthur Schopenhauer, also in nineteenth-century Germany, suggested that a single event could figure in two or more different chains of circumstance, linking the fates of different individuals in profound ways. He believed in a form of communication that took place between humans during dreams.[5] Walt Whitman, America's nineteenth-century bard, proclaimed, "All these separations and gaps shall be taken up and hook'd and link'd together…Nature and Man shall be disjoin'd and diffused no more…."[6] His contemporary, philosopher-essayist Ralph Waldo Emerson, wrote, "There is one mind common to all individual men…[a] universal mind…." Emerson called this universal mind the Over-Soul which, he said, is "that unity…within which every man's particular being is contained and made one with all other….[W]ithin man is the soul of the whole…the eternal ONE."[7] Among the poets in Emerson's camp was William Butler Yeats: "[T]he borders of our minds are ever shifting, and…many minds can flow into one another…and create or reveal a single mind, a single energy….[T]he borders of our memories are…shifting, and…our memories are part of one great memory…."[8] As Post reminds us, the Swiss psychiatrist Carl G. Jung's concept of the collective unconscious and the collective conscious paralleled the views of Emerson and Yeats. Bottom line: everything is connected, including minds.

It is not widely known that some of the greatest physicists of the twentieth century were aligned with the concept of a single, collective form of consciousness. Astrophysicist Sir James Jeans observed, "When we view ourselves in space and time, our consciousnesses are obviously the separate individuals of a particle-picture, but when we pass

---

4   G. W. F. Hegel. Quoted in: Inglis B. *Natural and Supernatural*. Bridport, Dorset, UK. Prism Press; 1992: 158.

5   Lyall Watson. *Dreams of Dragons*. Rochester, VT: Destiny Books; 1992: 27.

6   Walt Whitman. Passage to India. Quoted in: Nicholson DHS, Lee AHE, eds. *The Oxford Book of English Mystical Verse*. Oxford, UK: The Clarendon Press, 1917. Bartleby.com. http://www.bartleby.com/236/. Accessed 10 June, 2015.

7   Ralph Waldo Emerson. The Essays of Ralph Waldo Emerson. Illustrated, reprint, revised edition. Cambridge, MA: Harvard University Press; 1987. 160.

8   W.B. Yeats. Quoted in: D. Pierce (ed). *Irish Writing in the Twentieth Century*. Cork, Ireland: Cork University Press; 2000: 62.

beyond space and time, they may perhaps form ingredients of a single continuous stream of life. As it is with light and electricity, so it may be with life; the phenomena may be individuals carrying on separate existences in space and time, while in the deeper reality beyond space and time we may be all members of one body."[9]

Erwin Schrödinger, whose wave equations lie at the heart of quantum physics and who was awarded the Nobel Prize in Physics in 1933, wrote, "To divide or multiply consciousness is something meaningless. In all the world, there is no kind of framework within which we can find consciousness in the plural; this is simply something we construct because of the spatio-temporal plurality of individuals, but it is a false construction…. The category of *number,* of *whole* and of *parts,* are then simply not applicable to it.[10] …The overall number of minds is just one…. In truth there is only one mind.[11] [I]nconceivable as it seems to ordinary reason, you—and all other conscious beings as such—are all in all. Hence this life of yours which you are living is not merely a piece of the entire existence but is in a certain sense the *whole*; only this whole is not so constituted that it can be surveyed in one single glance."[12]

The eminent physicist David Bohm agreed, observing, "If we don't establish these absolute boundaries between minds, then it's possible they could…unite as one mind…. Deep down the consciousness of mankind is one. This is a virtual certainty…and if we don't see this it's because we are blinding ourselves to it."[13] Bohm and his colleague Basil Hiley further stated, "The notion of a separate organism is clearly an abstraction, as is also its boundary. Underlying all this is unbroken

9   Sir James Jeans. *Physics and Philosophy.* New York, NY: Dover; 1981: 204.

10 Erwin Schrödinger. *My View of the World.* Woodbridge, CT: Ox Bow Press; 1983: 31–34

11 Erwin Schrödinger. *What is Life? and Mind and Matter.* London, UK: Cambridge University Press; 1969: 139, 145.

12 Erwin Schrödinger. *My View of the World.* (Cecily Hastings, trans.) Reprint edition. Woodbridge, CT: Ox Bow Press; 1983: 21–22.

13 David Bohm. Quoted in: Renée Weber. *Dialogues with Scientists and Sages.* New York, NY: Routledge & Kegan Paul; 1986: 41.

wholeness even though our civilization has developed in such a way as to strongly emphasize the separation into parts."[14]

Therefore, *God and Love on Route 80* is more than an enchanting, beautiful book about a boy's recurring dream and the life journey that followed from it; it is a recapitulation of both ancient and modern insights, including the conclusions of a variety of Nobel laureates. Route 80 is well paved. It has a firm foundation.

Above all, *God and Love on Route 80* indicates the kind of awareness that is required if we are to survive the challenges we face as a species— the awareness of our connectivity and unity with all else, the knowledge that our world is sacred, holy, and worth saving. As novelist Alice Walker has said, "Anything we love can be saved"—including ourselves, our children, generations yet unborn, and the environment itself. And when we sense our intrinsic unity with one another, we can upgrade the Golden Rule from its customary expression, "Do unto others as you would have them do unto you," to "Be kind to others because in some sense they *are* you."

Post's infinite Mind helps us resacralize the world, to see it as intrinsically holy. Thank you, Stephen Post, for reminding us of this essential truth and for sharing with us an amazingly entertaining journey; this is above all a spiritual classic about the meaning we all seek and the possibilities for spiritual awakening that lie within.

—Larry Dossey, MD
Author: *One Mind: How Our Individual Mind Is Part of a Greater Consciousness and Why It Matters*

---

14   David Bohm and Basil J. Hiley. *The Undivided Universe.* Reprint edition. London, UK: Routledge; 1995: 389.

Prelude to a Journey

Synchronicity, Not Luck

What you seek is seeking you.

–Rumi

T he boy had no astonishing spiritual experiences like seeing a blazing bush on a rocky mountaintop, nor had he ever heard the voice of God telling him to do this or that like some prophet of old. He was modernly skeptical of such things, although not dismissive. It was only a simple recurring dream that started him off on a different kind of road trip that no one could ever have anticipated, much less condoned. The dream felt like a premonition, and from it many episodes of synchronicity followed. We all have had surprising encounters that are much too perfectly "set up" by the universe to come from chance and that point the way to a destiny of which we know nothing yet, but looking back we can connect the perfect dots.

***

The dream came to him about a half dozen times over a couple of years, identical in its details: *It was early morning, misty and silver-gray, at the end of a long road to the unknown west. High above the sea, a long-haired blond youth leaned outward over a ledge about to let go, when out of the mist appeared the light blue image of an angel's face. Speaking softly and with great love, the angel said, "If you save him, you too shall live." Then she faded back into the silver-gray mist.*

The boy understood that some special dreams can express divine intent, but he was no big believer in literal angels. He rarely remembered dreams at all. Yet each time this dream flowed into his sleeping mind, the boy remembered it vividly, and he quietly meditated on its details while seated on his favorite wooden pew in the back of the old chapel at St. Paul's School in New Hampshire, where he was a young student both whimsical and spiritual. Was the dream a vision calling him out on a journey to the unknown west? Was he invited by the cosmos to head off on a mysterious pilgrimage to a sacred place he knew not where? But the boy never strained to find an answer because he assumed one would flow toward him at the right time if there was one and there was no rushing it. He did wonder if the dream was just a creative delusion his brain tissue had concocted in order to make life more meaningful because beneath any happy human veneer emptiness is always a threat, and we are all desperate meaning-making creatures. But on the other hand, maybe the dream flowed from infinite Mind of which all our minds are some small part, and, if so, it was a gift and calling.

Surprisingly, the answers would come three thousand miles away, at the Pacific end of Route 80, and then a few months afterward up in Oregon. He had to travel far before he could know what the words *"If you save him, you too shall live"* meant, although he had not been sure they meant anything at all until some powerful westward events unfolded.

The dream recurred in the boy's sixteenth and seventeenth years. He had felt all along that normal pursuits were pointless. He did not want to be another J. P. Morgan, the most illustrious graduate of what everyone called "the" school, and he disliked every form of class elitism. God calls who God calls, regardless of money or family. There was nothing competitive in the boy, and he figured that it is better to always be kind than to always be right because most people are struggling with things hidden from view. More than anything, he feared being slowly digested by an immoral world at the cost of his soul; evil meant giving up on his sense of inner connection with the infinite Mind in a world where a lot of people wrongly assume that Matter came first in the universe and explains all. The boy could see that Mind came first and from it all things derive.

This book describes a wild spiritual adventure for anyone who wants to reclaim their soul from the doubts imposed by a materialistic culture and by those who insist that our minds are derived from matter and brain tissue, devoid of any unique nonmaterial spiritual substrate. It is a book for those who hold onto the deep mystery of divine original Mind "in the beginning," sustaining all that exists, and within in us all. It is about God, love, and synchronicity experienced in a new way, framed around an uncanny series of episodes that began with the dream and its alluring message: *"If you save him, you too shall live."* This is a story about synchronicity, not luck; *it is about perfectly timed occurrences that flow along too miraculously not to be planned by a cherishing universal Mind, with which the boy felt a secure oneness.* Statisticians contend that even the most improbable event will at some point eventually come to pass, but they rule out the way divine Mind whispers and winks at us through synchronicities as we move in faith down the highway of life, reassuring us that the journey is meaningful after all, even when we fall for a while into some downward-sucking negative vortex of nothingness. We take the journey so that we can encounter others who are placed in our path and through whom God works. Encounters can be routine, but some are absolutely pre-arranged.

Boy questers tend to be footloose, open-minded, easily bored, irreverent, defiant, mirthful, likely to make big mistakes, and embarrassing to their families. They sing songs to the open road like Whitman to celebrate feeling connected to the universe. They trust the road come what may; they do not pretend to make their lives so much as they respond creatively to what lies unexpected over the horizon waiting to be found. They believe in an established destiny that finds them more than they find it. They know that those who make no mistakes make nothing, so they make them with a smile. They can take gambles and squander a few worldly opportunities along the way. Their journeys are as confessional as they are inspirational, and as dubious as they are certain, depending on perspective and on how they work out in the end. By their fruits you shall know them.

Read on if you sense a universal creative Mind underlying our beautiful universe, a Mind that also exists in a small but special way within each of us in the form of a peaceful eternal soul, although we must slow down to awaken to it. The world constantly pulls us away from our souls with constant distractions and pressures. Read on if you think that Mind precedes Matter and is distinct from it. All the great scriptures teach of an eternal Mind or Consciousness beyond time and space, creating everything in a Big Bang, beginning from absolutely nothing other than itself.

Read on if you have had a premonition about a loved one imperiled far away, or suddenly encountered someone who was the perfect person to give you, at a desperate moment, exactly what you were praying for at the time. Read on if something that turned out to be absolutely true dropped into your mind as if from heaven, because you had no reason to think of it and it was way beyond anything you ever studied. It felt more like an invasion than an intuition. These things occur because our minds are part of the one cherishing Mind, but we have not yet fully awakened to this so we doubt our spiritual essence.

Read on if you have suddenly felt surrounded by an overwhelming energy of love that warmly and surprisingly revealed the innate dignity of a person near you for whom you had no personal affection or friendship, so that afterwards you determined to be kinder to that person than ever before, and you in fact became so enduringly. Any legitimate experience of infinite Mind has to become active in creative love, and never in destruction or hate.

Sometimes what happens is so completely unlikely that it can only have been caused, although not in the usual sense of a material causation. It is *pre-arranged* so perfectly with such unbelievable timing and love that it could not be mere coincidence. It even feels spooky, like that lost letter you were searching for everywhere and right after a prayer it slipped out from inside the pages of an old lost book that fell off the shelf into your hands. You begin to gain faith in an infinite Mind indwelling in the universe that cherishes each of us, with synchronicity its *modus operandi*. The boy was still a tad uncertain until he followed the dream west.

When a young boy who does not believe in angels has a blue angel dream and actually follows it on a journey to the unknown, it is bound to be disruptive of settled expectations, especially for a Swarthmore-bound St. Paul's graduate. For those who doubt God and a love-enchanted universe, this book can be read as an honest statement by a boy gone wildly wrong on a wasteful detour who was just lucky enough to stay out of the gutter. The boy was fifteen when he first had the dream, a natural-born starry-eyed child wanderer surrounded by colorful fall leaves at a prep school that he loved—a nice pricey orphanage where he was preparing for nothing, since nothing seemed worthy of preparation. He was happy up there in the North, where he studied hard and learned much. No one had ever told him he could amount to anything, but truth be told he appreciated being just a tad overlooked and keeping a low profile. This left the boy open to his kind of journey, when he might otherwise have ignored the dream and gone down Wall Street or to a prestigious law firm.

The boy considered the blue angel to be a symbolic expression of infinite Mind trying to break through his worldly consciousness and awaken him into awareness of the vast nonlocal Mind that underlies the universe and of which our minds are some very small part. This Mind is also a field of love in which we are all interconnected with God and one another, and it is the sole source of all that is perfectly wise, enduring, energetic, and pure. Such spiritual love is *not* comprised of the same uneven emotional "stuff" of human love, which is always making exceptions, and lacking in wisdom, reliability, and purity. Mere human love turns easily to indifference and even hatred or violence, which is why the world keeps burning. We need something higher.

Take this Route 80 dream-driven trip to reclaim your soul. Read on.

Interlude

The boy (left) in 1969 on his E.T. bike with friends Paul and Hap at St. Paul's School, in the days of the dream

The total number of minds in the universe is one.

—Erwin Schrödinger

Synchronicity is an ever-present reality for those who have eyes to see.

—Carl Jung

Faith is the bird that feels the light when the dawn is still dark.

—Rabindranath Tagore

How to Follow a Dream The boy, in his Sixth Form Independent Paper for Rev. Rodney Welles, wrote: "What really is spiritual love? When the happiness and security of others means as much to us as our own or sometimes even more, we love them. When any human being loves everyone who they actually do encounter in this way no matter who they are, they have far transcended the limits of human emotional love and entered the spiritual love field of the infinite Mind." The boy received Honors.

The boy in the yearbook

You must learn to get in touch with the innermost essence of your being. This true essence is beyond ego. It is formless; it is free; it is immune to criticism; it does not fear any challenge. It is beneath no one, superior to no one, and full of magic, mystery, and enchantment.

–Deepak Chopra

The Dream and the Car: How the Journey Began

We wake, if ever we wake at all, to mystery.

—Annie Dillard

*I*t was early morning, misty and silver-gray, at the end of a long road to the unknown west. High above the sea, a long-haired blond youth leaned outward over a ledge, about to let go, when out of the mist appeared the light blue image of an angel's face. Speaking softly and with great love, the angel said, "If you save him, you too shall live." Then she faded back into the silver-gray mist.

The boy's dream was vivid after he awoke, and it stuck with him over the course of the day and beyond. It started with a silvery-gray luminosity like a Tiffany stained glass window, and then came the leaning youth. Slowly it brightened into light blue, and out of that blue appeared the beautiful angel's face. Then spoke her deeply soothing and peaceful voice, after which she faded into silver-gray.

The boy was asleep when he dreamed this dream but felt as though he was in a state different than mere sleep, though nothing like usual wakefulness. It was a strange feeling of being beyond place and time, and, when he awoke from this dream into the quiet of the dawn, he was unsure of where he was but felt secure and in oneness with something mysterious and peaceful. But then his sense of time and place would come back, and the day was upon him with all its chronological demands, and he would get dressed for breakfast and eight o'clock morning chapel.

The boy had a fabulous sacred studies teacher, Rev. Rod Welles, an Episcopal priest who loved the Buddhism of Alan Watts, and the boy told him about the dream over a formal Sunday dinner in the school's large North Upper dining hall. North Upper was as elegantly constructed as the great dining hall in a Harry Potter novel, with sweeping varnished wooden beams pointing skywards, and oak tables and chairs in which sat five hundred young boys—a dozen boys per table—all suited up and just returned from mandatory Sunday chapel. Rev. Welles listened carefully, nodding his head, and said, "Well, in scripture an angel is a symbol of protection and brings messages, and light blue stands for purity and truth." The other boys rolled their eyes and smiled, but no one actually laughed because they agreed that the boy was an okay kid, even if a bit ethereal and independent.

"Who knows, maybe there is synchronicity at work, and a youth on a ledge awaits you somewhere in the future," Rev. Welles added. "Anyway, it's just a dream. But it could be from God; it could have a true message and reflect something more than your own classroom worries about that 'swirling downward vortex slowly sucking you into an immoral universe,' as you tend to put things."

"Maybe," the boy responded, and now his friends around the table nodded in wide-eyed approval.

The boys of St. Paul's called their teachers "Sir" at the time. They dressed in jackets and ties, lived simple and disciplined lives, and studied hard. It was a pure and good place to be, and Anglican in style and litany as it was a school still firmly rooted in the Episcopal tradition. He had just a few close friends because he preferred to remain self-possessed and simple. There were lots of people he got along with well, but they knew they had to give him space to be himself, and that was all he wanted. He figured it was simple to be happy but hard to be simple, and not everyone valued simplicity.

These were not tough times in the boy's life—he was not spending long afternoons under a hot sun raking fall leaves for Mr. Chapin to work off his very occasional demerit points, nor was he eating dyspepsia-inducing hotdogs or flunking courses, and he had not been bullied or abused by anyone. Though he was surely outclassed up there because he was from Long Island and not New York City, St. Paul's was a beautiful place that got him out of Babylon. Rev. Welles came to refer to the boy as "the Babylonian dreamer" and would mirthfully mouth *Namaste* with palms touching and fingers pointed upwards when the boy walked past his seat in the Chapel of St. Peter and St. Paul each morning. The boy was really from Babylon, literally, but not the ancient one with hanging gardens, rather the one on Long Island by the Great South Bay, which was for the boy an isolated commuter town far away from anything interesting other than the clamming.

He took to reading about ancient Babylon because all the other boys in history class knew about the great city in Mesopotamia, yet the boy knew nothing of it, drawing gasps from his more sophisticated peers when he proclaimed before all in his first class as a freshman Third Former, "Oh, I know all about Babylon because that's my home town. We have hanging plants in Argyle Park on Main Street. And I snag herring in the little waterfalls."

Sometimes Rev. Welles would seek the boy out in the crowd of "Paulies" scurrying from the chapel to the main schoolhouse along ice-covered, winding red brick paths in the cold New Hampshire mornings and ask, in a tone of pastoral warmth, "So, Babylon, any more blue angel dreams?"

"No, Sir. It's just once every few months at most, but nothing for a while, no, Sir."

Rev. Welles enjoyed hearing about the dream because he was always spiritually curious, and sometimes a good Episcopal priest needs a whispered hint that "God" is not dead. Kids can sometimes have spiritual experiences that adults can't even begin to understand. The boy had tea on occasion with Rev. Welles and his lovely wife Julie in their dorm apartment, and they were a bit mystified by the spiritual side of him but found hope in the idea that maybe there really is an inspiring universal Mind and they really had eternal souls. The boy was entertaining in his simplicity, telling only tasteful light jokes and keeping things memorably mirthful. He was a natural starry-eyed wanderer, and he felt comfortable speaking of the dream to the right sort of people to get their opinions. He was never overbearing or overly serious because he liked to see people smile, but he raised a lot of sincere, big questions without becoming unwelcome. He was the one who asked that one last big question when everyone thought the conversation was done and wanted to head out the door.

Over time the boy came to think that certain dreams are inflowing gifts from the infinite Mind that our little minds are a part of, like small points of light within an endless field of brightness, but we lack awareness of this. If we were more aware of this spiritual connectivity, we would harm no one, do good to all including ourselves, and we would be healed and healing in every encounter without exception. Some dreams can reveal destinies and should be followed, although following them brings testing…there must always be tests. He believed in destiny more than goals because if he had many goals he would never be open to destiny. He couldn't be filled with his own little goals and be open to having a larger destiny at the same time. This frustrated many of his teachers because they thought he had good potential but was markedly different from the other boys. He started to read about dreams and symbols, and he wore a simple silver ring with a green stone in it because a book said that green was the color of the Holy Spirit and comforting, like when you rest on a grassy field under the summer sun. He would wear that ring, which he purchased for five dollars in a little spiritual store in Cambridge, all of his life.

If the dream did nothing else, it awakened in him many questions and endless possibilities.

Why the Boy Was Known as "the Boy"

In the fall of his last year at St. Paul's School, the boy and Rev. Welles drove the four hours down to Yale Divinity School, where the Babylonian spoke of the dream in a class on adolescent psychology and pastoral care taught by one Professor James E. Dittes. Rev. Welles was a Yale Divinity grad and still very much a part of things there, and he wondered what these aspiring ministers would think about his Babylonian boy. The boy was happy to get out from classes for the day and take such a special trip. The Rector of St. Paul's, Rev. Matt Warren, thought this would be a great educational adventure so he supported it, although he himself did not know much of the dream.

And so Rev. Welles and the boy drove through New Haven along Prospect Street to the Divinity School and sat down in a seminar room around a wooden table with about twenty students, and the boy described the dream in detail, concluding only that maybe God was calling him to an unknown western ledge. This scared them a bit. To everyone's consternation, the boy revealed that the dream had prompted him to apply to a far-out West Coast college in distant Portland, where the Jungian Beat poet Robert Bly taught the musicality of words and no St. Paul's boys dared to venture. The boy would sometimes quote Bly and veer off into a stream-of-consciousness word flow like Beat poets do, like his favorites Kerouac and Muhammad Ali, and later Maya Angelou.

"Yes, the ledge and the angel and the road to the west, and the feeling that the road will find me when I stumble on it," the boy summarized, after telling the students about his dream. The students were cordial and asked many probing questions until the two hours were over. The boy had a few of them on the edge of their seats. They took notes.

"So what does it all mean to you, spiritually?" asked one of them.

"Well, I think it is about finding my destiny. It is Emerson's *Over-Soul* reaching down and saying that my destiny lies within its wisdom, not mine, limited as it is. We all read Emerson up at school because it's required, but no one really takes him seriously. I do though. He inspired me to read Hindu scriptures a bit. The Hindus write about the "Supreme Mind" or "God," and we are all of us a part of it because each mind is a precious drop of this infinite Mind, plus it underlies the whole universe. It is infinite, universal, and supreme. So we are free but connected with one another, and that explains a lot of why we have spiritual feelings of oneness. It makes the blue dream I had maybe something that was given to me rather than something I just imagined after a long day."

Professor Dittes asked, "Well, that's what Jung would say, more or less, with his collective unconscious. The Hindus get it, too. Western folks think it's a little crazy. We in the West have no idea what Mind is all about. So what is God to you? Mind?"

"Sir, God is an infinite universal original loving Mind that is all around us and within us, and all of our individual minds are a part of God's mind like small flames in an eternal fire, which means we are all connected with God and one another and even with nature, and that explains spirituality," answered the boy. "So I sometimes call God 'IM' for infinite Mind, but it so happens that in the Hebrew Bible it says God is the unnamed 'I am,' so it works out. Maybe universal Mind is better in some ways. It sounds less far away, and I agree with the idea that Mind is right within everything. But infinite Mind seems to work best. And when I stare into the fireplace, I see all the little shoots of flame flickering around in the big flame: they are parts of it but also distinct. God is the big flame and we are the little ones, but all is one. I like the passage from Acts 17, 'For in God we live and move and have our being.' "

The professor was a bit startled. "That's a little fuzzy. Do you think that there is just this single Mind?" he asked.

"Well, Sir, I feel it mostly. But yes, Mind is one, and we all have this indwelling Mind that is beyond place and time like Emerson wrote, and this explains why we can have blue angel dreams and intuitions and premonitions and feelings for the oneness."

"Anything else?" asked the professor.

"Well," said the boy, "I also think that, because of this oneness of Mind, when we help someone else we also help ourselves, and that may be what the blue angel was saying with 'If you save him, you too shall live,' but I do not know for sure and I do not know how I will find that out."

"So are you okay? Did Grandma Emily tell you too many times not to put your peas on your fork with your thumb? Did she teach you too much etiquette?" one of the Yale students asked with a laugh.

"Ah, Rev. Welles must have mentioned that," and the boy nodded toward the Reverend.

"Hey, I feel great. And Emily wasn't really my grandmother because my granddad Edwin divorced her when he got involved with a great-looking Broadway chorus girl in 1906 who became my real grandma, most likely. I don't know for sure because my folks are never very explicit about these details. That's when Emily started writing those books about manners because *Etiquette* paid the bills. I only met her once in New York when Dad was visiting his half-brother. I was a little kid. But Ned Jr. wrote me a letter to get me into St. Paul's. Grandfather Edwin lost all his money and his seat on the Stock Exchange in bad railroad investments, so Babylon was really the end of the line for him. But she got her last name from him and a couple of sons."

Everyone cracked up.

"So what's the blue angel message?" asked Professor Dittes.

"Well, like I said, maybe there is a message in the words 'If you save him, you too shall live.' Maybe the words will find me before I find them. But I am not headed for a gray flannel suit à la Sloan Wilson or drinking martinis."

"But all Episcopalians drink martinis, and Jesus drank wine," the students responded collectively, with smiles.

"Well, folks, if I were living back in the days of the Old Testament, I would have been a Nazarite, one of those people who abstains from wine and alcohol by some sort of vow. The idea is that you want to keep your mind clear and open to the infinite Mind, to divine inspiration, to intuitions and things, and drinking just gets in the way. It's an obstacle. Jesus did drink wine, but that was all they had back then, and he got to a point where he said he would no more drink of the fruit of the vine in Mark 14 as he got closer to the end. And John the Baptist was a lifelong Nazarite. St. Paul was too. *Nazar* means "set apart," but it really means staying clear-headed and mindful of spirit. It doesn't make me better than anyone else, but different. See, my Uncle Gary, for whom I was given my middle name, died of liver failure, and I went to his funeral in Groton. He was only forty-five or so. I don't look down on people who drink, but I don't understand why they do, and I wish Uncle Gary was alive. He gave up so much in life for one thing when he could have given up that one thing and had everything, including a good nephew. I drank beer a few times a year ago, mainly to try and fit in with the Long Island Babylonian guys that summer, or even once last fall with some St. Paul's guys on a long weekend in Boston at the Statler Hilton Hotel by the Commons, but it just made me feel blocked and stuck, so I am now officially a lifelong Nazarite and plan to stay this way. I don't want to miss true inspirations of Mind. Why should anyone give up a feeling of the living presence of the infinite Mind to drink?"

The Yale students looked shocked and wide-eyed, and one responded with a "Well, whatever floats your boat. But it isn't our culture."

"So how do you fit in with people up there in New Hampshire?" someone else asked.

"Well, okay. I am mostly happy to have escaped Babylon and for being up there, but those guys are really into big financial goals and Ivy League schools and I just don't think about those things. I fit in really well with nature up there—I love the woods and the architecture and the sermons on Sundays. I am lucky to be there, and people treat me better than on Long Island. The Babylon that I know is pretty rough. There are a lot of hoods and bullies, and St. Paul's is like a really cool orphanage and folks leave me in peace, even though I don't go to hockey games because they are mostly violence interrupted by long unnecessary meetings and guys blowing whistles all the time."

"What about the dream's ledge?"

"Who knows, but aren't we all a little on the ledge? Aren't we all running on empty a little and that's why you're here listening to a kid like me? I'm not actually on the ledge in the dream, it's the other guy. But this whole world is on the ledge."

"Do you play sports?" the good professor asked.

"Well, I run cross-country well and do cross-country skiing, because that's more me than the team stuff, and it keeps me independent. People call me 'the boy' because that's what the cross-country coach, Señor Ordonez, calls me when we're out running. 'Okay, Boy, up the hill,' he yells out. He never calls the students by their first names, only 'the boy so-and-so,' like 'the boy Smith.' But he just calls me 'the boy' and says that's all I need, because my older brother was in school there a couple of years ago and he already claimed 'the boy so-and-so.' Plus, he and I are not much alike, and Señor Ordonez liked my brother a lot."

"So people just refer to you as 'the boy'?" asked the professor.

"Yes, they do, or at least many do, and I like that because Rev. Welles says that we should all go through the whole course of our lives staying a little childlike, keeping connected with the child within us all, like Jung wrote. That's our true self, the self that isn't beaten down by disappointments and loses the mirth and joy of the child. Plus, I look a little more boyish than some in maybe a slightly mischievous, half-Irish kind of way, and as I grow older I want to stay a little immature to balance out aging. Even when I am an old man, I will still be the boy, and that is how I want it. I don't want to grow up if that means losing the boy. I almost think of growing up as an illness and aging as a disease, just because look at what happens to people, all bent over and stuff! I still like old folks a lot, but they have hard times ahead."

The students all smiled and discussed this inner child, and they said that if he could stay spiritually young all his life it would be great.

Rev. Welles chimed in, "You just have to put aside all the pressures of life and look deep into your soul and remember yourself as an innocent happy child and connect with that image. We all are only here a while anyway, and we are spiritual children so long as we don't get completely bogged down."

"And that drop of the Mind within us that we talk about in philosophy class that is beyond time and place, that is really the child within," offered the boy.

Professor Dittes was, like Rev. Welles, a Jungian, so he understood the boy. The boy was fun for all the Yale folks, and he helped them reclaim their souls in a way that all their theology books could not. He liked to challenge people to reclaim their souls, and that's why he spoke of the dream when he might just have easily pretended that he never had it. Being a blue angel dreamer does not quite pack the resume like hockey does, and it is no way to begin a college interview.

After a couple of hours, the professor thanked the boy, saying, "Well, some dreams happen for reasons we do not know. We are all connected in the collective unconscious, which Jung thought was the core of all spiritual experience and symbolism. So for next week, everyone, write a little reflective essay on the boy and his blue angel dream."

"Yes, we are connected," added the boy. "I mean, Alan Watts says even physically. Look at my glasses—thousands of people helped make these. Someone gathered the sand and melted the glass, and someone made the machine to do it with, and someone had to mine iron ore to make the steel to make the aluminum frames, and someone drove a truck to deliver these but there has to be a road and workers and it just goes on and on and on. We depend on the kindness of countless others for every detail of our lives. But, Professor, what I believe is that we are also all connected spiritually, all part of the divine Mind and so all kinds of spiritual connections are possible that completely go beyond the limits of time and place. The problem is that we think we are more separate than we are, so bad stuff happens."

"Do you think anyone will ever prove that this God, this infinite Mind, is real?" he asked the boy.

"Well, Sir, I would like to be more certain of it myself. And that is what the dream may be about. So I am inclined to follow it…who knows where, but west, somehow. I almost want to go on a westward pilgrimage, but I have no real idea of where to. Otherwise I might."

Then the whole group walked down the hallway to an early evening chapel service. The boy played *Jesu, Joy of Man's Desiring* on his classical guitar, and Rev. Welles gave a little sermon on how the pelican is a Christian symbol of love because it plucks its breast vein if it has to in order to feed its offspring. The pelican is the school symbol at St. Paul's for that reason, explained the Rev. Welles. Finally, they all had dinner in the dining hall before the boy and his teacher drove back up Route 91 to New Hampshire.

Sometimes at the start of his philosophy class, where the boys read about psychology and religious experience that can shift emotions toward tranquility beyond time and place, Rev. Welles would ask, "How real does that dream feel?"

"Well, like more than just any dream. It has a glow to it, and it feels real enough to puzzle me. It calls me, it pulls me," the boy answered, to the delight of his accepting peers. After all, the boy had visited Yale Divinity School and taught the students there about universal Mind, which to them was kind of wacky but also impressive. They wondered why the boy did not want to apply there for college, but he didn't want to. Nothing Ivy would do.

"It feels a bit like I am actually headed west to do something. It's only a dream, and I don't really believe in angels, and then I wake up and it's gone, but I remember it clearly. It's hard to explain. It's like I am sleeping but not really, kind of in some special zone. Sometimes I think this is infinite Mind telling me something that I don't understand yet, something that I have to discover and not give up on, because in the long run I might find out where I am headed. Guys, you know you are all trying to get to someplace or other like Harvard or Yale, but not me. If I have a goal, I am going to be lured to it by divine Mind, because it isn't coming from me. Goals are desperate detours from destiny."

The other boys were not at all surprised to hear this, because they knew the boy. "Well, if you are into this infinite Mind stuff, who really needs school?" one asked.

The boy answered, "Good question."

There was a beautiful life-size bronze statue of St. Paul outside the chapel, and the boys would pass by and touch its outstretched hand with a smile on their way to dinner at the Upper.

"For luck," they would exclaim, but the boy had read enough Jung to reply, "For synchronicity, not luck."

"Hey, whatever floats your boat, Babylon!" his classmates said. "So where does Jesus fit in?" they asked in class.

"Well," answered the boy, "we are all sinners and can't get to high goodness on our own, but there is a power of goodness in the universe that we could all draw on and use if we let it come our way. Something needed to happen to close the gap. Jesus had complete God consciousness, and this explains his amazing healing and creativity and love; it made his sacrifice very special and far more spiritually transformative than anything anyone else could do to open a window into the divine. I don't recite Creeds much in church, but I believe that Jesus had the unique spiritual calling that got him betrayed and nailed to a cross while maintaining the dignity of perfect love and forgiveness, so that God could overlook the fact that human nature is not a pretty thing and cherish us all anyway despite ourselves. The test for infinite love is the manner of response to infinite adversity."

In the library, the boy read spiritual classics and Frankel and Huxley and Bly and Kerouac. At Rev. Welles' suggestion, he devoured the ancient philosopher Plotinus because he was into the One, the infinite Mind and its continuity with every human mind. He dug into scriptures of the world's religions and wrote essays about how material things, competition, and glory do not constitute success, but that an awareness of our connection within the divine Mind can spring from sensing the emptiness of it all.

"Thoreau-like," his English teacher, Mr. George Carlisle, called him more than once. "The boy is a good kid, but not in a very useful sense." Occasionally, instead of going to watch the teams play soccer or hockey on a Saturday afternoon, the boy would wander the wooded paths up at Turkey Pond, pondering some passage from a book by whichever mystic he was reading that week. And he would read while walking around the library pond, uplifted by the magnificent fall colors or the snow, sometimes tripping on a rock. His good friend, the poet Ned Perkins, who edited the literary magazine and whose grandfather Malcolm Perkins was the editor for F. Scott Fitzgerald, referred to the boy as a "peripatetic spiritual road duck." "Peripatetic" means that you walk around reading stuff on paths, and road ducks sometimes get run over.

Most Sundays the boy joined a handful of other students with a Catholic history in the cab ride to attend Mass at Concord Carmel—short for the Carmelite Sisters of the Monastery of Our Lady and St. Joseph—down Pleasant Street from St. Paul's. They practiced silent prayer there and seemed to get the idea of a connecting Mind that we become more aware of when we stop talking and thinking, when we get away from reason and logic and go deeper into a still awareness of the divine Mind.

The boy was a natural-born Carmelite mystic, and sometimes also stopped by Carmel on Saturday afternoons on the way to Charlie's Pool Hall in downtown Concord, which was about a three-mile walk. He liked the nuns a lot, and often spoke with the sisters when they were out on the grounds and not sequestered about how they experienced what they called the Mind of God in their quiet rooms.

He then would continue on to Charlie's because he thought pool was Zen à la Kerouac, bumming cigarettes from the townies to look Bogart-cool in his old trench coat, even though he didn't smoke them really. It was just to blend in at Charlie's. They liked the boy because he tutored their little brothers and sisters at the Millville School, a red brick grade school across from St. Paul's on Pleasant Street. The students were mostly poor and lived out in the country. In his last year the boy tutored math and reading most afternoons for a few hours and got to know a lot of the parents. He liked the Millville School and it felt like his kind of place, where he could be who he was. Giving was living. He felt a giver's glow.

Then there was the mandatory Sunday mid-morning Mass in the school chapel, a thing of beauty to the boy, with sermons and music and common prayers that shaped him and made him who he was and would be.

Working with Rev. Welles, he had written his Sixth Form or senior paper on this infinite Mind and love that pervades the universe, and from which our individual minds at least mostly originate. That was a core belief for the New England Transcendentalists, who borrowed it from Hindu metaphysics. Our minds, wrote the boy, are more than matter; they have their origins in a Mind that preceded the universe and matter. Plato and Plotinus both thought so, and the boy agreed. "My mind," he wrote, "is a very small part of the infinite Mind such that I have a separate identity and individual destiny, but without ever being separated from the wholeness of a universal Mind that includes all other minds as well. We are all small points of light in the endless field of divine luminosity."

"Honors in Ancient History and Sacred Studies" was the sole distinction conferred on the boy at graduation, except for *La Junta*—the Spanish club—and cross-country. The other boys had a lot more items listed under their photos in the class yearbook because they were aiming high. The boy wasn't aiming at all, which made all the difference. He was runner-up for the math prize. The boy kept it simple.

At graduation, when Rev. Welles asked the boy about his plans in life, he answered, "Well, Sir, I am supposed to go to Swarthmore College, as you know, and thanks for the letter of recommendation. Gerry Studds wrote a good one too for American History class. They let me in off the waiting list a week ago. But I really just am not sure I need college. Maybe there is some westward road. Sir, you have been the best, the best—and Julie too."

Rev. Welles smiled, shook his head a bit, and raised his thick dark James Bond eyebrows a little pessimistically. "Well, keep us posted and stay in touch. Do some good, that's all we can ask. And stay off Wall Street, Babylon."

"Yes, Sir, I will. Thanks for everything. There's a road out there somewhere."

"All right, Babylon. It will find you."

And the boy returned to Babylon, from whence he had come.

But now things get a little confessional. The wild side of life—including the *mea culpa* part—is always there waiting, and the boy was about to experience it in a way that would alter his path forever. He really was heading west.

Why the Boy Took the Car, the Big Argument, and the Journey West

Most boys who are honest and trustworthy have at least one big argument with their dads growing up. That doesn't mean that they should seek it out, but if it finds them and involves defending their integrity, the confrontation must be accepted with courage. This doesn't mean that dads are bad, or boys either. It's just about growing up.

It was early July, and the boy was home in Babylon after graduation, thinking that college made no sense. One Saturday evening he drove out to Westhampton Beach, a seaside town filled with lively young people and quite a few St. Paul's guys celebrating the end of school at a class graduation party. The boy felt so removed from the scene and the drinking that he walked away. It just seemed like such a waste of minds.

That evening did not find him struggling to escape from some dark valley of despair. But he saw no meaning in going to Swarthmore anymore, where he had in the end decided to go because it was supposedly more acceptable and East Coast than heading out west to Reed, where he had received an offer that he turned down.

After returning home late that night the boy was feeling claustrophobic, stuck on a too Long Island, and, thinking about his dream, determined that he just might journey to the west after all. Now, anyone who would follow a blue dream as though it were a direction sign is trusting the universe more than most, but the boy sort of wanted to do just that. He had no worldly goals, but he was open to surprises.

Anyway, St. Paul himself was always on the road, and so were Kerouac and Whitman, he thought. Sometimes that early July he would drive over to Huntington along the North Shore and stop at Whitman's birthplace on Route 110, or to Northport, the next town over, to visit Gunther's Tap Room where Kerouac spent years drinking heavily after he wrote *On the Road*. The boy would hang out there, ordering Cokes and asking the fishermen about Kerouac. Some remembered a guy jotting words down on napkins at a corner table while others just drew a blank. The bartender knew a lot about Kerouac and hung old news articles about him on the wall.

"After all," said the bartender, "Kerouac coined the term 'Beat Generation,' so we give him most of the wall space on that side."

It was heaven-sent that, in the middle of that July, the boy and his dad got into a fierce argument; otherwise he would never have had the audacity to follow the dream to the west in the way that he did. There had to be a push as well as a pull, and it really helps if the push is strong when the pull is as vague as a recurring dream. Why the argument? The boy had been offered a great summer job tutoring inner-city kids in the Bronx, building on his Millville experience. But his dad thought the location was dangerous. He said he'd had someone check it out, but the boy doubted it. The bottom line was that his folks did not have any sense for who the boy was, and anyway he was overshadowed by two superstar older siblings.

"It's dangerous in the Bronx, and your mother is against it," Dad said over his standard whiskey on the rocks. It was mostly Mom who'd pressured him to take a stand against the Bronx.

"Dad, this is something that I planned on and it means everything to me," said the boy. "Rev. Welles pulled a few strings and set it up, and it is one thing I really want to do."

"Look, you can't do it. I won't put up with it. That's it. No further discussion." The tone was terminal.

The boy managed a few words of defiance: "Look, folks, this just makes no sense. It confines me, and I am going to do this."

"You will not," said Mom, in a serious throaty tone, red lipstick covering her cigarette, martini in hand.

Dad stood up angrily and thundered, with all the strength of the WW II Navy Commander that he had been, "You are upsetting your mother!"

"I am not dropping this job, that's it!" the boy repeated.

Then, Mom, having had her several drinks, and Dad too, raised the stakes. "I'm paying for Swarthmore, so either you drop this job or you're paying on your own."

He paused. "Okay, but I am not thinking of you as good parents. So what am I supposed to do this summer?"

"I can call Bill De Bono," Dad said. "Bill's got a lampshade factory. You can make lampshades in Patchogue." At the time Dad was the VP of W&J Sloane's Furniture Store on Fifth Avenue, so he knew a lot of people around New York who were in the lamp business.

"Oh, what the heck!" the boy relented. He had nothing against hard work, but it would be empty manual labor.

So now he had a job in Patchogue, a town about half an hour farther east, in Bill De Bono's lampshade factory. The boy tried it for a couple of weeks. Old Bill, cigar in hand, stationed him on an assembly line, cutting cardboard forms between two large Italian women, Maria and Cassandra. These were hardworking, salt-of-the-earth women, and the boy got along with them okay; the boy got along with everyone. But the factory did not have air conditioning, so it was hot and sweaty and smelly. And with each passing day he became angrier and more ready to head off to greener pastures in a way that might just declare his total and complete emancipation from his parents' influence forever and ever.

Dad still had that second-hand gray Mercedes 190 that he had bought to look good when he visited St. Paul's. One hot, muggy Friday, two weeks into his factory job, the boy drove the 190 to the factory as usual and put in a solid day of hard labor. Then, that evening, he drove out to Westhampton again to spend a few days with friends—good old Livy, a buddy from St. Paul's, and the boy's nice blonde girlfriend Lee, whom he liked a lot because he could look into her eyes and see the universe as the waves were crashing into the dunes. The folks were okay with his borrowing the 190 because they could drive the other car. The next night, a Saturday, was the fateful night the boy finally decided to set out on an unspecified quest west.

That evening the boy sat on the bench pondering his favorite book, Aldous Huxley's *The Perennial Philosophy*, about "Ultimate Reality" and dharma, and knew he was worried that everything he was doing was pointless and that at his dying breath he would be filled with regrets over a meaningless life. Putting aside his copy of Huxley, he pulled his heavily underlined copy of Hesse's *Siddhartha* out of his backpack. It tells about a young man born into a rich family—a.k.a. the Buddha— who took to the road on a spiritual journey of self-discovery, seeking meaning and authenticity.

At eleven that night, feeling the need to resist the downward vortex of family life, he got into the Mercedes 190 and said goodbye to Lee and Livy without telling them anything about his plans. He just started driving west. He followed the Sunrise Highway (Route 27) to the Long Island Expressway (I-495). He drove through the Midtown Tunnel and up the FDR Drive and over the George Washington Bridge and just followed the signs for Route 80 West. He did not have a road map, but west is west, and the only other sign was for I-95 South. There was nothing about "south" in the dream.

Route 80 runs from the George Washington Bridge in the east to the Bay Bridge in the west. But when you're following a dream any long highway will do, so you can pick your own.

After a couple of hours on 80, rationality kicked in a bit and the boy began to have real doubts about taking Dad's car, although he was pissed about the job—and maybe he even lost a little faith in the dream for a few minutes. He decided to turn around and head home, like any respectable kid should, and try to renegotiate things—although communication with his parents had never been good. If he turned back now, no one would ever know that he had even been out on Route 80. That was the boy's thinking at the time, but the divine Mind had other plans.

Synchronicity intervened, gracefully but with awesome power. The boy was close to making a U-turn across the midway when something totally uncanny and unexpected happened that changed his life forever—and ultimately for the better.

Rather than crossing over the median, the car barely made it to the right shoulder of the highway as the generator failed and the entire engine went dead. It was still dark, but the sun was beginning to rise. The boy had all of fifty dollars in his wallet, no credit cards, and there at the intersection of Route 80 with Route 215 near Milton and Lewisburg, Pennsylvania, there was nothing visible for miles but wheat fields and cornstalks. The boy felt like the generator had broken as an act of God, and for one good reason: the universe was now forcing him to live out his dream. And since he was now pretty far from home, there was no turning back.

So the boy did what only an adolescent male with limited management skills and a typical underdeveloped frontal cortex might do. He took a pencil from the glove compartment and carefully printed in large block letters the following note on a scrap of paper:

> To the Pennsylvania State Police:
> Please return this car to Henry my dad,
> 44 Davison Lane East
> West Islip, New York
> Call 516-669-5655.
> —His son, who just quit the lampshade
> factory for good

Just as the sun was rising, the boy stood on the side of Route 80 with his thumb out, his classical guitar case and backpack full of spiritual books at his side, and prayed for a ride. The very first vehicle that came along, a big white truck, pulled over and the driver yelled out, "Okay, kid, where you headed?"

And the boy responded, "Thanks, sir. Goin' west, looks like!"

"Well, how far?"

"Far, sir!"

"Well, not sure where far is, but I can get you to Chicago, so jump in. My name is Gary."

"Okay, I had an uncle named Gary, but his liver failed. He almost drank himself to death in Africa and came home to live in Connecticut. He visited the house once or twice but was falling all over the place. He was too far gone to take any interest in me, even though I got my middle name to honor the guy. Those heavy drinkers give up everything for one thing when they could give up one thing for everything."

"No drinking here, kid, not on the road." Gary had a Bible on the seat and a wooden cross hanging from the big mirror in front of him.

"So what are you doing out here, kid?"

And the boy told him about the lampshade factory and then a little about the dream. Gary was very quiet as the boy spoke and looked deeply pensive. He was a good listener, and very present in the moment. After the boy finished, there was a long silence.

"Well, kid, that Mercedes 190 back there and the note, it should make its way back to your dad, but he won't be happy. That's a long way from Long Island. You sure you want to head west? You should at least call home."

As Gary spoke, he pointed to the towering mountains and steep, rocky granite cliffs right at the edge of Route 80 after you pass that Lewisburg/Milton exit.

"Did you ever see mountain cliffs like that, kid?"

"No, but wow! They are amazing," answered the boy.

"Up on that one over in the distance you can see a big white cross at the top. People along Route 80 have all done things that they probably shouldn't have. We all do. But down here below the cross we are all still okay, because even when we don't look up and think about that cross as we drive on by, we are always covered by it. Still, you need to call your mom," he said, without sounding judgmental.

"Kid," he continued, "you still have to try to do your best and someday, somehow you will make the most of things."

"I might have handled this better, Gary," I replied. "But the car broke down and there was this dream and the world needs dreamers. Plus, I really wanted that tutoring job. Dad, he will get the car back somehow. I should be okay heading west. I will get back at some point, I guess. Anyway, the car breaking when it did was some kind of quantum alchemy. It happened for a reason.

"Well, you never really quite get back to where you left from in the same way. But that's not too bad, kid," said Gary. "And your dad will eventually get his car. So let's head to Chicago. But it's early morning, so I will say a prayer. Yup, way kind of leads on to way."

And Gary improvised a prayer out loud for the boy and his journey to the west, ending with, "Now Lord, wherever this boy goes and whatever he does, let your Light shine on his highway, and protect him from every kind of danger because he could get in trouble. So take care of him please, and take care of his parents, and let him learn from all this.

Amen." It was deeper than anything the boy had ever heard, heartfelt rather than formulaic.

***

As the morning sun started to shine brightly and puffy white clouds filled the Ohio skies, the boy began to feel tranquility. Forgetting about the car and how angry Dad was going to be, he fell asleep and woke up in Indiana.

Around noon they pulled into a McDonald's and Gary treated the boy to lunch. Gary was tall and thin and dressed in Western style, his well-worn jeans and red-and-white checked shirt topped with a brown leather vest. He carried himself with grace and was careful about what he said. He was kind to the boy.

"Kid, maybe you could call your mom now from that booth," he suggested.

"Not now, maybe later for sure. I'm not certain what I would say," answered the boy.

The boy didn't take the journey so much as it took him. We are all more taken than in control, and the journey finds us even if we are not quite clear about seeking it. That includes mechanical failures on Route 80. Sure, we have some control over our lives, but so much that happens to us is a surprise. The boy had no idea, for example, that the generator would break near Lewisburg. Okay, you can say that, when it happened, he should have waited for the police and called home. But he was so tired of cutting cardboard, so mad about not doing his summer tutoring job, that he was ready for a big escape. Was it infinite Mind that caused the generator to break down and stopped that big white truck as soon as the boy stuck out his thumb? It all happened so quickly, it felt like a perfect divine setup. A lot of things that happen are much more set up than we realize, but we need to notice this and listen to the whispers.

Backtracking to Birth

As far as the boy was concerned, even his conception smacked of synchronicity.

He owed his embodied existence to a car crash on the LIE, the Long Island Expressway or I-495, which at the time was known as the Queens-Midtown Expressway. It runs east from Manhattan, a stretch of highway packed with big trucks in a hurry and tense commuters snarled in traffic jams—drivers so stressed-out by trying to make ends meet in the glittery pressure cooker that is Greater New York that they cut you off, cursing or gesturing obscenely in the process. In 1948, two perfect strangers in two separate cars were driving east out of Manhattan after work. Henry was a lamp buyer and Molly was a saleslady at Macy's. It was a Friday afternoon and traffic was bad. Somewhere in Queens, Henry's Chevy rear-ended Molly's Ford.

Now the boy's Irish Catholic mother, Molly, who was raised on a Bridgehampton potato farm, used to say that the crash and the meeting that followed was an "act of God, a bit of grace." Like a lot of Irish folks, she tended to attribute divine meaning to things. Otherwise, when the boy asked Mom how she met Dad, she would only be able to say, "Well, Dad plowed into my car on the LIE and he looked pretty good."

When the boy was at St. Paul's, he had to give a chapel talk one morning about how little control we have over how we enter this life. So he told the story of how his parents met, which was shocking to the elite student body who were a little too high-brow to think well of marriages born on the road, and especially on the LIE.

The boy said, "Yup, Dad just rear-ended Mom on the LIE." Everyone laughed, and the boy couldn't figure out why until Rector Matt Warren, the imposing headmaster, tapped the boy's shoulder and asked, "Would you possibly be referring to her automobile?"

"Yes, Sir, her automobile, of course, Sir!" he responded.

"That's better," said the Rector. "Be careful with words."

The boy had no love for the LIE, that noisy, ugly, congested slab of concrete covered with fumes, and he avoided it for the most part because of the trucks. But he had to affirm it as key to his conception. If there had been no crash, he would not have gotten his start as a zygote a few years later. He tended to view that crash as synchronicity in action; there was clearly nothing rational or normal about how his parents met.

How Mr. and Mrs. Muller Taught the Boy

Wise old Mr. Karl Muller and Mrs. Muller saved the boy in every way that a kid can be saved, especially spiritually.

The boy at age five

The boy's family lived a very long seventy miles east of Manhattan where culture mostly meant boats, clamming, and drinking on the beach or at yacht club parties. The sand at the end of Oak Neck Lane was littered with beer cans and broken bottles, so kids would sometimes slice their feet when they went swimming and have to head to Good Samaritan Hospital.

When the boy was six years old, there were no kids his age on the lane. Mom worried that he spent too much time by himself and encouraged him to "go out and do something for someone."

"Okay, Mom, I'll go to Mr. and Mrs. Mullers' place."

He was gone for the rest of the day. He headed down the street about a quarter mile to the Mullers' little white house, walked up the back steps to the second story over the garage, and knocked on their door. The Mullers had no children of their own. They were well into their seventies and more quietly reflective than effusive, but there was a depth about them, and they always welcomed the boy. They kept a cross on the wall in their kitchen and a Bible on the table just below it. They did not drink, but Mr. Muller smoked some. The Mullers didn't have a lot of wealth, but they were at peace: simple folks, unpretentious, plainly dressed, like in a spiritually evocative Rembrandt painting. Mr. Muller had a pension because he had worked for years building airplanes for Grumman, which was a big deal on Long Island before it moved away.

"Mr. Muller, I'm here to do something for you, like maybe rake leaves or rake the gravel on the driveway. Is that okay with you? Mom sent me."

Karl Muller rose and walked down the steps with the boy to find something for him to do. The boy got two nickels for his work.

"Save it so you can go to a good school one day," he told the boy. That seemed like sound advice, and the boy thought that Mr. Muller seemed like he would be a good manager for a young kid to have.

Mr. Muller also told him, "Boy, you get a lot done, but you seem kind of old for a kid of six. That's good, but you've got lessons ahead of you, and hard lessons are learned hard. That's the only way. No one can learn your lessons for you."

"Why can't I learn from other people's mistakes? Do I just have to learn from my own?"

"You can learn from others, but not the hard stuff."

Mr. Muller was a Presbyterian who believed rightly that human nature is a mixed bag. He smiled some, and when he did it was a warm, generous smile, but he didn't smile all the time.

"Smiling is okay. Be cheerful, but never trust people who smile all the time," he said. "They are just after your nickels. The thing about people is, they're never all that good, none of them, and you have to tolerate them as best you can and forgive them because you can't change human nature."

Mr. Muller was quite pessimistic in a nice way.

"What does 'tolerate' mean, Mr. Muller?"

"You can't expect anyone to be too good. If they are real good it isn't actually them, it's God in them."

To be good at clamming, you have to know where the clams are. When Mr. Muller and the boy went clamming in the Mullers' little flat boat, Mr. Muller's method for finding the clams was to offer a brief, improvised prayer: "Dear Lord, we have faith that there are clams out here today, but we don't know where they are. Please guide us to the best spot, if it be Your loving will, because we can't clam unless we know where they are just like You do. Amen."

When they did very well and harvested a lot of clams, they figured that prayer was the reason why.

They also raked hard, standing on the deck.

Mr. Muller taught the boy that "God does the finding, but you do the digging."

He also had the boy memorize Bible passages, and they burned some of them into wood planks and then varnished them before nailing them to the trees all around Mr. Muller's property. They did the same with lines from Robert Frost poems and read aloud together pretty much all of Frost's stuff in the living room by the fireplace.

"Are you reading the Bible I gave you every day at home?" Mr. Muller asked the boy.

They read a lot of Bible passages and talked about them. Mr. Muller gave the boy extra nickels for knowing Bible quotes, King James style, including book, chapter, and verse. The boy went home and underlined them, including the words of the prophets and Jesus and St. Paul, and that explains a little why he was attracted to St. Paul's School, and why he knew the blue angel dream was more than a reaction to dyspepsia.

Mr. Muller taught him a lot of other things, including, "Don't expect gratitude for helping people out, don't expect people to clap for you."

He also taught that "God loves a cheerful giver."[15] They burned that passage into a piece of wood, did the varnishing in the garage, and up it went on an oak tree along the driveway.

"It's good to give, and don't ever be sad about giving," Mr. Muller told him. "If you can't be cheerful about helping your neighbor, then the spirit isn't in it. When it is, you give and you glow."

Mrs. Muller was always kind. The boy never heard from her that loud, annoying, out-of-control kind of talk that he considered pointless and had learned to dislike a lot. The Mullers never screamed. Mrs. Muller

---

15   St. Paul, 2 Cor. 9:7.

wanted him to be prayerful and peaceful in his mind all the time. "The Bible says 'pray without ceasing,' " she reminded him, and the three of them burned that into a plank as well and nailed it to a tree down the street, right next to his mailbox.

The boy's favorite afternoons were when Mr. and Mrs. Muller had him in for clam chowder and warm, homemade bread, especially in winter after shoveling snow from their steps and the long gravel driveway. The three held hands and Mr. or Mrs. Muller said grace in a sincere and beautiful way. How different this was from his home, where there was no everyday spirituality, although he and his family did make it to church some Sundays. The Mullers were deeply spiritual people, so they did not need to get rowdy or out of control. They practiced temperance and were joyfully close to God. The boy felt peaceful with them.

"Don't expect people to come to your funeral, I don't expect them to come to mine," Mr. Muller told him. "But you should come."

"Okay, I will," the boy promised. And a few years later, he did.

Looking back on Oak Neck Lane, it seems that the Mullers were the perfect people in the right place at the right time to be the boy's spiritual mentors. It seems as though they were put there to shape the boy's youth. This is what it means when people say that sometimes we only recognize synchronicity when we look backward and connect the dots.

But then came the big move, and the boy and his family landed at 42 Dorset Lane in Babylon, on a creek so Dad could keep his boat in the backyard, and there were more kids around.

The downside was losing Mr. Muller, who was now about ten miles away. The boy rode his bike over there to say hello every once in a while, but Mr. Muller died not too long after the move. The boy was nine when he rode his bike all the way back to the old street one afternoon in summer and Mrs. Muller said, "I'm sorry, but Mr. Muller passed away the other day. He died of lung cancer." They said a pretty emotional prayer for him, and the boy cleaned some junk out of the garage, for old time's sake.

The boy went into the Mullers' old tool shed, where he sawed a big pine plank and burned a passage across it before he varnished it and nailed it to a tree: "Thank God for Mr. Muller."

Mom took the boy to Mr. Muller's memorial service—his funeral, which the boy just had to attend. There were maybe two dozen people there from Mr. Muller's church, and Mrs. Muller. The boy said a few words.

"Mr. Muller taught me the Bible and we prayed and we clammed, and he taught me how to use tools. He was always there, and he taught me to save my nickels. He taught me to be realistic about people and not to expect a lot, but he believed that God could still inspire them to do good."

At age twelve, the boy got his first job in Dave Southard's Boat Yard, building small wooden-hulled sailboats. That too was thanks to Mr. Muller, who made the boy into a carpenter. When the older guys at Southard's would ask the boy where he learned how to use all the tools, he always answered, "Good old Mr. Muller." But his dad was an excellent carpenter too and a hard worker, so the boy learned from him as well.

Synchronicity as Protection—A Risky Moment in Mexico

Things happen that you don't control, like your parents' car accident on the LIE or the Mercedes breaking down on Route 80, and all that remains is the journey forward. Truth be told, though, in general following dreams on Route 80 can be quite dangerous for a boy. Maybe the Mercedes could have died lightless right in the middle of 80 and gotten plowed into by Gary's truck with the boy inside, or maybe he could have been hit trying to walk over to the shoulder. But the car had just enough to make it over to the side before it went completely dead. But the boy had always been protected by God, like when he was hitching through Mexico at age thirteen.

The summer of his Third Form year at St. Paul's (ninth grade), the boy took an Areonaves de Mexico flight with a one-day stopover in Mexico City, en route to a school in Saltillo to study Spanish and guitar. After landing, he walked for most of the evening and spent the night in Chapultepec Forest, Mexico City's large and very dangerous park where people got robbed, kidnapped, and killed a lot. The next night he spent in a small motel called *Agua Caliente,* "The Hot Water Motel." They did have a hot shower and he took one, but he slept in his jeans because the sheets looked pretty well used. The next day he flew from Mexico City to Monterrey and hopped on a bus to downtown Saltillo, where there is a beautiful plaza, a nice but not magnificent cathedral, and an okay university.

It took five minutes to walk from the university to the family home, where he shared rooms with two college students from Florida who were studying Spanish literature. He liked the family, ate meals with them, and went to the outdoor market for shopping, where he learned a lot of Spanish about the physiology of the bull. All over the city, radios blared music by The Kinks or The Animals, contemporary '60s rock bands that were taking the US by storm. He frequented a movie theater downtown that showed mostly old black-and-white films, dropping coins into the palms of the native Mexican Indians sitting around in large groups out in front, begging in the shade.

It was a productive summer. The boy played music on his guitar and received a Spanish Language Certificate from *La Universidad de Jaime Balmes,* which made him quite proud.

But when the time came to depart for home, the boy screwed up. The young male mind is not worth much when it comes to advance planning; it is a disorganized mind at best. He woke up that August morning around ten o'clock, packed for the flight home, and only then did it dawn on him that he had forgotten something crucial—he needed to catch the Saltillo bus to get to Monterrey airport, about ninety minutes away, but he had just missed it!

"Whoa!" he thought. "The flight for New York leaves at noon!"

He quickly picked up his little tan suitcase, grabbed his guitar case, said goodbye to his host family, and ran a couple of miles until he reached the edge of town and the two-lane highway. He had been warned that it was a dangerous place, though, and as he stood there two really big, bad-looking guys with bats started walking his way. Quickly the boy stuck out his thumb and prayed. Behold the miracle: An immediate act of divine synchronicity! A nice old farmer wearing a straw hat pulled over in his rusty, greenish old truck filled with chickens in crowded cages. Now the two bad *hombres* started running toward him, so this had to be quick.

The farmer asked the boy where he was headed, and the boy told him, *"Monterrey Aeropuerto, por favor, y muy rapido! Veinte dolares para usted!"*

Then he jumped into the back of the truck and the farmer took off as fast as that old truck would go, with the chickens going crazy as he sat beside them in the truck bed and shouted at the two guys disappearing in the distance. By the way, all the other Mexicans he met that summer were really nice people.

And he made it to the airport in time! The boy gave that farmer every bill and coin he had, thanked him profusely, and ran across the parking lot of the little airport—the whole place was only about fifty feet long. The boy showed his ticket and passport, and the attendant told him to run because the plane was just about to close its door.

So run the boy did, screaming out *"Por favor, espera para mi!"*

Well, it all worked out. He shoved his guitar into the space above his seat and crammed his suitcase under his feet.

When the boy arrived at JFK, Mom and Dad met him at the gate. Mom looked really anxious, and blurted out, "You're safe! Here you are. Alive!" As we drove home, the boy gleefully told them about hitching to the airport from Saltillo, the two really bad-looking *hombres* coming after him, and the kind chicken farmer who saved him. Mom was turning green and even Dad was ashen. The boy should not have told the story.

But ever the Irish mystic, Mom declared, "Only God could have arranged that ride along the highway, because otherwise you would be dead in the desert!"

"Mom," the boy responded, "something in the universe was at work."

What a perfect moment of synchronicity. The boy could have died, but somehow the right truck driver came along, chickens and all, at the right time, and saved him.

Julie's Big Worry

One day in April of 2015 the boy, now an adult and considerably older, went to Boston to see Julie Welles, his second-year dorm mother at St. Paul's. He found her still vibrant and thriving despite her eighty-five years. She remembered how her husband, Rev. Welles, had wondered about the boy's future, and the boy asked her to try to write down how she remembered him as a teenager. A few weeks later he received an email with her response: "I met you more than forty years ago, upon your arrival at St. Paul's School. I was surprised by your openness and innocence. You wore your heart on your sleeve, and your lack of sophistication was a rarity at St. Paul's. I remember hoping it would survive. I have never seen you compromise that 'goodness.' Many times, as a student you dared to take the road less traveled, and it has led you to a career as a beacon of thoughtfulness and integrity in a complex society. You worried me because I thought you would fail miserably or succeed plentifully."

Clearly, Julie had picked up on things.

And she was right to worry about the boy. Meaning is everything, and when boys—and girls—don't find meaning, they get pretty desperate.

The boy had decided to take Route 80 in the direction of his dream, but he doubted himself until that misty silver-gray morning, high above the western sea, just like in the dream. This is where he reclaimed his soul for good, despite modern skepticism.

Interlude

The boy pondering Jung in study hall at St. Paul's

Hold fast to your dreams for if dreams die life is a broken-winged bird that cannot fly.

—Langston Hughes

Caminante no hay camino, se hace camino al andar.

Wayfarer, there isn't any road; you make the road as you go on.

—Antonio Machado

The spiritual journey is individual, highly personal. It can't be organized or regulated. It isn't true that everyone should follow one path. Listen to your own truth.

–Ram Dass

How to Follow a Dream—The First Lesson: Boys can follow a deep recurring dream if they pray about it and come to feel a spiritual trust in its meaning over time, but some dreams are just made up, so careful discernment over time is the key. A boy has to feel that the dream is more than likely a calling, but that does not allow him to have absolute certainty. If he follows the dream on a highway pilgrimage he does so in faith until he arrives at he knows not where, and there he will know that he really was guided, and he will feel validated in believing that there is an infinite connecting Mind of cherishing love. This experience of arrival need only happen once to shape the course of a lifetime. A boy may feel strongly about a dream but resist following it because he does not want to upset family expectations, but discovering a destiny usually means setting aside acceptability and little human goals.

Once a boy sets out on such a pilgrimage and if he starts thinking he should turn around before it's too late, the way will somehow be blocked. The car will break down. Otherwise it was not really his destiny after all, but at least he would have tried.

So many young people pursue materialistic goals that disappoint them in the long run. It is better to give all that up early and follow a pilgrim's path because we need to know ourselves as in essence eternal spiritual souls connected with others, with nature, and with the universal Mind to truly flourish. Every day young people die of emptiness and affluenza. Following a dream can save them. Be free. Only the worldly will laugh.

Evil is the absence of the good. It happens when we get out of spiritual touch with the infinite Mind of love, and break into a free fall of emptiness, ego, and self-destruction.

The boy in art class at St. Paul's (top row, fourth from left)

Let yourself be drawn by the strange pull of what you call love. It will not lead you astray.

—Rumi

The main school building after chapel

The Youth and the Ledge: "If You Save Him"

The biggest adventure you can take is to live the life of your dreams.

–Oprah Winfrey

G ary dropped the boy off in downtown Chicago, along Lake
  Michigan on Lake Shore Drive.

"Here, kid, take these forty dollars in case you need it, and you will, but
let's pray before you go." And Gary said a second prayer, but not until he
paused and quoted a passage that the boy remembered from Mr. Muller
years before: "The Lord is with you wherever you go."

"That was Joshua 1:9," said the boy. That had been one of Mr.
Muller's favorites.

"Not bad, kid." Gary prayed for safe travels and grace.

"Okay, thanks Gary, you were there when I needed you and now we go
our separate ways." Then Gary and the boy shook hands and the boy
jumped out with his couple of books and his guitar case, which included
a toothbrush and a few pairs of underwear crammed in next to his
instrument. It was summer and no time for socks. He had ninety dollars
in his jeans now, the fifty he brought from Westhampton Beach and the
forty that Gary had added.

"Okay, kid, but call home," Gary said, as he waved goodbye. "You can
walk a couple of miles to Grant Park and grab a bench."

The boy watched Gary pull away and then he walked to Grant Park
along the shores of Lake Michigan near the Art Institute. There was an
antiwar protest going on there and lots of people handing out literature.
The boy sat down on a bench and started to play some slow and simple
ragtime and a little Villa-Lobos, and people started to drop dollar bills
into his guitar case. He slept next to a hedge for a couple of nights. By
the third day, he had earned over a hundred dollars from his playing,
so now he had one hundred and ninety total. The boy befriended a
group of five hippies who were part of the protest and told them that
he was headed for someplace in the west otherwise unspecified, so
they invited him to jump in their blue VW minibus because they were
California-bound.

As they drove, his companions got a little curious about the boy so he shared his experience working in the lampshade factory. He also told them about taking the Mercedes and about Gary the truck driver. They smoked weed, but the boy did not because he was happy with his clear natural mind, which he considered to be a simple, sacred state. After listening to his story, they encouraged him to call home like Gary had. Finally, about a week after leaving Westhampton, the boy called Mom collect from a telephone booth along Route 80, just east of Lincoln, Nebraska.

"Hi, Mom, it's me! I'm in Nebraska!"

"Nebraska? Well, thank God, you're alive. We can call off the Pinkertons!" she exclaimed.

"What, you called the Pinkertons? You mean the detectives? Mom, why did you do that? Didn't you get my note?"

"Well, now we know you aren't kidnapped," she said. "Your father got the car. He had the car towed all the way from Lewisburg to the repair shop in the village. We got the note… We realize we weren't listening. We figured that out. So where are you headed?"

"West, Mom. Yup, I was really finished with the lampshade thing. Two weeks was all I could take. I might have turned back, but then the generator broke and that wasn't my fault. It was an act of God—at least that's how I see it. Anyway, I managed to get off the road with it before it broke down. Heck, if that had happened to you or Dad, you might not have been so lucky. Your lives probably just got saved thanks to me. I'm headed west to San Francisco, because that's where this highway ends. It's all Route 80."

"Well, thanks for saving us," she offered.

"Mom, do you have cousin George's address? I could use a cousin with an apartment out there."

Mom gave the boy the address—4 Chenery Street—and then told him, "Well, now you're on your own, but I will call George and let him know to expect you."

"Okay, Mom. I may do some tutoring in the Mission District, which is not as safe as the Bronx. And I am going to play music in the Hispanic bars and restaurants," he teased.

"Okay, just try to stay alive," and then she hung up.

The boy's cousin George was working as superintendent of an apartment building in the Mission District in return for free rent following two tours of duty with the Green Berets in Vietnam, including a stint in Laos that he never discussed. He also had a day job, off and on, in an office downtown. A hospitable, low-key guy, George had gotten a degree in Chinese from the University of North Carolina, Chapel Hill, and now was immersed in the Vietnam vet subculture that had grown up around the Bay Area.

The boy showed up at his place after a few days wandering the streets around Telegraph Avenue in Berkeley, where the hippies had let him off. He said hello, and George generously offered to let him spend the rest of the summer sleeping on the living room floor of his big one-bedroom flat, located a few blocks from Market Street.

***

Walking down Market Street the next day, the boy stumbled on a storefront Buddhist temple and wandered in. He had been reading a lot about the Buddha over the years, and Buddhism was on his mind. He liked the idea that if you live according to spiritual and moral principles (dharma), mainly the positive Golden Rule of "do unto others," you will be rewarded in surprising ways at some point in this life or the next according to karma. For the most part, good things actually do happen to good people in this life, but they have to be living in a decent and functional community. But, regardless, it always feels good inwardly to be good in accord with divine conscience. Moral conscience is a manifestation of the infinite Mind within us and seeing that inalienable dignity in others.

So during the couple of months he lived on Chenery Street, the boy was a happy daily practitioner of Nichiren Buddhism. He met many amazing Asians in that community, mostly Japanese Americans. They were amazing because of their devotion to chanting the mantra *nam myoho renge kyo*, which means something like "devotion to the mysterious ultimate reality." The boy thought it was awesome and had never seen anything remotely like it before. It was so loud, deep, and powerful that it was like living in an alternate reality.

The Nichiren community is nowadays known worldwide as *Soka Gakkai*. A central teaching is that the chanting enhances your karma— your eternal spiritual track record of good or bad deeds—although you have to follow through with good actions. The boy signed on and, during that summer, he briefly became a member for those couple of months, in addition to being an Episcopalian. He knew that *Soka Gakkai* was a little controversial, mainly because it was new in America, and foreign.

One older member, a slender, gray-haired, seventy-year-old Japanese Buddhist named Gus, became the boy's spiritual mentor. Affirming the Buddhist (and Hindu) idea that the mind is a gift over which we have stewardship, Gus confirmed for the boy that alcohol and drugs make a mockery of the pure natural soul, and that practices such as meditation and chanting are designed to increase our spiritual awareness so we don't need help from anything from outside of us. That suited the boy perfectly, because for him happiness had always come from feeling a certain oneness with a power of mind and goodness greater than himself, from which he could draw, and in which he felt peace. When he watched all the "happenings" erupting in San Francisco at the time, and saw people walking around "high" on chemicals, he was saddened because every mind is a divine gift, another small flame in the divine Mind, and we need to be good caretakers of our minds. Our minds are gifts given so that we might act in creative love in the very image of God.

The boy loved chanting, because the boundaries between himself and others disappeared as the group, all seated on the floor and fingering their meditation beads, raised their voices simultaneously in a great deep chorus. The boy learned that it is only when you turn off your thinking by chanting for quite a while—sometimes even for a few hours—that you can become aware of your oneness with the universal Mind of which you are a part and shift into a zone where time, place, matter, and ego dissolve. In those high-volume chanting sessions, as the smoke from burning incense wafted upward, the boy left the lower mind behind and was absorbed in the higher Mind. This is where he learned that the dignity of being human lies not in linear reasoning or being super smart or clever, but in honoring our Consciousness free from thought, the pressures of chronological time, and the demands of the material world. And in those loud group chants, the boy sensed the deeper human connectedness that flows from awareness of the one Mind.

The boy also paid fifty dollars for a *Gohonzon* scroll inscribed with Japanese characters, the main object of devotion in Nichiren that you take home and use to create your own little temple and focus on when you are chanting. It is to be treated with reverence and is supposed to add to the chanter's success, for it can trigger the Buddha nature. Mornings the boy arose early, when things were still quiet and people were still sleeping. In those early hours he felt beyond time and place because he was not yet locked into the day's routines, and he figured that if he was ever going to pray deeply and connect with infinite Mind that would be the time, because God is beyond time and place too. Plus, like Gary had said, people haven't had time to screw up the world, at least for that day. The best Route 80 prayers are prayed early.

With old Gus sometimes accompanying him, the boy spent the rest of his time that summer playing his guitar in Hispanic restaurants around the Mission District, where he earned about forty dollars a night in tips, which was plenty. The Mission District was a big, exciting cultural leap beyond Bill De Bono's old lampshade factory. Plus, he had found a meaningful spiritual community. Why would he ever want to go to college now? Besides, he was earning—and saving—a fair amount of money, and George was not going to kick him out.

He would have just kept going to the Buddhist temple on Market Street and maybe gotten a real job for a while, but everything changed when he drew a bad number in the draft and was likely headed to Vietnam. Neither the boy nor cousin George saw any value in that. So he called the admissions office at Reed College in Portland, where he'd applied with the blue angel dream in mind and to study with the poet Robert Bly. He asked them if he could have his place back in the freshman class, even though he had turned them down six months earlier. Amazingly, they said okay. They understood his predicament.

As he set out to make his way northward, the boy was about to discover the meaning of the blue angel dream.

The Youth on the Bridge and the Dream Fulfilled

Very early that morning, in the final days of August, the boy was up praying before packing his motley few possessions into his new backpack, grabbing his guitar case again, and saying goodbye to George, Gus, and the other Buddhists who had gathered at seven o'clock in the temple to see him off. "Take care of that *Gohonzon,* boy, remember that happiness comes from chanting, and be kind to everyone regardless," said Gus, as he bowed respectfully to the boy and the boy bowed back.

"Be careful among those Oregonians." Then the boy caught a bus to Golden Gate Park.

From the park he started to walk toward the Golden Gate Bridge, heading north. Usually the bridge shone orange-gold in the sun, but it was too early in the morning, maybe about eight or so, and there was no sun, just thick silvery-gray fog. He walked along the wide pedestrian path on the west side of the bridge, its edge rimmed by nothing but a breast-high metal fence, and just below it a thin ledge buffeted by a swirling moist wind over the Bay. He could only see about eight feet ahead through the thick silvery mist as the walkway flattened out when he neared the center of the great span. He felt very high up and much removed from the world.

The boy was startled when he glanced to his left and saw somebody just a few feet away, on the other side of the railing, standing on the little ledge and leaning outwards. He looked just a few years older than the boy, with stringy blond hair and a thin face, and he was staring intently downward. All was quiet.

For one intense moment, the boy's eyes and those of the youth met, and then the boy spoke softly, "I really and truly hope you don't plan to jump."

"Why not?" lamented the youth. "Life is just nothingness."

And then, desperately shouting at the top of his lungs out across the miles of empty space, he impressively recited Shakespeare's monologue about despair:

> Life's but a walking shadow, a poor player,
> That struts and frets his hour upon the stage.
> And then is heard no more. It is a tale
> Told by an idiot, full of sound and fury,
> Signifying nothing.

The boy clapped and smiled. "Wow, kid, great job! *Macbeth*, I believe. That was awesome. You do it better than the guys back in school in New Hampshire. I mean, it sounds a lot more serious when you are hanging out there ready to jump than on a stage in Memorial Hall!"

The youth bowed slightly on the ledge and nodded, acknowledging the compliment.

"We have the same problem," said the boy. "We could trade places more or less. Nothingness, chatter is all there is out there. Nothing is real. It's all idiotic, whatever side of the railing you happen to be on. Your feeling this way is a good thing! It means that the infinite Mind is at work, cutting you off from silly goals so you can be free. We are both free. Look at me. All I'm doing is following a blue angel dream all the way from New Hampshire via Long Island and a stolen car on Route 80 for the express purpose of running into you at this very moment and in this very place. What a setup. This place right here is a holy place, a sacred place, and this is where I was going on my dreamy pilgrimage. What's your name?" the boy asked.

"Harry," the youth responded, looking confused but curious. Still, he leaned out from the ledge. "Don't touch me or I jump."

"I've got zero interest in touching you, Harry, zero. I get why you are out there. I mean, aren't we all wondering what it all means? But we don't all jump. Suicide is pretty reasonable if there is no God and love on Route 80."

The boy paused, waiting to see if Harry would actually jump or keep talking, and thinking about what he could do to save him. The answer came in the form of a question.

"What the hell is a blue angel dream and what do you mean about following it across the country? You are weird, man. And what the hell is this Route 80 business? Maybe you really should be out here, and not me!" Harry exclaimed, smiling just a little.

"Hey, Harry, we are all out there at times, just like you," replied the boy. "Let me tell you about the dream and how I got to be standing here talking with you. Just promise that, if I tell you this story, you won't jump while I'm telling it. I need about a half hour."

"Okay, deal. What's your name, by the way?"

"Back at school they called me the boy or sometimes Ho because I always told pretty clean little jokes that made people laugh."

"Okay, Ho, tell me a joke."

"All right. Question: What did the fish say when it swam into the wall?"

"No idea, man."

"Answer: Damn!"

The youth burst out laughing, and the boy sensed that he was connecting a bit.

"Okay, what's the Irish definition of hospitality?"

"What?"

"You make someone feel perfectly at home while you be a-wishin' they were," said the boy.

The boy built on the moment by proceeding, over the course of the half an hour, to tell Harry every last detail about the blue angel dream he'd had up in New Hampshire, about Rev. Welles, about going to Yale Divinity School and meeting Dr. Dittes, about the infinite Mind, the big argument with Dad over the lampshade factory, leaving Lee and Livy, driving west, Dad's old Mercedes 190 and how the universe intervened and busted the generator, about that note to the Pennsylvania State Police, about Gary, about the hippies who asked him to call Mom collect from near Lincoln, Nebraska, how she was crazy enough to call the Pinkertons, and so forth, all in a run-on monologue reminiscent of Arlo

Guthrie's *Alice's Restaurant* and with a little movement and gesturing, like an actor on a cloud, or a dancer in the mist.

Harry was mesmerized. "That's really something. Did that blond kid really look like me?"

"Well, pretty much. I mean, not exactly in every detail, but more or less. You do seem to fill the bill pretty well because you certainly are leaning outwards on a ledge in the west!"

"Really, like me? You can't be sure. Maybe my life is not a cosmic mistake after all! Maybe if you came here out of a New Hampshire dream to meet me, there is something somewhere that loves me and wants me to live. So are you supposed to save me?"

"Hey Harry, if anyone's life is a cosmic mistake it's mine, because my folks met when Dad rear-ended Mom on the Long Island Expressway. I mean her car, of course."

The youth started to laugh, just like all the Paulies had in morning chapel a year ago.

"No, your life isn't a mistake. In fact, you are so special that it looks like the infinite Mind set up this whole Route 80 trip. I am supposed to save you so I can live…I don't know what that means exactly, but probably something. Remember, the blue angel said, 'If you save him, you too shall live.' "

"You can't save me!" the youth retorted and leaned out defiantly as if to let go.

"I have the answer! Harry, you don't need to jump because in the name of God, physics, and the universe I've got something for you that will solve all your problems. I mean *all*. It is perfect! I mean it only cost me fifty dollars and you can have it for free. It's guaranteed to help someone like you who is out on a ledge because it's the luckiest thing in the universe," the boy offered. "It absolutely works! Trust me."

"You have no idea what the hell you're talking about, but what do you have to give me?" he asked.

"Harry, get off that ledge and come on over here and look at the beautiful magical *Gohonzon* in my backpack because it brings whoever possesses it a lot of good fortune and blessings. It fixes their karma and helps them in the presence of infinite Mind," the boy responded. "You need to take this!" he offered excitedly, with a big smile.

And he pulled out the *Gohonzon* and unrolled it. He figured that if *Gohonzons* can really solve life's problems he would know for sure in a moment, because Harry would move away from the ledge.

Then the big moment came. Harry glanced at the scroll.

"Okay, I'm coming over to see this thing," Harry said, and he stepped over the railing onto the walkway. The boy was now himself just a little more convinced that *Gohonzons* work.

"Awesome!"

"Okay, let me see that thing. What is it? By the way, what's your real name?"

The boy said, "Just call me boy, like Stevie Boy." And he and the youth shook hands.

"It's a scroll written in Japanese. It says that if you possess it and chant every day your fortune will change for the better. I'm not supposed to give it away—bad luck if I do. But you can have it and see if it works. It got you from the ledge to here, anyway. They say that if I give it away it's bad karma, but that's okay if you use it well. We are kind of connected anyway—like through the dream. Anyway, if we are all in the Oneness, then when you benefit so do I, so we both flourish."

So Harry held the boy's *Gohonzon*. He was fascinated. He looked at it for a few minutes, traced the nicely printed Japanese calligraphy one symbol at a time, and suddenly he smiled wider than before. "Wow! What's it mean?"

And the boy proceeded to explain that the *Gohonzon* is a sacred object in Japanese Buddhism, and that you chant in front of it for luck. "It means something like Devotion to the Mysterious Mystic Principle, or something close to that anyway. I don't know that exactly, but it is about living as part of the infinite Mind and energy of love, or thereabouts," said the boy, and then he added, after a long pause staring at the object, "but I don't know Japanese. Maybe someday I will." He went on.

"It's all yours, Harry, but you have to do one thing if I give it to you. You have to walk through Golden Gate Park with this *Gohonzon* in your hand and take the Market Street bus straight to the Buddhist temple on the corner of Market and Chenery in the Mission District, and you have to ask for old Gus, and Gus will guide you. Tell him I sent you. Gus can help you to accept the emptiness, which is real, but then help you to find your own way, the dharma, the path. Running on empty is a great way to get to something deeper. It's your stairway to heaven, Harry. He can talk with you and teach you to chant and pray and live for others to get away from yourself. That's what I did all summer and look, I'm not outside the railing."

"You really think he can help me?"

"Harry, I know he can, and he can keep you on this side of the rail," replied the boy.

"And Harry, when you chant with them, it is a real experience where you forget about self and the problems of the self, and you don't have to seek meaning because you feel that you have found it in your awareness of the infinite Mind that you have within. It's like diving deep into the sea, and when you surface everything looks different and you won't be hanging out here on the ledge," said the boy.

"Harry, we are more connected than we know. Let me teach you to chant a bit."

Right there along the rails, the boy taught Harry to chant and together they called out loudly together across the San Francisco Bay as the sun burned away all the mist, *Nam myoho renge kyo, Nam myoho renge kyo...*

After about five minutes of chanting, Harry gave the boy a big hug, and intoned, "In-A-Gadda-Da-Vida," which the boy knew was a song from a band called Iron Butterfly.

"That means 'In the Garden of Life,' right?" the boy asked.

"Harry, I want your absolute pledge. Find Gus. And here is my cousin George's address. You can sleep there on the floor for as long as you need. He gets it, too. George was in Laos and he knows emptiness too. He has a cool motorcycle. Promise me, Harry."

And Harry looked out over the light blue as the sun burned off the fog, and yelled out, "I promise!"

The boy wrote down George's address for him and added a little note:

> To Cousin George Lamont,
> This is Harry. Please let him sleep in my spot on the
> living room floor while he gets it together. Make sure
> he meets Gus today. Take him over there, but he needs a
> shower first.
> Thanks Cousin. See you at Thanksgiving.

Harry walked slowly away from the boy and down along the bridge toward the park. Then he paused, turned around, and said, "Hey, man, you really are a dreamer. Good luck up north."

"World needs dreamers, you too," said the boy, with a smile.

The boy never saw Harry again, but over Thanksgiving break from
Reed, when he was down at George's, he learned that Harry had spent
a few weeks there, went to see Gus every day, loved chanting, stopped
doing drugs, and then headed back home to North Carolina somewhere
with his *Gohonzon* in hand. He had not been heard from Harry since or
ever again.

As the boy continued walking north along the nearly two-mile-long
span, suspended over the swirling waters of the Bay below, the sun
began to shine and the red-orange of the bridge came alive. It really
was not golden, but in the bright sun it looked fiery. Fire, he knew, is
often indicative of divine presence—a smoking firepot was the sign of
a covenant God made with Abraham, and then there was the burning
bush, and the Lord leading the Israelites disguised as a pillar of fire. As
the boy thought about those things, he felt the presence of the universal
Mind. He also thought about how fire is used to refine, and how the
bridge, where he had met Harry, had become a place of refinement
for him, too.

So the boy's soul was changed on the bridge because he felt that his
mysterious dream had come at least half true. Now he was living a new
life, having found the presence of the Lord on the bridge, and feeling
more guided in his journey. It was the closest thing to a burning bush
that a young, imaginative boy could experience. He felt uplifted and
very grateful. Now he knew what a great and awesome thing it was that
the Mercedes 190 broke down back on Route 80 when it did, and that all
was well. Now he was really going to sign up for Alchemy 101 at Reed
because it combined the history of science with quantum physics.

And in the years to come, the boy would stay changed. He would
sometimes tell his story about the dream, the car, 80, the ledge, and the
perfect synchronistic encounter with infinite Mind that occurred there
on the Golden Gate Bridge. But he only told the story if he encountered
someone who, like Harry, had to reclaim their soul in order to live.
There was no doubt in the boy's mind: that encounter had not just

happened by chance. It was, as the theologians say, a strangely *numinous* experience—one with such a strong spiritual quality that it could only have been holy and blessed. The boy was thankful for this moment on the bridge, and he knew that if he remembered to have gratitude, then other opportunities would come along because he was acknowledging the infinite Mind.

He also learned what "If you save him, you too shall live" means. It means that, if you follow a blue angel dream because you have faith that it is a holy lure into the unknown of Route 80, and you manage to do what it asks of you through a series of incredible synchronicities despite traveling three thousand hazardous miles on a pilgrimage to you know not quite where, you are going to begin to live anew, or be born again, and be truly alive. You passed the test.

***

Earlier, when he'd read up on them, the boy had learned that blue is one of the seven "angel colors," based on seven different light rays. The theologians of old said that blue angels protect and defend people. The boy knew nothing of what they call *angelology,* but he knew that angels are in the Bible, and he knew that old Mr. Muller believed in them, so he'd figured that maybe his blue angel was real or maybe it was not. For the boy meaning was something real and objective but it was also something we create, a little enchantment to help us survive.

After his experience on the bridge that morning, never again in life did the boy struggle for meaning. There were some ordeals here and there, peaks and valleys, but never again did he himself ever feel even a little on the ledge. He realized that we think we are more separate from each other than we are, and that, even if we are not fully aware of it, we are connected in the mystery of a Mind that ultimately holds us close despite all. Hope is being open to the surprises of graceful synchronicity that echo themes of connectedness.

All the pieces fit together, at least almost. The boy's discussions with Rev. Welles, reading of world scriptures along the wooded paths of Turkey Pond, and this entire astonishing escapade on Route 80 was just to set up that one meeting with Harry, to bring one person back from the ledge. This was why the generator broke so the boy could not turn back even though he wanted to and thus he continued on the road west to the end, not knowing what he might find but hoping that somewhere he might discover the ledge. Even that bad lottery number he had drawn in the draft had to happen, because otherwise he would never have walked across the Golden Gate Bridge early that morning headed north for Oregon. It was all synchronicity, not luck, although those with a disenchanted materialist worldview will have a different perspective than the boy.

And now that he had found the ledge and the youth, he could also grasp the simplest and most universal source of meaning possible, *If you save him, you too shall live.* The whole encounter was so gratifying and reassuring.

By the time the boy reached the end of the bridge, it was gleaming in the sun with spiritual Rx: Give and Glow, a daily vitamin for the soul.

But something felt incomplete to the boy. He wondered if he had really lived out the whole dream because, while he had saved the youth on the ledge, as the dream foretold, and experienced the sweetest oneness with infinite Mind as it had now surely manifested in this uncanny encounter, would he himself be saved in turn from some unforeseen perilous episode of fear and trembling? Had he to be saved, literally, or just metaphorically? He was not certain how the words, "You too shall be saved" were meant. What awaited him in Oregon? He sensed that this pilgrimage did not end at the Golden Gate.

Interlude

Dad's Mercedes 190 in the driveway at home

Normalcy is a paved road. It's comfortable to walk, but no flowers grow on it.

—Vincent Van Gogh

Being love, rather than giving or taking love, is the only thing that provides stability.

—Ram Dass

You can only come to the morning through the shadows.

—J. R. R. Tolkien

How to Follow a Dream—Lesson Two: There is a ledge, but the ledge isn't such a bad thing. Once we are out on it, we have to set aside all pretensions and false sources of meaning. Then God can inspire us early on in life so there might be real spiritual meaning over the course of our entire lifetimes, rather than only after many wasted decades pursuing meaningless goals before having a midlife spiritual crisis, or before regretting our entire lives at the sad moment of that last dying breath, having never figured out what success really is. Being out on the ledge young may not be easy and it can be dangerous, but at least we ask the right big questions. Some never do. So it is best in the long run to trust the wayward spiritual dream when we are pretty sure it is deeply meaningful, come what may.

When we take desperate detours in growing up, infinite Mind can awaken us in wonderful ways that are not possible if all we are doing is collecting all the perfect pedigrees and toeing the line. Often our depth of need calls the surprises of synchronicity into being. God sometimes tests us with different kinds of dreams but is already there down the highway waiting for us with uncanny encounters and divine whispers that tell us how cherished we are despite our doubts.

Boys who make no mistakes make nothing. Synchronicity is proof of Oneness.

A Gohonzon scroll

The world is full of magical things, patiently waiting for our sense to grow sharper.

—Ralph Waldo Emerson

The Biker and the Premonition: "You Too Shall Live"

Deep down the consciousness of mankind is one. This is a virtual certainty.

–David Bohm

T he boy wondered that morning, as he stood with thumb out on
Route 1 headed north to Portland, if another big white truck like
Gary's would stop immediately, like a powerful white horse whose rider
was on some holy quest. No white truck showed up, so he had to wait
for an hour in the sun at the northern end of the bridge until he finally
got a lift in a beat-up, rusty green pickup truck owned by Mr. Dwayne
Dill from Santa Rosa.

"Hey there, boy, you headed north? My name is Dwayne Dill, yup, D-I-
L-L just like in dillllll pickle, and this here is my wife Dorothy Dill. We're
driving to Oregon from Santa Rosa." And the boy climbed into the truck
with his stuff and sat down beside Dorothy to enjoy a wonderful ride
north that took pretty much all day.

The Dills were people of faith, and they read some Bible verses to the
boy who, thanks to Mr. Muller, already knew a lot of them. Green is
thought to be a color of life and healing,[16] and the boy recalled the
green farmer's truck that had picked him up back in Saltillo, Mexico.
It was a healing drive along Route 1, comfortable and a lot like being
back in the Mullers' kitchen. The Dills wondered why a boy with his
knowledge of the Bible was going to Reed College of all places, but the
boy said he would be fine, and that "The Lord is with you wherever you
go."[17] This is true, and a lot of people can stay home and do not need
to take a Route 80 pilgrimage, but for some reason the boy chose to
follow a dream.

It was at Reed that the boy had another profound, lived experience of
infinite Mind. That experience would stick with him just as much as the
youth on the ledge because through it he was very literally saved from a
certain death, completing the second half of the prophecy, "If you save
him, *you too shall live.*" He too would live, but just barely. From then on,
he was on borrowed time.

---

16   Rev. 4:3.
17   Joshua 1:9

Kesey and Bly

The boy arrived at Reed around six o'clock that evening. He had never been there before, and he was surprised to see a white plastic bubble-tent about a quarter the size of a basketball court on the college green, with a few hundred kids hanging out inside and outside. Loud rock music was playing, and bright colors projected onto the tent lit up the surface in the early evening as dusk approached and the sun was setting.

A stocky man with curly red hair and a large bald spot on the top of his head sat holding a can of beer in one hand and a cigar-like entity in the other. The boy approached him and, speaking loudly over the music and the shouts of the crowd, asked in the fashion of a good St. Paul's boy, "Sir, is this Reed College?"

The man smiled, exhaling smoke in the boy's face and simultaneously revealing a full red, white, and blue American flag permanently ensconced on his upper-right front tooth. He pointed to it with his pinky, cigar-like object in hand.

"Yeah, little buddy," he answered. "And you don't need to call me sir. No one calls me sir. Call me Ken."

"Okay. It's just a high school habit, Ken. Glad to know I'm here."

"Well, you were supposed to be here and that's why you are, otherwise you would not be here but instead over there, or maybe just everywhere." And with that, Ken blew a second blast of smoke in the boy's face. That was quite an encounter, and maybe it too was synchronicity. Sometimes you encounter people to teach you how not to be. The boy wandered away and asked a young bearded kid who that man "Ken" was.

"Ken Kesey," he responded.

"Damn, I called Ken Kesey sir! How cool."

Kesey was no role model. Quite the contrary. But Kesey was in Oregon writing his second novel, *Sometimes a Great Notion*, having decided that the world of San Francisco hippies was too superficial. He had grown up near Eugene and still had family there. He was visiting the college campus that afternoon with some of his notorious followers, known popularly as the Merry Pranksters in large part for their psychedelic shenanigans.

The boy was more for Kerouac than Kesey, anyway. He loved Kerouac quotes like "All human beings are also dream beings. Dreaming ties all mankind together," or, "But no matter, the road is life," or "I had nothing to offer anybody but my own confusion." Kerouac drank himself to death, but he sensed something profound. "Dreaming ties all mankind together." The boy knew this to be true.

Around seven in the evening Pacific coast time, the boy called his mother (collect) in New York and told her he had made it to college, so to speak. She was relieved, until he told her that the very first person he ran into was Ken Kesey.

"Mom, I just met Ken Kesey and he said I could call him Ken! What do you think about that? The guy blew smoke in my face too, but I'm okay!"

Mom was silent for about two minutes, possibly because she was experiencing a bout of anxious dyspepsia. The boy recalled that she'd read Tom Wolfe's account of the Kesey phenomenon, *The Electric Kool-Aid Acid Test*, because she had mentioned it earlier in the summer, and the boy had leafed through the first few pages as it sat on the kitchen table among the ashtrays.

"Gee, Mom, maybe I shouldn't have said that."

"Oh, my God! Are you really okay?" Mom asked.

After a brief pause, the boy responded, "Don't worry about a thing, Mom. He had no influence on me whatsoever! Besides, I'm sure I'm safer here than in the Bronx."

"You want me to send you anything?"

"Nope, I'm good. Thanks for covering a bit of the tuition after all. Just letting you know that I made it to Portland."

The boy never again saw Kesey, who was headed for the Willamette River to write about the lumberjacks.

***

When the boy finally met Robert Bly, he saw he was true to form. A migrant to Oregon from Minnesota by way of San Francisco, Bly was by far the most musical of the poets. The boy considered him the true poet laureate of the country, though he was a little far-out for most. That summer Bly had spent a few evenings at City Lights Books, the classic bookstore in San Francisco where all the great poets gathered and read their works, and it was said that no one performed their poems better than Bly.

Bly sometimes had his students sit in a circle on the floor of the seminar room and as he plucked his one-string, turtle-shell instrument he asked them to sing a word: fast, slow, high, low, loud, soft, and with periods of silence that were as important as periods of sound. These axes of contrast, all working simultaneously, are what give emotional power and depth to words, like great music. Those were days when they could easily spend a whole hour simply repeating the word "tranquility" or "murmur," all together, or not at all. Bly was a poet who really lived in another world as well as this one. He put himself into some deep inner state, so that his poems seemed to emanate from divine Mind, and he encouraged the boy and his classmates to cultivate their own spiritual consciousness. He read sections of his *The Light Around the Body.* And when he read his poems, it was as if he made every word blaze across the sky; his phrasing was like Copeland's *Fanfare for the Common Man*, full of intensity and enduring impact. Just hearing him was worth the quest west.

Bly was a spiritual man who believed in Jung, archetypes, and the collective unconscious mind that connects us all; he believed that Mind is more than matter, and that we all share in it. In short, he was an infinite Mind kind of guy, and so was the boy, who now had nothing to live for but a blue dream that had already come true.

So when the boy told Bly about his blue angel dream and about the youth on the ledge and the *Gohonzon* and how he was not overly certain about the nature of "God" but that the idea has something to do with an infinite original universal Mind in which we are all connected and cherished, and that is a force for goodness, the bard simply said, "Sounds so."

But the boy's next encounter with connectivity was not about Kesey or Bly. It was about a mad biker and Mom's premonition from almost three thousand miles away. It is what sealed the deal for the boy on the reality of nonlocal infinite Mind, and affirmed conclusively for him that an infinite Mind indwells in all of us and is playing the loving conductor behind the scenes—in this case revealing itself so powerfully that the boy would never forget its living, loving reality throughout his life, and moving him to share it with others.

You Too Shall Live: The Boy's Near-Death Experience and Mom's Premonition

This is about Mom's "nonlocal" long-distance phone call, prompted by her equally long-distance participation in infinite Mind connectivity—participation intensified by the fact that motherhood also means the anticipatory extension of anxiety beyond oneself, so that it includes at least the immediate family. That's why moms tend to have premonitions when their children are endangered, even in faraway places. They sense the danger. But it is also about the fulfillment of the dreaming words, "you too shall live."

That winter, late in January, the boy came to take the idea of nonlocal mind completely to heart—because of a memorable experience that involved his mother.

Reed's student coffeehouse tended to fill up on the weekends. One rainy Saturday night at about ten o'clock, the boy was drinking a cup of tea and talking with a couple of folks from his Alchemy 101 class, comparing quantum models of connectivity with models devised by medieval minds. Suddenly, in walked a thin fellow with a mustache who was about twenty-six or twenty-seven years old and wearing a black leather jacket. He was on the flamboyant side, his eyes were on the wild side, and he yelled out over the room:

"My name is Andy from LA, and I have a brand-new Harley. Who wants to take a ride?"

No one responded.

"Please, someone? It's a super-fast Shovelhead engine, as fast as they make 'em."

"Damn, I will," declared the boy. "Why not? I haven't ever ridden on a bike before, much less a super-fast Shovelhead. And no one else is going to ride with this guy."

So they went out to the parking lot and the boy jumped on the back of a very large and heavy motorcycle that looked like some sort of Batman special. The night was not snowy or especially icy, but the asphalt of the parking lot was wet from the light rain that was still falling, making it slushy and slippery. That was not good, but the tires on this thing were really wide.

To the boy's great shock, no sooner were they on the bike than Andy stomped on the gas pedal and within about thirty seconds they were doing 120 miles an hour and headed for the highway, ignoring all the red lights and stop signs. They got out on the Pacific Coast Highway and skidded south on the wet slick of the pavement. The boy hung on for dear life, with the cold rain beating on his face and his wavy brown hair streaming behind him in the wind, like a flag in a hurricane.

He screamed, "Stop, let me off now! You are going to get us both killed! It's too slippery!"

But Andy just laughed like a drugged-up sociopath.

The boy considered himself dead, and he quickly repeated the Lord's Prayer and anxiously chanted *nam myoho renge kyo,* all with his eyes closed tightly and the rain beating painfully against his face and hands.

After speeding down the highway for about half an hour, Andy did a wild 180-degree Evel Knievel turn, jumping the bike across the muddy midway, and finally headed back toward Portland, hitting 160 miles an hour.

The boy almost wished he hadn't given away his *Gohonzon.* He wondered if this was some sort of punishment. But he only gave it away to save a life, so it should be okay.

At last Andy skidded back onto campus and pulled up to the exact spot where he had picked the boy up less than an hour before, although the boy felt like he had been clinging to the back of that cycle for much longer than that. He jumped off, totally shaken and pulverized, as Andy laughed loudly into the dark sky before accelerating off, engine blasting in the night.

The boy had had an absolutely frightening near-death experience and knew that he had been delivered from the darkness to live the rest of his life in the light.

Now here is the nonlocal infinite Mind part, where Mom comes in.

The boy walked slowly back across the bridge over the ravine to his dormitory and stumbled into the common room, headed for his bed. Just as he entered the building, the pay phone on the wall started ringing. For no reason, he felt an urge to walk over and pick up the receiver—something the boy never ever did, ever. It was impossible at that time to reach the boy by phone unless he made the call. But he had given the pay phone number to Mom when he talked to her after his Kesey encounter, so she was able to call that night and call she did, in a total panic, at about two o'clock New York time, sounding petrified.

"You're alive! I had the most terrible feeling that you were about to die. I was sound asleep, and I woke up with this shock and fear in my soul and I knew for sure that you were deader than a door nail."

"Mom, you got that exactly right, but I didn't quite die! Close enough, though. I was just out on the Pacific Coast Highway, on a motorcycle driven by a crazy guy at 140 miles an hour in the sleet and rain. I am surprised to be alive. He was probably drugged up. His eyes were on fire like Roman candles in the dark and he must have been sadistic or something, because he really enjoyed almost killing us. He was screaming and laughing like the devil. How did you know?"

"Mothers just feel these things. They know them. It's a mystery."

"But Mom, you're almost three thousand miles away."

"Distance doesn't matter, sometimes moms just know. I was sound asleep and then woke up with a terrible feeling and heard you scream out and so I called."

"Okay, Mom, well…thanks. You are kind of like a radio picking up a wave, aren't you?"

"Maybe we all are. Get warmed up and try to sleep."

"Okay, Mom. But let me just tell you that when I was back at St. Paul's, I had a recurring dream and deep down felt that I had to come west for something destined to actually happen."

And the boy told his Mom about the blue angel dream for the first time, and why he thought the Mercedes broke down just when it did, and that he had saved a youth on a ledge. Mom listened without interrupting.

She responded, "Well, you know your great grandfather, Cast Iron John the Sag Harbor harpoonist, came to America with his father after his mom had had a dream that the English were coming to hang them both for sedition. So sometimes dreams do save lives."

"You know Mom, you have been telling us that story for many years and I never fully appreciated it until now." The boy continued:

"But, Mom, the thing about the blue angel dream is that I couldn't really figure out the words 'you too shall live.' I mean, sure, I could realize that in helping others we help ourselves too, and in this sense we live more fully. But I was not exactly certain that I too had been saved. But after tonight, with the death ride of a lifetime, I feel that I really should be dead. Mom, I should be dead after that crazy Andy ride. But I was saved by God to live because after all I had saved the youth on the ledge, and now I could be saved too. This may sound like a stretch, but I think that the two things are intermingled. So now I finally really know what it meant when the angel said, 'If you save him, you too shall live.' "

The boy was realizing then that he was destined to head up to Oregon, because how else could he have encountered crazy drugged-up Andy and come so close to death on the Pacific Coast Highway that his mom could have a fear-filled promotion that night, all those miles away and prove once and for all that the human mind has a mysterious nonlocal aspect that is beyond matter and place. The boy also was able to have fulfilled the blue angel prophecy because he had **both saved** on the

Golden Gate and then six months later **been saved himself** on the icy
wet roads of the great Northwest.

Yes, the mystery of Mind. He was shown with vivid clarity that the
human mind is not just a conglomeration of chemicals, cells, and tissue
from which it is entirely derived. Rather, there is a mysterious nonlocal
aspect to the mind, an aspect completely beyond time and place, which
is to say that we are all interconnected within the mental field of an
infinite divine universal and original Mind, like millions of points of
light, like the Hindus teach so well.

The boy went upstairs to his dorm suite, still shaken, and fell asleep
thinking that a mom's mind is a mysterious thing, and for that matter,
so is every human mind, because there is something about a mind that
is beyond time and place. The boy had written about this Jungian idea a
year earlier for Rev. Welles's class in Concord, and hanging around with
Bly made it easier to write about. But now his Mom had helped him
understand it even better. In her phone call to the boy that night, she
had confirmed the message of his journey to the west—infinite Mind
connects us all.

Mind Is Not Matter

Matter is local, like cells, tissues, and brain existing in one place at one
time. But Mind is not restricted to locality, and the miles between New
York and Oregon mean nothing to it. Therefore, Mind is not derived
from matter, but is something entirely different. The Greek philosopher
Plato proposed the existence of *Nous*, of Mind existing separately from
matter, over two thousand years ago, although without the attribute of
divine Love that expresses itself as personal caring and concern.

Indeed, it is likely that all matter and energy derive from the singular
Mind that precedes and underlies all. Lao Tzu, the ancient Chinese sage,
simply referred to it as "The Way"—"The Tao that can be told is not the

eternal Tao. The name that can be named is not the eternal name. The nameless is the beginning of heaven and earth…."

Mom intuited that the boy was about to die, from 2,972 miles away, in a different time zone. There is absolutely no way that a materialistic model of mind can explain this because, whatever energy a brain might generate—or transmit—that energy could not extend outward more than a few inches or so. Only the highest-powered electronic tower can communicate that far.

In other words, a brain may be located in some specific physical space, but each mind must possess a dimension of nonmaterial substance that is beyond locality and concrete physicality. Between Mom's premonition and meeting the youth on the ledge, the boy knew the divine Mind was giving him private lessons on how limited a materialistic and "closed-off" view of the mind is, because Mind cannot be derived from matter or explained by it. It is a different nonmaterial reality beyond time and place, and it is truly a part of God, a spiritual gift, what some call a soul. The neuroscientists are always trying to figure out the origins of Consciousness in the matter of the brain, but none of them can explain this. The more logical view is that matter and energy all derive from infinite Mind, which was there eternally before things began unfolding from it in a Big Bang with perfectly rational mathematical principles, constants, and thermodynamics to perfectly set up the platform for our being and becoming. In this sense, this beautiful planet earth gives testimony to divine synchronicity, but we miss such an obvious truth and maltreat our land, oceans, and skies.

Is this really such a strange idea? Not to most people who express their spiritual and religious intuitions. But others have been too easily swayed by a materialist view of the universe that insists that every aspect of the human mind and the of the universe can be reduced to matter.

Consider those intuitive moments when you just "know" something, as if tapping into a higher level of knowledge. Consider the synchronistic encounters that seem to happen as the explicit answer to a prayer. Consider the surprising premonitions that people have, and the dreams that turn out to be true. Consider the significant numbers of creative people in the sciences and arts who have worked hard to master their fields and develop their expertise, but who also describe their most innovative breakthroughs in terms of a visionary moment when they felt like they were participating in the omniscience of universal Mind.

Premonitions and Moms

The boy thought about how a mother's deep love and concern had allowed her mind to transcend locality and reach out across 2,972 miles of space through its connection with the one Mind. Maybe the Mind as a reality that connects us all becomes most evident when selfless love is intensely felt and urgency is great. After Mom's premonition, the boy never again believed anyone who claimed that our minds are walled off from each other. Separate and individual—fenced off, yes—but walled off, never.

Mom prayed for the boy and said her Rosary like a good Irish lass from Bridgehampton does when her son strays into dangerous territories. Premonitions, meaning literally "forewarnings" from the Latin, are so typically experienced between parents and children, between spouses, siblings, and close friends. This is because there is something about deep, anxious, and selfless love that moves us so far beyond ego and selfishness that we can most powerfully enter the field of the infinite Mind, which is also a field of infinite Love. When premonitions occur, it is a sign that the walls between "I" and "You" have been replaced by oneness, and at that frequency of love the miracles of premonition and synchronicity are most likely to happen.

In case you're still not sure about this idea of a higher Mind of oneness and connectivity, here is an account that Jo-Ann Triner, a school administrator in Columbus, Ohio, sent to the boy in 2014.

My mother was a firsthand witness to the encounter below. She was still a young girl when the event occurred and told the story to me countless times with the utmost conviction:

My dearly beloved grandfather, his wife, and their five children slept soundly most nights, warmed by the coal furnace that he so lovingly tended each evening. In both a physical and a spiritual sense, he was the keeper of the fire, a man of unusual love and warmth. But on this particular occasion, as all slept peacefully, that cozy family feeling was interrupted when he arose from a vivid dream in a deep state of anguish, distraught enough to throw on the house lights and awaken the entire family from their slumber. He was a man of steel and not easily shaken, but on this night he was inconsolable, overcome with emotion, recounting the horrific images in his dream of his brother in Poland, trapped in a barn fire and crying out for help. Convinced that something dreadful had actually happened, he marked the date on the wall calendar in the kitchen. Months later he received a letter from family members in Poland, disclosing the violent death of his brother in a barn fire on that very same night.

This tragic incident again suggests that, under the right circumstances, we can connect with those we love through nonmaterial Mind. Love is a feeling that the happiness, security, and well-being of another is as real and important to you as your own, or even more so. In some way, the energy of such pure love may respond to feelings of fear and alarm in those we care deeply about and, in so doing, transcend the apparent limits of time and space.

Someday, maybe we will all become aware of our Oneness within the infinite Mind, and then we can know that when we help another we also help ourselves because we are more connected than we are aware, and that when we hurt another we also hurt ourselves. And then in Oneness peace will come at last, and all of our journeys will be complete in joy. We will have reclaimed our souls.

Interlude

A college boy awakening

You are not a drop in the ocean. You are the entire ocean in a drop.

—Rumi

Become a good noticer. Pay attention to the feelings, hunches, and intuitions that flood your life. If you do, you will see that premonitions are not rare, but a natural part of our lives.

—Larry Dossey

Where there is great doubt, there will be great awakening; small
doubt, small awakening; no doubt, no awakening.

–Zen Proverb

How to Follow a Dream—Lesson Three: Boys are especially prone
to do crazy things sometimes because, in most cases, their brains
are undeveloped when it comes to future-mindedness and executive
function, at least until they hit twenty-five. If they evolved to be short-
lived spear throwers, this makes sense. Girls are a little less crazy on the
whole because, if they become moms, they will have to be protective
and future-minded when looking after kids. A boy's mom is always
thinking of him, and mother-love is to some degree the vicarious
extension of anxiety, because you were born from your mom while
your dad just hung around watching. Your dad is less likely to wake
up three thousand miles away in a fearful premonition because you
did something crazy risky. Boys should in general avoid motorcycles,
especially when the drivers are pretty clearly drugged-up, but the fact
that boys might not do so indicates a real neurological deficit.

Moms have that deep sort of love which means that your happiness
and security as a foolish boy mean as much to them as their own
and probably even more. That is exactly what love means: when the
happiness and security of another is a real to you as your own, you
love that person. Dads love too, but not quite like moms. Their love
goes way beyond the limits of place, time, and local mind. Their love
demonstrates in comprehensible terms our participation in the shared
nonmaterial, and therefore nonlocal, one Mind behind the many.

Boys should be grateful for the unconditional love of their moms, which
is always there even when a boy leaves a family car out on Route 80 and
doesn't call home until he hits Nebraska.

A super-fast Harley-Davidson Shovelhead

Something very beautiful happens to people when their world has fallen apart: a humility, a nobility, a higher intelligence emerges at just that point when our knees hit the floor.

–Marianne Williamson

Mom's painting of the blue angel dream

The Patients and the Rice Balls: Route 80 in New York

No one knows the weight of another's burden.

—George Herbert

W hen he got back to New York City, the boy was still following the dream, but dreams can grow dim when you are under pressure to pay the bills and navigate the long gray shadows cast by the concrete buildings with the massive crowds rushing past them too busy to say hello. New Yorkers are kind people, but that fact can get lost in the relentless pressures to survive with the thin line between having a tiny apartment to call home and sleeping on the street. In short, New York City is a place where kindness can be overwhelmed, and dreams can fade. But it can work well if you can preserve your soul wherever you go, and New York wonderfully tests the depth of our spirits.

Out on Route 80, the whole open highway before the boy was enchanted and sustained by the one Mind. He had been on a marvelous pilgrimage to the unknown west and he had found the sacred spot on a bridge. But New York posed a challenge and a test. Could it be a place of spiritual growth, rather than an invitation to anxiety?

The boy really had no choice. He had to do something to stick with his dream so as not to abandon his spiritual journey and lose meaning. Why not work with more people on more ledges, and then he would flourish not so much as directly intended but as an acceptable side effect or by-product of helping others? So in faith and synchronicity the boy meditated while seated on a bench in Brooklyn Heights near the Hotel St. George, said a prayer and opened up the jobs section of the *New York Post* that he had just bought at the subway entrance on Clark and Henry Streets. This was one of those moments when he was going to check out whatever advertisement involved helping other Harrys of any age on ledges.

The Dream and the Dialysis Patients

And so the boy's first job was as a dialysis technician at the Manhattan Dialysis Center on 30th Street in midtown, as advertised that morning in the *Post*. The boy had read about these kidney machines in the Northwest because of the "God committees" in Seattle where respectable people gathered in a small circle to decide who should be saved since there were not enough machines to go around. Needless to say, they decided to save other respectable people just about like them—white, educated, married, professional. The Pacific Northwest would have been a bad place for a blue angel dreamer with kidney failure. Kidney machines were still pretty new then and dialysis was a challenging ordeal for patients, but now they were free for everyone, thanks to the US Congress, and there were plenty of them.

Within two weeks, the boy was numbing up the skin over the bovine graft in countless wrist veins before slipping in the butterfly needle and watching the blood flow red through a clear rubber line, destined for a white plastic coil surrounded by warm water for osmotic cleaning inside a white tub that looked like an old-fashioned washing machine.

So he could connect a little better with the patients, the boy kept a journal about their experiences. He asked them what was hardest for them about dialysis, what worried them most about getting hooked up, about how they coped, if they felt that they were being treated well, and if they ever had days when they didn't want to come in. He observed that sometimes they were treated with respect and kindness, but sometimes not, and this made a big difference. The ones who were treated unkindly were more likely to stop showing up for their appointments, meaning that within a week or so they were dead. So the boy really understood that love truly heals when patients are undergoing a demanding procedure with no end in sight for a chronic condition.

So, after a few night shifts, the boy determined to treat everyone kindly, like VIPs at a fancy hotel, and to welcome the most difficult patients. This worked pretty well, and he tried to sound a little like Mr. Rogers when he talked with them because anyone can be hostile when dealing with such a harsh illness. He tried to be a steady role model for his coworkers and focus on the little things when interacting with patients, like tone of voice, listening well, and being a clear communicator.

The number of patients leaving for good dropped, and the director, the distinguished Dr. Dean from Columbia University Medical Center, complimented the boy and suggested he think about becoming a physician one day. The staff noticed too and asked the boy to spend more time talking with patients and not to worry quite so much about actually putting them on the machines, getting heparin shots into their lines, cleaning plastic coils, and all of the more technical things, though he still did those things too, like everyone else. He was learning that healing never happens without loving-kindness, and everyone working with these patients has to understand that. Even if his colleagues were not as naturally empathic and present in a heart-centered way as they could have been, they still had to say the right things. They might not have a natural emotional connection with patients, but going through the motions is still better than treating them like biological slabs. The boy noted that the dialysis technicians who provided kind and more personalized care tended to be happier and made fewer errors.

The room where the patients were treated was large, about a hundred feet square, with about ten dialysis machines lining each of the four walls and a comfortable brown recliner next to each machine because those were three hours when a patient needed to be able to rest and relax while experiencing physical and emotional struggles.

Sometimes the techs got so busy that they forgot to inject heparin into the lines to keep the blood from coagulating. They were not just the uncaring ones, but mostly. This caused the plastic coils to form a bubble and explode, spraying blood all over the white ceiling and nearby patients. Hepatitis B infection was a constant danger, especially when the blood splattered around. But dialysis technicians accepted the risk, and some did get sick—that came with the territory.

The boy managed to explode a coil and felt guilty about it as elderly African-American patient Fred went into a severe BP drop, all the buzzers started buzzing wildly, and the system crashed. Fred got through it, and the boy sincerely apologized.

"Fred, I forgot the heparin because I was so busy. I am really sorry. Please forgive me."

"That's okay, don't worry about it. Those who make no mistakes make nothing," he said.

"I like that. It makes sense. Those who make no mistakes make nothing. Did you make that up?" asked the boy.

"Actually, a lot of people have said that or something like it, even Einstein and Dr. King," answered Fred. "Anyway, you are doing your best and we all like you."

The boy became a full dialysis technician almost right away because no one else much wanted to take the risk, and because there weren't that many regulations at the time. The whole idea of helping others at some risk to oneself was a big part of the job, and yet no one in their right mind ever wants to get sick. You just have to accept the possibility and try to be careful. Risks come with the territory, but that doesn't mean that you are looking for them. If you were looking for them, that would be really strange. The techs talked a lot about the risks, and some got really ill. The boy tried to avoid sticking himself with needles but did so at least a dozen times. Still, he stayed well.

It was about midnight on Christmas Eve, during the thirteen-hour night shift with a cheap tape player echoing "The Little Drummer Boy" and other carols, when a coil exploded in the middle of the big treatment room.

Things got pretty emotional and chaotic that night after the coil popped, and everyone needed to calm down. Blood pressures were dropping, with beepers going off left and right, and the stress was on everyone's faces. Adding to the uproar, Edwina, a poor, thin, heroin-addicted African-American patient, was naturally in withdrawal during her dialysis and started loudly singing the old Negro spiritual: "I got a sister in Beulah Land, she outshines the sun. I got a sister in Beulah Land, way beyond the stars." Beulah Land means heaven, and Edwina was thinking about following along on that final journey. The boy sang with her a bit, because he knew the song from listening to Mississippi John Hurt at Folk City on West 4th Street.

The technician who was responsible, a nice young gal from Rye, started weeping. The boy took her to the middle of the big room and quietly told her what Fred said to him about making mistakes, and she calmed down.

The boy, unable to think of any other options, stood by the long black lab table in the middle of the room and asked if everyone wanted to hear a story, because it was Christmas, and—even if they didn't celebrate Christmas—would it be okay? They all nodded their approval. Most of them kept some of the symbols from their particular religious tradition near their chairs, and it was easy to see that faith and prayer were how many of them coped with their profound challenges. Religion and medicine have such historic synergy.

And so with a smile the boy told them about his blue angel dream and going to the class at Yale. He told them about the lampshade factory, the argument with Dad, the Mercedes 190 and Route 80, calling Mom from Nebraska, George, Gus, the youth on the ledge, Andy the wild biker, Mom's premonition, and why he believed in universal Mind. He walked around the big center table, making eye contact with everyone in the room. There was total quiet during the entire forty-five minutes that the boy spoke—sometimes quietly and sometimes more loudly, sometimes quickly and sometimes slowly, but always trying to make the story engaging, involving…even captivating. It was a Christmas performance.

People were mesmerized, and all the anxiety in the room evaporated. Everyone calmed down, and you could hear a pin drop.

When the boy finished his story, an elderly Jewish woman said, "Oh, my God, that was some note you left out there on the Mercedes! Your dad must have been really mad at you!" while smiling mischievously like it was really okay. "You're still a very nice boy, but please don't take his car ever again. It's bad for your reputation. You sound kabbalistic, by the way—very. You sound like Chagall, running off like that after a big argument with your poor dad."

The boy had not heard that about Chagall's life yet, but he knew who he was.

Others chimed in with countless questions about the details of the story, and one patient even wondered if the boy's parents weren't right about the Bronx being too dangerous. That sparked a huge debate. But mainly they asked about the dream itself, and if it ever recurred after the boy turned seventeen, which it didn't.

"It doesn't have to return. I just have to follow it," answered the boy.

The boy asked them if, when they came in for dialysis, they felt a little close to the ledge and thought about not coming back again for treatment, and how the staff could help with that. At this point things got really deep, revealing all the struggles that people went through day by day, and what they still hoped for in life, especially if they were waiting for an organ donor.

"Well, everyone, we are all always close to a ledge. But if we can create a little community here, and be kind to everyone else, it should help. Here with these machines we can't fool ourselves about the ledge, because every couple of weeks there is someone who goes missing for one reason or another, but it will happen less if you can all think of yourselves as wounded healers, as people who can help other people with kidney failure just based on your experience of it."

So the boy asked the patients to openly share with one another the things that they struggled with most, were still grateful for, and hoped for. And one by one the patients started talking, with the help of a little microphone that the boy passed around. It was astounding to hear about those hopes, of every sort, and how people saw a pathway to a better future. Hope for some was just the idea of seeing family on Christmas, and for others it was looking forward to a transplant. They all had hopes. And they all had fears. This went on for about two hours. And early on that Christmas morning, half the patients spoke of hope as knowing that God loved them, and about experiencing God's love directly or through others. And even though the other half said nothing about this, spirituality was in the air.

Then Edwina started singing the song "Amen" from the movie *Lilies in the Field*, and everyone joined in, patients and staff. There were some great voices among them that we had never heard before.

And Fred had a great deep voice and he was standing, now fully recovered, and singing like he was in the Riverside Church choir.

So the boy—patients came to refer to him as "the boy"—became someone they called on to sit down by their big chairs and steady them, often by just listening, which was mostly all it took. Patients want to be listened to. It got to the point where, before he poked some bovine vein graft with a butterfly needle, seeking access on a deeply needle-scarred wrist or leg, folks would ask for a prayer. Sometimes the boy brought his classical guitar and played quiet pieces like Tarrega's *Recuerdos de la Alhambra* late at night, or other calming music. The Spanish stuff does that for people. Music heals too.

***

After his Christmas Eve experience, the boy realized that he could share his encounters with God and love on Route 80 with pretty much any imperiled person at the right time and in the right place and give them a way to smile and be open to happy surprises. "*If you save him, you too shall live.*" Here he was with so many seriously ill people on a different ledge, using his wits and creativity to get folks through their dark nights of the soul. So even in New York City, around a lot of really suffering people, he could re-create an enchanted Route 80 world and bring the Golden Gate east.

Some of the alcoholic and addicted patients had not showered in a long time. A few cursed, and they could lie a lot. When the machines pumped the drugs from their blood they moaned sadly, although the machines did not pump out all the heroin molecules because they are large. The boy asked those patients if they hoped to go straight one day, and they all did. That was when he learned from them about twelve-step programs and Narcotics Anonymous and AA, and one patient brought in the AA "Big Book" about the steps and how to recover by humbly trusting God and serving others. So the boy got a copy of the Big Book and late at night he would read passages from it with these especially endangered patients. Sometimes he spoke of Gus and how he just liked to keep a clear mind.

"See, your mind is God's gift, it is a little drop of the infinite Mind, and there is a mystery to it," the boy explained, and people wanted to talk about that. Most believed that they had an eternal soul, a spiritual mind, that was more than matter.

The boy would take the late afternoon subway into Manhattan from Clark Street in Brooklyn Heights and think about all the patients he was going to be putting on dialysis machines that night. He envisioned their faces, imagined their voices, and asked for guidance from the divine Mind about what they needed. Was it attentive listening, compassion, mirth, guidance, "carefrontation"? Sometimes he would tear up just a bit on that subway ride back to Brooklyn, or as he walked through Clark Street station past the flower sellers, because he felt grateful to have been out on Route 80 and to be able to tell about the experiences he had there.

Those nine months pumping blood with people on the ledge, telling them about Route 80 and playing his guitar for them, meant a lot. He came to view the blue angel dream as a lifelong gift. But then he decided to move on, just because he had witnessed a lot and learned much, but he needed a break. Many of the patients brought him little gifts, and they all spoke with him warmly and wished him well. To this day, the boy sometimes visits dialysis centers to do clinical pastoral care.

Rice Balls on 71st Street

The boy got a job working in the lab of a Dr. New, a wonderful pediatrician researcher at New York Hospital. He moved from Brooklyn Heights to East 71st Street, three doorways west of York Avenue, to an old five story walk-up apartment building that is still there. It had an old tub but no shower. Having finally majored in biology in college, mostly because of a crush on a blonde girl named Eliza from Minneapolis who was pre-med, he was now a "research assistant" helping in the lab to measure the hormone levels of intersex children.

Still the teetotaler, the boy avoided bars but frequented all the lectures on spiritual thinkers and practices of every tradition that he came across in Manhattan, east and west, north and south, and visited and observed spiritual communities throughout Greater New York, from Hasidic Jews to Krishnas to Rastafarians to Spiritists to the Unity School of Christianity. He also read everything he could find about spirituality, just like he had as a student at St. Paul's, walking around Turkey Pond. The boy did not just tolerate other religions, he celebrated them in all their differences and tried to learn as much as he could from each one.

Still, the elegance of the Episcopal prayers and liturgy stayed with him, but not in some empty formulaic way. The boy felt that Jesus was fully one with the one Mind and aware of its responsiveness to him in every moment, and that is how he could heal people like he did. He was unique in his degree of awareness of oneness with infinite Mind, and in his ability to teach, heal, and love. Somehow Jesus drew on infinite Mind in every encounter. Someday we would all have that oneness of spiritual consciousness in an age of pure unlimited love. Mr. Muller had often reminded the boy of John 14:12, "Whoever believes in me will do the works I have been doing, and they will do even greater things than these, because I am going to the Father." And they talked about Mark 9:23, "Anything is possible if a person believes."

The boy often made Sunday Mass at St. Thomas's on Fifth Avenue, something he had not done since leaving New Hampshire. The boy needed beauty to worship. Beauty is a window into the divine, and few places are more beautiful than St. Thomas's. For the boy, it was always good to receive Holy Communion, because one thing Jesus clearly asked was that we "do this in memory of me."[18] He was so complete and good in his oneness with infinite Mind that people wanted to eliminate him rather than confront their own flaws. Human nature is such a mixed bag that people resent pure and loving individuals. If greatness of soul is measured by how a spiritual figure responds to adversity, then Jesus had truly great last words, "Forgive them, for they know not what they do."[19]

But this basic Christian loyalty never kept the boy from seeking and finding jewels of spiritual insight in lots of other places. One Saturday morning in early spring of that year, the boy took a walk down 71st Street toward Central Park and the Frick Collection, one of his favorite art museums. A block from the park on Madison Avenue and two doors before the Frick Art Reference Library, at 18 East 71st Street, he glanced over to read an engraved brass sign on the wall of a white marble building. The sign read "Holy Spirit Association."

"What is this?" he wondered, as he pondered the sign and its symbol, which looked like something from physics with orbits and rays shooting outwards from the center.

---

18   Luke 22.
19   Luke 23.

The insatiably curious boy walked through the door, a free soul always eager to learn. Seated at the entrance desk was the kindest and most gracious Japanese woman imaginable, who introduced herself as Keiko. She had a soft, serene way of smiling that seemed deeper than most, was professional in her dress, pure, dignified, and hospitable. He had never met anyone nicer, more beautiful, more dignified, or more spiritual. She invited him in, and the boy could see a few other people there in the foyer and living room, Japanese and Americans mainly. He was introduced to them as well. Over the next few months, he went to meals at the association every week or two and heard presentations about how they hoped to bring eastern and Western traditions together in a new teaching that would also merge science and the world's religions. It was different than what he had experienced some years earlier on Market Street in San Francisco, and there was no *Gohonzon* on the wall, but he felt peaceful and at home.

In Keiko's eyes he saw great depth. They prayed together. Soon she invited the boy to a weekend retreat, and he took the association's crowded van to the three-day retreat in upstate New York, along the Hudson about two hours north of Manhattan. But he lasted exactly one day before walking away and hitching back across the Kingston-Rhinecliff Bridge into downtown Kingston to catch a bus back to Manhattan. There were a lot of long lectures, and the boy was more of an independent learner, so he got fidgety and restless. Still, he greatly admired the group's spiritual intensity and commitment to a cause beyond themselves, and he believed that people could find the infinite Mind in lots of pathways.

But there was something of a very respectful theological disagreement too. The boy could see how someone as holy and perfectly one with the infinite Mind as Jesus might be able to close the obviously wide gap between God and humanity by enduring the worst persecution in absolute forgiveness and with the kind of reluctance that meant it was a hard pill to swallow. Keiko and the boy quietly disagreed about this.

She simply did not understand it. Christianity just never got much of a start in Japan because the emperors repressed it so viciously. The boy understood that.

He did not see Keiko again until about three weeks later. She rang the street-level bell to his apartment early in the morning as he was about to leave for work, announced herself, and he buzzed her in. After climbing the five flights to his floor, she knocked on the apartment door.

Keiko looked a great deal thinner than usual and handed the boy a paper plate with seven rice balls on it. The boy had never seen rice balls before, and they looked a little strange to him.

"Do you like rice balls? I wanted to bring you some so you could start your day well," she said weakly.

The boy quietly thanked her and took the plate. "Keiko, I will have these later. You are here so early, and you have never come to my place before. What a surprise. What's up?"

"I have been praying so much for you. For every one of the seven rice balls, I fasted on water alone for one day. That is how much God wants you to come to another retreat and stay this time. And I am going to keep it up until you come back."

Keiko spoke with such urgency, and while she was naturally quite petite, now she looked much too thin and her cheeks were sunken. The boy had never seen anything like it, although he knew that Gandhi had fasted for a long time. Talk about dedication to a cause! That was something he respected greatly.

She whispered in her broken English, "Will you please come to another retreat and stay?"

And the boy thought of that youth on the ledge, and the words "If you save him, you too shall live." It was another blue angel moment. There was no way on earth that the boy was going to let Keiko fast herself to nothing just to resist a weekend workshop.

"What will you do if I don't?" he asked.

"Just keep fasting until you do."

"Okay, Keiko, I'll come, but you need to eat something today, all right?"

"Yes," she agreed.

"Promise? Right now, okay? Not later."

"Yes."

They each ate a rice ball after she offered a brief prayer, and then she descended the stairs and went on her way. The boy headed to work impressed and amazed at such devotion. He had fasted himself once when he was living in San Francisco, just drinking plain tea for a week. But Keiko was planning to go on and on, and she seemed so weak.

A few days later, when he saw Keiko again at her community on 71st Street, she appeared both joyful and serene, so he decided, gratefully, that he didn't have to worry about her quite as much. As he had promised, the boy went back upstate the next weekend, but was still not able to become a real believer. The good news, though, was that Keiko was also there enjoying miso soup and sandwiches, and that is what mattered to him.

Deep down, the boy could not fully connect with these new teachings. He was never critical of Keiko because she had a great soul, wept when she prayed, and had only the very best intentions. She deepened him in many ways, as did her friends. But Route 80 people like the boy tend toward Walt Whitman's open road and are more experimental than doctrinaire. So he learned but moved on with nothing but appreciation. The boy was never one to dismiss someone else's faith. Back on Market Street, old Gus used to tell the boy that if one person believes something unusual people think they are crazy, and if a bunch of people begin to believe it, they call it a cult. But if a whole society comes to believe it, they call it a culture.

Maybe the boy had stumbled on something that was just too deep and true for him to comprehend at that point in his life. The boy was too independent a soul for pretty much any organization anyway. Still, in Keiko the boy found a nobility of soul that he would always admire gratefully. Those were after all seven rice balls straight from the heart. Journeys are all about discovering who we are destined to meet, and Keiko was destiny. And, after all, living on 71st Street just blocks away was synchronicity to begin with.

When the boy dies one day, he will not have failed to prevent at least one instance of semi-starvation.

Unity

A few weeks later the boy started to go from East 71st Street to the Unity School of Christianity on West 58th Street, where he liked the meditation-focused services and events. The message of Unity was that our thoughts are carried forward into manifestation in our daily living. And, as free individuals, we are each ultimately responsible for what we allow into our minds and, hence, for creating our lives. The best investment any of us can ever make is to mold a mind full of thoughts that build up our lives and the lives of others, rather than thoughts that tear us down—thoughts that clearly envision the future we want to achieve and how we can creatively contribute to the world around us.

This idea of controlling our thoughts is found in the writings of Emmanuel Swedenborg and Emerson, and in Hinduism, Quakerism, Theosophy, and so many other systems of life enhancement. The *Upanishads,* a collection of sacred Hindu texts, declare that "What you think you become." It was all philosophy that he had imbibed in

Concord in his studies with Rev. Welles. Mastery of one's thoughts is mastery of one's soul and fate. It is by practicing concentration that we achieve unity with our thoughts, and that enables us to unleash the deeper levels of energy that lie within us.

But it is not merely the human mind that is at work here. The power to use our mind to create our future reality depends on, and demonstrates, our continuity with the infinite creative Mind, which wants to help us express creative love in the world. Infinite Mind can be relied upon for guidance and empowerment because God, the original Mind, of which we are a part, always wants to respond to us, and support us, at the right time and place for the right purposes.

This is what synchronicity is really all about. We can turn over our problems and obstacles to the one Mind and all that is needed to solve them will eventually flow our way. The universal Mind, which is always a force for good, is perfectly reliable if what we ask for is creative and loving. We need not be anxious because the answers and solutions are already on their way to us. This was good, solid Route 80 thinking.

From a Blue Angel Dream to the University of Chicago Divinity School

Blue angel dreamers and Route 80 questers eventually have to end up at the Divinity School of the University of Chicago, the global center for the study of world religions. And so the boy dropped out of an all-expenses-paid NIH doctoral program in microbiology at the University of Pennsylvania and headed west again by Amtrak to the city where he had landed years earlier, with just his guitar and backpack, after a long drive in Gary's big white truck. Even after giving a lecture at Penn's famous Wistar Institute, the boy realized that what he really needed to do was to study spirituality and religion in their many forms across the globe, and maybe later connect it with science and speculation about the nature of ultimate reality.

He spent five great years in the Divinity School's Swift Hall. Once he shared the story of his dream and trip west and the youth on the ledge with Joseph Campbell in the Swift Kick Coffee Shop. Campbell was visiting from New York to give lectures on *The Hero with a Thousand Faces,* his essential book about spiritual journeys, and when the boy told him about how he only got to Swift Hall because the generator broke years ago, Campbell smiled and said, "It was synchronicity, not luck." Mircea Eliade, the noted scholar and author of *Shamanism,* was also at the table and listened quietly, staring into his coffee shaman-like and nodding in agreement. With a smile on his aged face and lots of thick gray hair shooting out from his ears, he asked the boy, "Is all of spirituality synchronicity?"

"Not all," responded the boy, "but you have to notice it and be open to surprises. You need spiritual observational skills. When something is too good to be true, look carefully and trace the lines."

Come summer of 1983, the boy was one of just seven doctoral students to be elected by the Divinity School faculty to be a University Fellow and a Fellow in the Nuveen Institute for Advanced Studies in Religion. He was awarded a full scholarship and a stipend. He was now also teaching humanities in the medical school, focused on how careful listening to the patient's story is the beginning point of empathy, and how love heals along with good technical skills. He was connecting healing and love, spirituality with health, and goodness with flourishing at a truly excellent university.

When people at the Divinity School asked him where he was from, he sometimes told those he had gotten to know well, "Babylon, but I am really just from Route 80." Then people would get really curious, and the boy might tell them a little about the dream if he trusted them. But these were folks who were so intellectually serious that the boy felt he was inadequately skeptical.

Hyde Park, where the University of Chicago is located, was not far from Grant Park, just a quick trip on the number 6 Jeffrey bus, and sometimes the boy went there to stand for a moment on the spot where Gary had dropped him off so many years ago. He remembered stepping out of that big, powerful white truck, walking to the park, and sitting on the bench playing his guitar. He tended from time to time to reconnect with the dream by going there and reflecting while seated on the bench. How profoundly grateful he was that his journey was just as it came to be, and he knew it was God's work. Everything he did and everyone he encountered was love made visible on a Route 80 journey open to surprises.

He also liked to go over to the Chicago Art Institute, where he stood mesmerized before the huge *America Windows* by Marc Chagall, with blue angels floating in stained glass. He would have more experiences with the angels in Chagall's windows later, but he knew nothing of this at the time.

***

Mitsuko was a ballet dancer from Japan whom the boy met in New York at an ethnic performance festival. She liked his performance of Villa-Lobos, and she was an impressive dancer. She was also beautiful. To make a long story short, they got married in 1982 at the Daley Center in the Chicago Loop. The three-minute ceremony cost fifteen dollars and was performed by a retired African-American justice of the peace. Afterward, she looked at them and said, "I bet you are not going on a big honeymoon."

"No, ma'am, I'm just a poor graduate student making ends meet," the boy answered, "and Mitsuko is working in a restaurant."

"Well, I got just what you need. Listen to this!" she said. And she opened a music box on her desk that played the theme song from the famous old musical, *Around the World*.

"Oh wow!" responded the newlyweds.

Then everyone laughed, and Mitsuko and the boy headed back to Hyde Park.

Their first child, a little girl, was born at the University of Chicago in July of 1983, two weeks before they set out for Ann Arbor, Michigan, the next stop on Route 80.

Interlude

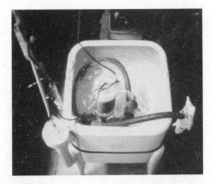

The old-style kidney dialysis machine that the boy knew well

When people are overwhelmed by illness, we must give them physical relief, but it is equally important to encourage the spirit through a constant show of love and compassion. It is shameful how often we fail to see that what people desperately require is human affection. Deprived of human warmth and a sense of value, other forms of treatment prove less effective.

—Dalai Lama

If you truly loved yourself, you could never hurt another.

—Buddha

The mind is its own place and in itself can make a heaven of hell and a hell of heaven.

—John Milton

How to Follow a Dream—Lesson Four: Route 80 boys never forget that love heals all hurts and illnesses with time, but there is so much social pressure on boys to be tough and hard-hearted that they tend to resist this universal truth. But love heals those who give and those who receive, and we all need to place it at the very center of our lives. This is not the love of chocolate or designer jeans, but the kind of love we give we feel when the happiness and security of another is as real and meaningful to us as our own. To have this kind of love consistently, we need to be connected with the infinite Mind of cherishing love as the true dependable source, and we are all connected with this because it lies within us in the form of an eternal soul. But we lack awareness of our true essence, of who we really are. The material world distracts us. But divine love can flow through us to all the people we encounter when we get out of its way and remove all the obstacles of resentment and materialism that block the channel. Whether we are looking at a patient in a bed, having tea with an old friend who is disappointed with life, or feeding homeless folks at Thanksgiving, when we are possessed by the spirit of God we feel a boundless love that is more enduring, more wise, more expansive, and more energetic than anything that mere human nature disconnected from the infinite Mind can ever achieve.

When you share your deepest spiritual intuitions of divine love, disregard the skeptics because you have been awakened into awareness of the Mind that dwells within you. Speak freely and awaken others who are scared to openly discuss the cherishing energy of the eternal original Mind that they feel in their souls.

Playing Villa-Lobos before the night dialysis shift

*Some changes look negative on the surface, but you will soon realize
that space is being created for something new to emerge.*

–Eckhart Tolle

The Synchronicity Whispers and Chagall's Blue Angel: Finally a Fellow Traveler

There is a voice that doesn't use words. Listen.

–Rumi

T o follow the dream, the boy was one to listen for the whispers of synchronicity. He became someone to notice things that seem so cherishing and improbable that they unveil the hidden causality of God. He came to observe with care. Not that everything is synchronicity, but there are those startling occurrences so perfect as to be obvious, especially when in answer to a heartfelt and prayerful need.

Jung described synchronicity as "uncaused causality"—a causality that has nothing to do with material sequences of action and reaction. The boy sometimes spoke of the "synchronicity whispers" as the very underpinning of spirituality for all people. But to hear the whispers, we have to turn down the volume of the external distractions of the world.

Some instances of synchronicity are like a bell tolling loudly and unmistakably, like the youth on the ledge or Mom's premonition. But most occurrences are quiet, subtle whispers from a cherishing God to remind us of our being loved when we are otherwise preoccupied with our struggles, the pressures of everyday life, and the feeling of aloneness in a disenchanted universe. When the whispers come and we hear them, they carry us beyond our immediate place and time and into the flow of infinite Mind.

The boy's Route 80 journey began as nothing more than a spiritual whisper that most would have missed entirely as the by-product of frigid New Hampshire snows and possible hypothermia from skating fast on pond ice. But this whisper echoed over time. Dreams like that are trying to tell you something. The boy had developed a spiritual ear from silent meditative walks around the library pond, and from being more introspective than some—introspective in the sense of turning his gaze toward the stillness of inner being and finding meaning in relative detachment from the outer world. He assumed that if enough people had experiences of dreams like his then the new dark ages, captured in the copy of *Atlas Shrugged* that some philanthropic St. Paul's alum had just distributed to the entire class, would fade into something better.

A Synchronicity Whisper and a Hundred-Dollar Bill

After two years in the fabulous university town of Ann Arbor, Michigan, the boy was offered a new teaching job in world religions and ethics at Marymount-Fordham in Tarrytown, New York—a truly lovely village along the Hudson that borders the town Washington Irving described in "The Legend of Sleepy Hollow." So he and his wife and toddler daughter were back on Route 80 headed east. The boy's mom was a Marymount grad from years before.

But rents in Tarrytown were so high that the boy spent every penny he had to get the little family of three into a decent apartment on the corner of Main Street and Route 9, just across from the noisy bus stop and all-night 7-Eleven. After paying the rent plus a security deposit, they were running low on food and needed a hundred dollars desperately.

So the little family of three sat in their car in the parking lot of a Howard Johnson's restaurant across from the entrance to the Tappan Zee Bridge and the Tarrytown Double Tree Hilton, counting quarters to see what kind of meal they could scrape together without using the American Express card, which was already overloaded. It was about noon, and they were mainly interested in getting a little lunch.

That's how the need arose for a hundred-dollar prayer. At the boy's suggestion, he and Mitsuko prayed for someone to flat-out give them a hundred dollars to tide them over for a couple of days until his first paycheck arrived. The boy was always suggesting prayers, but in the middle of this prayer they felt a very slight *bump!* The car shook a tiny bit, and while the boy didn't think anything of it, Mitsuko said someone had hit them.

As soon as the boy got out to look, a large African-American guy in a white suit, white hat, blue shirt, and tie adorned with a blue angel image came over to him, smiling apologetically.

"Sorry, boy," he said, pointing to his Cadillac. "I think I might have tapped the corner of your car. But no damage, right? Why don't you just take this?"

It was interesting that the driver addressed him as "boy," which seemed to be a sign in itself. Then he handed the boy a crisp hundred-dollar bill that he had pulled from his wallet.

"Wow, thanks! Did you know that you are an answer to our prayer? Yes, sir, you are an angel in blue and white! We were asking God just now for a hundred dollars, so you came along at the perfect time!"

"Well, I am just coming from a Pentecostal service and felt like somehow the Holy Spirit has been with me, skin-touch-close, all morning," he said smiling, his voice deep and joyful. "I was definitely here for a reason!"

Then they laughed loudly, shook hands, said, "Thank the Lord," and he went on his way with a smile. The boy, wife, and daughter headed into the restaurant. Two days later his first paycheck arrived, and they were back in business. The incident was, for the boy, another mega-synchronicity "whisper" reassuring them that despite any ordeal they were in the hands of a higher Love. Infinite Mind reveals its loving nature in responding to our requests, and so long as our intentions are generous and wise, an answer will come in God's time.

But on this occasion, they needed an answer immediately—and miraculously it arrived. That was one hundred dollars from heaven. Sometimes in a pinch God works fast. And after that powerful affirmation from the infinite Mind, they felt that Tarrytown was the place they were meant to be, so they got off to a good start and thrived.

Now the materialists and statisticians will say that there was a probability of one in 1,000,000,000,000,000,000,000,000,000 (est.) that, in the exact place and at the exact moment of their deepest need, the perfect guy would show up, bump their car, and pull that hundred-dollar bill out of his wallet. In other words, it could just have happened by chance. Technically, this is true. But what a ridiculously forced explanation! Let's just acknowledge that it actually makes more sense to assert that the hand of God was at work, and that such a meaningful whisper is clearly much more than chance.

Dreaming with Chagall

The dream never recurred after those years at St. Paul's. Why did it have to? There were plenty of synchronicity whispers, intuitions, premonitions, and opportunities to live its message, "If you save him, you too shall live," and the boy remained in harmony with the dream. But he never found a true fellow traveler who could appreciate his journey and its challenges until Chagall came his way, though the great blue angel artist had passed away in March of 1985, just a few months before the boy arrived in Tarrytown.

August 1985 was a magical time as the boy arrived on campus to meet his new friend and office mate Dr. Gabriel Gomes. Gabe, who was bronze-toned from Bangladesh, had small E.T.-like size and awesome wisdom. He and the boy shared a passion for world spirituality. The boy told Gabe about the dream and whole Route 80 pilgrimage, including the car and the bridge and the motorcycle, and even the dialysis patients. After a solid half hour, Gabe laughed in amazement and congratulated him.

"Wow! What a journey! Classic! And after all," said Gabe, "it got you to the University of Chicago Divinity School!"

Then, with a warm smile on his face, Gabe added, "You must now walk just two miles up the road to the old stone Union Church in Pocantico Hills. Inside the church is the finest collection of spiritually themed Chagall windows on earth, especially the huge blue angel window titled *The Good Samaritan*, although his windows of the Hebrew prophets are spectacular, and you can touch them from the end of the pews. There is no other place in the world where you can be so close to a Chagall window. You remind me of Chagall because when he was a boy, he had a spiritual experience a little like yours, including the big fight with his dad. But he has a blue angel dream after the fight, and you had it before. Now go. Go. You go find Chagall. Go there now!"

Gabe was a highly renowned world religions scholar in the Religion and Philosophy Department, and he knew that the boy would like the Union Church immensely. A Catholic with a Spanish name due to the Jesuit missionaries of old who went to Bangladesh four centuries ago, Gabe also believed in spiritually significant dreams, and the two often spoke of the mystical experiences reported by practitioners of all the great religions and spiritual traditions. They sometimes co-taught undergrad courses on the varieties of spiritual experience, and Gabe added instruction in meditation.

The boy felt that encountering Gabe was itself deep synchronicity. What is the likelihood of being surprised by an E.T.-like office mate who would know so much about Chagall? So he walked over to the Union Church in the early August warmth with Gabe's words "Go there now!" in his mind.

The boy discovered Chagall at Union Church and returned at least every week for those three years, often jogging over from the hilltop campus, around the reservoir with its quiet pure waters, and then up past the Rockefeller mansion to sit in meditation before what for him was the greatest window on earth, the huge *Good Samaritan* that fills the entire back of the church wall with shimmering blue light. The window ranks as one of the most profound works of spiritual art ever created, and its symbols from every tradition all evoke a breathtaking ineffable oneness with divine Mind.

The Chagall window reminded him of his dream back at St. Paul's, and gazing at it the boy felt as peaceful as he had seated in his favorite wooden pew in at age sixteen in the old chapel. He could sit in the Union Church and be reminded that in the end he was just a blue angel dreamer living a life of faith following a path. The boy loved the exhilaration of writing in his journal while seated near this beautiful window, and he also began writing articles for some major scholarly publications on spirituality. When he needed to be inspired anew after hours of work, he visited those Chagall windows and sat quietly, carried along by the stream of ideas, somewhere beyond time and place, in a state of creative "flow."

Then, upon returning to his office on campus, he could gaze across the Tappan Zee on a clear day and absorb the beauty of nature, as the distant shore glowed with all the colors of autumn and the winds seemed to chase the clouds over the Hudson. Beauty was everywhere in Tarrytown and was always a path into the infinite Mind, as was his little family.

But the glorious windows of Chagall came to mean even more to the boy after he learned more about the artist's boyhood. Like Gabe said, *Chagall also ran away from home after a big argument with his dad, just like the boy.* At last the boy had someone he felt he could connect with closely, because the great Chagall too was a late-adolescent runaway who also experienced a transforming blue angel vision and did not much get along with his dad. The boy now studied Chagall for the first time, feeling that he had a spiritual brother of sorts, one who dared to carve out his own path rather than surrendering to his dad's expectations. Parental love is a good thing, but the infinite Mind matters more if you can hear its whispers.

Chagall's Vision

So we must take a slight detour to Chagall only so the boy does not sound quite as isolated and unusual as he otherwise might.

Chagall's *The Apparition* (1907), painted just after his dream

The boy learned that Chagall (1887–1985) was known as the "painter of angels" for a reason. Mark Shagal was born into a poor Jewish family on July 7, 1887, in the small Jewish ghetto of Viebsk, a minor city in northwest Russia, one of ten children. His father pickled herring and wanted his son to take over the business. (In learning of this, the boy remembered back to the job his dad found for him in the lampshade factory.) The odds were all against him becoming a painter. His family was, however, deeply grounded in the mystical tradition of Hasidism, an eighteenth-century Jewish movement that emphasized divine love and joyful energetic union with the divine and with one's neighbor through prayer, music, and dance. The Hasidim, or "pious ones," celebrated not mere happiness, with all its contingencies, but a deeper joy—in union with Being and community—that transcended materialism.

Chagall's father deplored the idea of his son being a painter. They had a furious argument and Marc—he now changed his name from "Mark"—ran away to St. Petersburg at the age of seventeen, where he studied for four years. He lived in small rooms, sold black-and-white sketches for a living, and shared cots with other street people.

Eventually the boy came to lecture about Chagall in his classes on spirituality and the arts, and on how creative essence can be grounded in a dramatic spiritual experience. For Chagall, such experience entirely shaped his artistic direction and turned his ethereal right-brain world blue. He had this experience at age seventeen, at the same time in life as the boy. Chagall was living in St. Petersburg, and captured this experience in his youthful autobiography, *My Life*,[20] which he started in Moscow in 1921 and completed the following year in Berlin:

> My means did not permit me to rent a room; I was forced to content myself with nooks and alcoves. I didn't even have a bed to myself. I had to share it with a workingman. It's true, he was an angel, that workingman with the very black mustache.
>
> He was so kind to me he even flattened himself against the wall to give me more room. Turning my back on him and my face to the window, I breathed fresh air.
>
> In those communal recesses, with laborers and pushcart vendors for neighbors, there was nothing for me to do but stretch out on the edge of my bed and think about myself. What else? And dreams overwhelmed me: a bedroom, square, empty. In one corner, a single bed and me on it. It is getting dark.
>
> Suddenly, the ceiling opens, and a winged creature descends with great commotion, filling the room with movement and clouds.

---

20 Boston: Da Capo Press, 1994.

A swish of wings fluttering.

I think: an angel! I can't open my eyes; it's too bright,
too luminous.

After rummaging about on all sides, he rises and passes through
the opening in the ceiling, carrying with him all the light and
the blue air.

Once again it is dark. I wake up.[21]

He immediately captured this dream in his first blue painting (1907)
of many, *My Apparition*. He also added a second "l" to his name to
proclaim his new life and declare his mission, because in Russian
Chagall means "to stride with big steps." Much of his art for the rest
of his life would be shaped by the color blue and by images of angels.
He would remain aloof from all the artistic movements of his time—
cubism, surrealism, and the like—because he was intent on capturing
in his creations the interface he had viewed between the material world
and a nonmaterial world. For him the ethereal was the real.

Famously, Pablo Picasso had it right: "When Chagall paints, you do not
know if he is asleep or awake. Somewhere inside his head, there must be
an angel."

One scholar, Johanna Skilling, captures the importance of the angel's
appearance to the young Chagall in her "Marc Chagall: Painter
of Angels."

> At that time, an amazing vision has a cataclysmic effect on his
> life and art. One night, drifting into sleep in his small room,
> Chagall thought he heard the rustle of wings. He opened
> his eyes and immediately felt pins and needles of pain in his
> forehead. The room was filled with an unearthly, brilliant
> blue light. As Chagall watched, the angel slowly floated

---

21 *My Life*. Boston: Da Capo Press, 1994 (pp. 81–82).

up through the ceiling; the light and the beautiful blue air
vanished with him.

After this vision, Chagall began a lifetime of work to portray the
wonder of the angel and the color of the beautiful blue air. Later
he would describe his work by saying, "My art is an extravagant
art, a flaming vermilion, a blue flooding over my paintings."[22]

***

Those were fabulous years (1985–88) in Tarrytown. Synchronicity was
everywhere—it seemed to flow down from the hills surrounding the
idyllic village like a river.

One problem remained. They were still living in that motley apartment
in an old Tudor building on the corner of Main Street and R0ute 9, next
to the Tarrytown Music Theater, and with that bus stop across the street,
right in front of the 7-Eleven, there was still a lot of noise late at night.
The village was nice, with lots of shops within walking distance and a
lovely playground down the road in front of the grade school where
they could take his daughter. But after a couple of years they realized
that they were going to have to look for a new opportunity outside of
New York, someplace where a dollar bought a lot more.

Not too far west this time, though! The boy was definitely not heading
back out to the Pacific coast again. Instead, he sat prayerfully at his
office desk up on the hill and drew a circle on a map. The circumference
extended to Pittsburgh, and Cleveland was a bit farther west, but it was
close enough. So it was that he came to write a letter to the School of
Medicine at Case Western Reserve University, applying for an assistant
professorship. No way did he think he could get the job, because he
knew that medical school was a big deal and he was just an angel
dreamer. But as things turned out he got an interview, flew to Cleveland

---

22   *The Big Book of Angels*. New York: Rodale, 2002 (pp. 318–320)

trying to make out the traces of Route 80 below, and met with the search committee.

The boy hated leaving Tarrytown, but in June of 1988 he was able to get wife and daughter tickets to Japan, where they would spend the summer before joining him in Cleveland when school started. He stayed behind, sold the Nissan Sentra for five hundred dollars, along with their few items of furniture, packed everything that was left into one small U-Haul truck, and headed west after a goodbye lunch with Mom and Dad, who never did understand that this move was one more episode on spiritual journey, which is what had made his life worth living. No one in his family could, so he did not blame them.

The boy decided not to drive south to connect with Route 80 West this time. Instead, he took Route 17 West, the New York Southern Tier Expressway, which, like 80, goes all the way to Cleveland, but runs parallel to it about fifty miles north of the Alleghenies. He spent the night at a Red Roof Inn in Erie, and by late the next morning he was cruising down Euclid Avenue toward a section of Cleveland Heights called Coventry. There he rented a top-floor, one-bedroom apartment on Hampshire Road. The summer of 1988 was really hot everywhere in America, and in this old building the ceiling of his apartment was right under a black-tar roof that reached 110 degrees daily and stayed there. So he slept little but had never needed much sleep.

Interlude

The Chagall *Good Samaritan Window* of Union Church

We do not create our destiny; we participate in its unfolding. Synchronicity works as a catalyst toward the working out of that destiny.

–David Richo

You may say me a dreamer
But I'm not the only one.
I hope some say you'll join us
And the world will be as one…

–John Lennon

The universe works in its own way to join those of us who need to be connected.

–Susan Barbara Apollon

How to Follow a Dream—Lesson Five: A boy may feel that he is all alone in the universe if he follows a blue angel dream that most of his friends think is a little bit odd. But the infinite Mind knows that we need some added support, and that it is not going to come much from other human beings. So God will answer a prayer by sending along an African-American guy in a big white suit who shows up perfectly in a HoJo parking lot with that hundred-dollar bill we just asked for. This is a synchronicity whisper, a reassuring hint that we are each more cherished than we may realize. We might even be told by the guy who just happens to be our office mate to visit a church we never heard of and discover the art of another human being who is not only a fellow blue angel dreamer, but one who ran away just like we did years ago, changing his life forever like it did our own. When we find someone who has had a spiritual experience like our own, we will feel that we have a companion on the journey at last.

Chagall's *Blue Angel in Concert*

One fine night in June 1933 I was sitting on a lawn after dinner with three colleagues, two women and one man. We liked each other well enough but were certainly not intimate friends, nor had anyone of us a sexual interest in another. Incidentally, we had not drunk any alcohol. We were talking casually about everyday matters when, quite suddenly and unexpectedly, something happened. I felt myself invaded by a power which, though I consented to it, was irresistible and certainly not mine. For the first time in my life I knew exactly— because, thanks to the power, I was doing it—what it means to love one's neighbor as oneself. I was also certain, though the conversation continued to be perfectly ordinary, that my three colleagues were having the same experience. (In the case of one of them, I was able later to confirm this.) My personal feelings toward them were unchanged—they were still colleagues, not intimate friends—but I felt their existence as themselves to be of infinite value and rejoiced in it.

—W.H. Auden

The Great Healer and the Deeply Forgetful Prophet: Premonition on the Highway

Each of us has a unique part to play in the healing of the world.

—Marianne Williamson

I t was a healing dream, and so the boy appreciated healers and spent many years among them.

The boy arrived for an interview at Case Western School of Medicine in the spring of 1988 and was offered the job a month later only because Joseph Michael Foley, MD, a senior neurologist of renown, wanted him in Cleveland after their astonishing conversation while sitting on a couple of frayed white vinyl chairs in the lobby of the old Hanna Pavilion, a psychiatric hospital. Dr. Foley had asked the boy an interesting interview question:

"Tell me, lad, what do you think about people who have dementia, how should we view them? How gone are they?"

"Dr. Foley, assume that deeply forgetful people have a consciousness that is of no lesser significance than the consciousness of all us 'hypercognitive' people who tend to disrespect them because we have more lucidity of mind," the boy answered. "It would help if we thought of them not as demented but as deeply forgetful. We are *all* a little forgetful, some of us are a lot more forgetful than we let on, and yet 'the demented' are mocked. Even when they have trouble communicating or remembering things, there is more there beneath the surface than we might think. They often surprise me with a few words, a smile, and other hints that as if to let us know that they are still there.

"Yes, these patients can be very surprising and often are, but you have to be open to it," said Joe.

"It's more than that, Dr. Foley. My grandmother died with dementia, and I used to visit her sometimes in the nursing home because we were close. I could sense that there was more of her there than met the eye. I have long felt that there is a mystery to the human mind that's not explained by the mere material brain with its cells and tissue. I think that mind at least in some ways transcends matter, that there's a kind of

Over-Soul or infinite Mind in which we all participate in some sort of great connectivity."

Dr. Foley was a second-generation Boston Irishman and a graduate of the Boston Latin School and Harvard Med who had read a lot of Emerson.

"Like Emerson, yes, Over-Soul, something that is just categorically different from matter," he responded. "I know neurologists who keep an open mind about that, and I certainly do, being Catholic."

So the boy explained what he meant a little more fully. "We may each have a spark of that Over-Soul within us, like bit of light flowing outwards from a Roman candle, or maybe like little inlets filled with water from the ocean. This is not derived from matter, because there are so many mental experiences people have that are mystical and take them well past time and space, and they have a consciousness of Oneness and of one Mind. Lots of great philosophers and theologians, from Plato to Augustine, have thought that Mind precedes matter in the universe, and that we each have a spark of it within. But we have to be so introspective to elevate our awareness of it, and not be focused on the body. And they believed that we have an original spiritual nature that is good and truthful and beautiful, and a source of inner peace and harmony. So even if the brain deteriorates from Alzheimer's or some other cause, like with my grandmother, she still had this spiritual essence within, and sometimes it became apparent depending on the day. In other words, we don't need to rule out the idea of an eternal soul."

Now the boy did not think that this kind of discussion was likely to get him too far in a sophisticated medical center while seated in the foyer of a psychiatric hospital where a materialistic view of the mind as nothing but cells and neurons is the only acceptable one. He expected that he would soon be heading back to Tarrytown for good.

Dr. Foley, however, surprisingly, agreed with him:

"Well, after all my years I, too, think that mind may well be more than matter, and you have to be open-minded about what lies beneath the chaos of dementia. I have seen too many cases of surprising lucidity when we thought there could be none. I'm Catholic and haven't given up on the idea of a soul," Dr. Foley said. "But in such a materialistic age, the idea of the soul is a huge stretch for many people."

"And, Dr. Foley, it is a pretty dark age because if all we are is tissue and matter, then what is the basis for believing in any kind of lasting human dignity? Aren't we then, in the end, as Bertrand Russell famously wrote, just complicated 'pond scum'? And then we sink into discussions about the 'life unworthy of life,' and 'useless eaters.' Materialism is never going to provide a firm basis for human dignity, especially when people lose their ability to reason and be economically productive. Dignity must be grounded in something sacred and eternal. St. Paul said that we are God's temple and that God's spirit dwells within us, and the Hindus say that within each of us is the Supreme Being. They say *Namaste*."

To the boy's continuing astonishment, Dr. Foley answered, "You know, it's refreshing to hear a younger man like yourself speak of a sacred dignity. I've never been convinced that all aspects of mind and even of memory are derived from matter. Open-mindedness is what we need. You are bringing joy to me in my old age! Our drives for truth, goodness and beauty strike me as spiritual in nature."

There in that lobby a relationship was forged between Dr. Foley and the boy that would last twenty-five years, until Joe died in the summer of 2012. Joe wanted to hire someone who was still open to the mysteries of the mind and spirit, who would be able to connect with the vast majority of everyday people who find mysteries plausible, and who rely on them when they are seriously ill. He wanted to hire someone who wanted to look respectfully on the deeply forgetful and spend time with them and those who cared for them.

After a few years on the job, doing medical ethics and working with deeply forgetful people and their families across Ohio, the boy told Joe about the blue angel dream. Joe responded with a story about a Catholic girl he once knew who, at the age of ten, was standing in a church in Boston, when she suddenly felt surrounded by a blue cloud and saw an angel. The vision continued for a few minutes, although she really had no sense of time or place. Joe said that she never again had a similar experience, but once was enough, and she was living out her life as though a divine Love was with her every moment, teaching in a theological school and serving as a successful inner-city minister.

Nothing the boy ever thought was too much for Dr. Foley, who was forever curious and open-minded.

The Deeply Forgetful Prophet Who Spoke of God's Love

During his twenty years in Cleveland, the boy assisted deeply forgetful people and their families whenever he had time. He visited family caregivers and stood in for them so they could take a break from their duties, convened support groups, conducted research, and taught, and wrote. The boy also organized healing arts programs at assisted living centers, where the residents took part in poetry readings, drawing classes, and musical events, and he conducted caregiver workshops in more than two hundred cities and towns across the United States and Canada. He brought medical students into the poorest inner-city neighborhoods to visit caregivers and deeply forgetful people who lived in very difficult conditions.

In the fall of 1988, just after the boy arrived at Case Western, he and Dr. Foley drove east on Route 80 for half an hour and then turned north, until they reached a nursing home called Heather Hill in Chardin, Ohio. They were there to visit the unit for the most deeply forgetful residents.

Joe and the boy made visits like this to many different centers all over the Western Reserve of Ohio for close to a decade. They spent mornings talking to individuals with dementia and their families, and lunchtimes with the professional staff, discussing practical issues but focusing on why we need to accept deeply forgetful people and learn from them that a human life has profound value, even when you have to look a little harder for hints of continuing selfhood. They emphasized this because deep forgetfulness does not mean that someone is a "husk," "gone," "dead," or "empty." The deeply forgetful are just more hidden, but still one with infinite Mind and infinite Love.

Joe and the boy met Jim that morning at Heather Hill. Jim was among the most deeply forgetful. When they arrived at his door and saw he was not there, they read his biosketch on the wall outside his room. Jim was about eighty-five years of age and had Alzheimer's. The sketch said that he had been successful in business, was active in his church, that his wife had passed away, and that he had two sons, Jim Jr. and David, who were both doing very well and came by to visit their dad from time to time.

Then they went back out on the unit and the boy asked the nurse if she would point Jim out to them. There were about a dozen people with advanced dementia sitting there or walking slowly around the room. The nurse pointed to Jim, a thin and frail man of average height who was standing up but moving slowly and hunched over a bit. Joe asked the boy to try communicating with him. So they approached Jim and guided him to a table, where they sat down.

"Jim, how are your sons? How are Jim and David?"

Jim did not say a word, as is usually the case with those who are this forgetful. He had clearly lost most of the temporal glue that connects the past and the present. He could not respond to any questions, although the boy looked him in the eye and called him by name, as an expression of respect.

Then they noticed that Jim was holding a brown twig about a foot long.

"Jim, do you ever pray?" asked the boy.

Jim did not respond, at least not for a minute or so.

Then Jim placed his twig in the boy's hands—and smiled with a warmth and joy that lit the boy right up. If love were electric, the room would have been on fire. Jim struggled to get out just three words, and they were all he spoke that morning.

"God is love."

The boy was amazed. The nurses overheard what Jim had said and looked at him curiously. Where did this come from?

It seemed to the boy that, despite his deep forgetfulness, there was still within Jim some sense of the infinite Mind—and a soul. Jim was like a prophet blowing through materialism.

The boy turned to Jim's nurse and asked about the twig.

It turns out that as a boy growing up on an Ohio farm, Jim had a father—a devout Christian—who loved him very deeply. Jim's father gave him a chore to do every morning, which was to bring kindling in for the fireplaces. Like many others with progressive dementia, Jim had journeyed back into his past and landed at the place where he felt the safest and most secure, embraced by love. That twig symbolized the love of his father and the joy that Jim felt in doing a small but useful chore early in life.

It also symbolized for Jim divine love, as he understood it.

There, in the desert of deep forgetfulness, Jim was coping with the chaos of the present through his abiding memory of faith and devotion. Even the ravages of forgetfulness did not fully eradicate these glimmers of an emotionally resonant past or the memory of a higher and sustaining Love.

They were discussing Jim as they drove home along Route 80, and Dr. Foley returned to a favorite theme: that on many occasions during his clinical interactions with individuals who had even the most advanced dementia, he had been surprised by moments when they might laugh a bit, or blurt out a relevant word, or even a little more. He told about visiting a priest he had studied with at Holy Cross College who was in his final days and struggling with end-stage Alzheimer's. Joe and a friend sat with the old priest and spoke with him as though he was fully lucid, not expecting any response. But all of a sudden the old priest exclaimed, "Those were the good old days, Joe!"

In Jim's case, it appeared that nothing could entirely separate him from the love of God, not even dementia. The boy recalled old Mr. Muller, who had him recite Romans 8:38–39: "For I am convinced that neither death nor life, neither angels nor demons, neither the present nor the future, nor any powers, neither height nor depth, nor anything else in all creation, will be able to separate us from the love of God and Christ." But this was too long to burn into a board and nail to the trees back on Oak Neck Lane.

***

Everyone on spiritual journeys these days talks about living in the Now. By this they mean getting beyond the busyness of running from point A to point B across chronological time. But whenever the boy connected with someone who was deeply forgetful, he was forced to live in the Now, because that's the only thing deeply forgetful people know. The deeply forgetful help us to be spiritually free in a place beyond time, where we can feel closer to the infinite Mind. The boy always made sure to learn the spiritual traditions of the deeply forgetful people he encountered, often recited familiar prayers with them, and always felt that they were soothed, even if they did not join in.

So it is that the boy discovered many wonderful things otherwise undiscoverable. For example, when looking after a deeply forgetful person, a caregiver's hope must rest mostly in being "open to surprises"—that is, to sporadic expressions of continuing self-identity in their loved one. The boy also learned to always be kind to the deeply forgetful, rather than always being right, for there is no value in pulling them back into our reality once they have settled well into their own and made a separate peace with it.

Once he came to understand these things, the boy began to write and publish articles to awaken others to this self-identity that still exists within the deeply forgetful, and to the hidden rewards of being with them that are obscured by the "hypercognitive values" that dominate our culture. As he had described to Dr. Foley, his own grandmother had taught the boy these things through her graceful silence, her quiet presence, and the occasional mornings when she called him by name. Dr. Foley and the boy wrote some wonderful articles together, though Dr. Foley was less into writing than into providing tender loving care to deeply forgetful people at the Foley Elder Health Center that was named after him. He was loved by all, and people were thrilled just to see him in the hallways.

Can we, as individuals and as a society, discover the equal dignity of deeply forgetful people? Can we stop thinking that "the demented" are a waste and using this word in insulting ways?

We live in a Western culture that is dominated by elevated expectations of rationalism and economic productivity, so clarity of mind is for many of us what makes life worth living. As a proof of our existence and key to our humanity, "I think, therefore I am" is not easily replaced with "I will, feel, and relate while disconnected by forgetfulness from my former self, but still, I am"—but it should be.

Another Youth on a Ledge

Some years after arriving in Cleveland, in that same Hanna Pavilion of the University Hospitals of Cleveland where the boy first met Dr. Foley, the boy was introduced to a local college freshman who was so depressed that he had attempted suicide twice that year and on the third try had swallowed twenty sedative pills. The doctors in adolescent psychiatry called the boy because they couldn't get anywhere with this kid, who—like Harry on the ledge of the Golden Gate Bridge— was quite brilliant and had formulated an excellent philosophical argument for total nihilism and self-destruction. Now he was under 24/7 supervision in the hospital and had brought his favorite books with him, including Dawkins, Sartre, and Nietzsche, powerful disciples of the emptiness and meaninglessness of it all. When Dawkins says that ultimately humans are just unwitting conduits of DNA coils that are using us to replicate themselves into the future through the trick of love, what remains of meaning? When any expression of kindness is discounted as just manipulation and power-seeking, what happens to hope?

So the boy visited the kid in his hospital room. They talked about all the kid's favorite authors, and the boy kindly disputed them one by one, trying to convince the kid that there is at least some good in human nature worth cultivating and that science agrees. But he got nowhere with this line of argument. So as a last resort, the boy told the kid about his own emptiness growing up, about how spirituality became important to him, about the blue angel dream, about the youth on the ledge out west, and about the motorcycle. The student was enthralled to hear something like this from a full professor—something the boy achieved in just six years after arriving.

"Well," he said thoughtfully, "maybe the emptiness doesn't mean I have to kill myself. Maybe I just need a *Gohonzon*."

The next day the boy returned, and the next, and the next. For three days they talked. During that time the doctors saw marked improvement in the student, and he was soon released under parental supervision and went home. A year later he was back in school and would stop by the boy's office every couple of weeks to talk about meaning and spirituality and how his life was changed now because he was spending a lot more time volunteering in a homeless shelter, which the boy had connected him with. The boy also told the kid to go to the local Buddhist temple on nearby Lee Road and chant *nan myoho renge kyo.* Although the boy had not done any chanting himself since his time in San Francisco, he figured it just might work. It turned out that the kid loved chanting, and the boy stopped by Lee Road to buy him a *Gohonzon.*

What chanting does, regardless of the tradition involved, is clear the mind of thoughts and worries so that we can connect with the Now and awaken a bit to our oneness with the infinite Mind of love, deepening our sense of security, our compassion, and our creativity. This Mind is a force for good, always desiring to support us in acts of kindness and creative vision.

We all know about the force of gravity. It keeps us connected to terra firma all day every day, and we completely trust it to be there at all times. But no one has ever seen gravity because it is an invisible force, however real. No one really understands its basic essence, although we see and measure its effects. The infinite Mind of kindness is like gravity, and we all need to have more confidence in it.

A Route 80 Premonition as Joe Lay Dying

Here is another amazing synchronicity shaped by a highway premonition.

In 2008, twenty years after they arrived, the boy and his family left Cleveland for Stony Brook, New York, and it was a hard move to make. He was leaving behind many good friends and colleagues—especially beloved Dr. Joe Foley, who had been his collaborator and mentor for all those years. Fast-forward to Wednesday, July 11, 2012. With their now teenage son away in Costa Rica for a few weeks, Mitsuko and the boy headed back to Cleveland for a vacation. They drove west on Route 80 that afternoon and about nine o'clock arrived at the Best Western in Lewisburg on Route 215, which is right off 80 at exit 210, halfway between the George Washington Bridge and Cleveland. After spending the night, they rose early and headed for Cleveland at sunrise, with four hours to go.

That morning, as they were driving past the spot where the boy left had left his dad's car so many years ago, *he experienced an overwhelming intuition that the first thing he should do in Cleveland was to visit his ninety-six-year-old friend and mentor Dr. Foley.* When they arrived at about two in the afternoon on July 12, they drove over to Joe's house on Berkshire Road in Cleveland Heights right away, even before checking in at the hotel. The boy knocked on the door and Joe's son, Stephen, answered and showed him into the pantry, where Joe was bedridden and looking very frail. He'd already been in decline when the boy had stopped in to see him a couple of months earlier. At that time Joe was unable to walk but was still fairly lucid, at least when the boy entertained him with about a dozen Irish jokes that he had taught the boy over the twenty years of their friendship. Today Joe could no longer remember much, so every joke was hilarious to him.

The jokes got Joe in touch with himself and his memories of Boston Latin School, his parents in Dorchester, his father the garbage collector, and his days at Holy Cross and Harvard Med. Humor seemed to touch Joe's soul and reconnect him with his life story.

But now, two months later, Joe Foley was clearly ready to deliver himself over to the care of God in Christ.

The boy was Joe's last outside visitor. He died at 5:37 the next morning, Friday, July 13, with his daughter Celia by his side. She, Steve, and their sister Mara were all there in their old home, looking out for their dad. Celia told the boy two days later that, for the last several hours of his life, Joe had stretched his arms upward and kept asking to be moved closer to the light.

He was ready for a new adventure.

On Tuesday, July 17, 2012, at St. Ann's Church in Cleveland Heights, where Joe had gone to Mass each morning in his old age, the boy attended his crowded funeral service. Joe had designated the boy to read at his funeral the passage from St. Paul's Letter to the Philippians.[23]

> This is my prayer for you: that your love will grow more and more; that you will have knowledge and understanding with your love; that you will see the difference between good and bad and will choose the good; that you will be pure and without wrong for the coming of Christ; that you will be filled with the good things produced in your life by Christ to bring glory and praise to God.

As he read the boy felt that he was speaking on Joe's behalf, for from their long friendship he knew that this was truly Joe's message to the five hundred gathered there from every background and walk of life. The boy teared up but breathed deep and stayed poised.

Driving back to New York on Route 80 that afternoon, he imagined Joe laughing a bit and remarking, "Well, my lad, just my Irish luck to die on a Friday the thirteenth."

---

23 Philippians 1:9-1:11.

Interlude

Dr. Joe Foley, the boy, Dean Nate Berger, and Dr. Bob Binstock of Case Med

There is no difficulty that enough LOVE will not conquer; no disease that enough LOVE will not heal; no door that enough LOVE will not open; no gulf that enough LOVE will not bridge; no wall that enough LOVE will not throw down; no sin that enough LOVE will not redeem.

–Emmet Fox

Whether you believe in an eternal soul or you believe that mind and memory are all merely brain tissue, we can agree on this: when it comes to the deeply forgetful LOVE is the question, LOVE is the answer, and LOVE is the way.

–Anonymous

For every minute you remain angry you give up sixty seconds of
peace of mind.

–Ralph Waldo Emerson

How to Follow a Dream—Lesson Six: Boys should always be willing to give Cleveland a chance. It is a good city where many good people are found. Getting out on Route 80 to experiment with a new place and new people can be life-transforming. And we should never give up on deeply forgetful old folks, because they too have souls and we can be present with them in peace. Give them a chance. Even the most deeply forgetful people can reveal their continuing oneness with the infinite Mind and Love. Our brain cells may deteriorate, and as a result our language may be lost, but we are all still eternal souls having a human experience, and ultimately each of us remains a drop of divine Mind. Mind is before matter, so matter cannot diminish Mind in any ultimate sense, although it may look that way. The deeply forgetful individual who seems so distant much of the time is just someone who has already headed to the railroad station and started to climb aboard that train bound for glory— it just hasn't quite left.

The boy with Dr. Jack Templeton being inducted into the Philadelphia College of Physicians for "distinguished contributions to medicine"

This is the real secret of life—to be completely engaged with what you are doing in the here and now. And instead of calling it work, realize it is play.

—Alan Watts

The Big Bold Prayer and Two Miracles: The Inner Road

In prayer, it is better to have a heart without words, than words without heart.

—John Bunyon

The boy was confident that a clearly worded prayer, stated with conviction for a good purpose, will with time elicit a response from the infinite Mind, a power so much greater than ourselves and upon which we can draw. He was not afraid to pray even for very big things, because this allows the infinite Mind to express itself more completely. The following episode is about a big bold prayer and two miracles that flowed from it, and they left the boy inspired to do more and more.

Prayer at the Harvard Memorial Chapel

In 1996 the boy was back up in New Hampshire visiting St. Paul's with his daughter when she reversed course and decided not to enroll there but instead to continue school in Shaker Heights, Ohio. He had some hours to visit the old chapel where he had had peacefully meditated all those years ago on the meaning of blue angel dream, but early in the afternoon the girl insisted on leaving. So instead of staying in Concord for the entire weekend, they spent Sunday touring Harvard Square before flying back to Cleveland Sunday night. His daughter went shopping. The boy felt inspired to visit Harvard Memorial Chapel and ask God for something big. He prayed quietly for an hour near the right-hand wall, the one with all the engraved names of famous graduates.

On March 28, 1996, he asked for the creation of an institute that would study the highest form of love in the universe—not flawed human love. It was a prayer for a research center that would take as its basic premise a belief in the divine love that prompted infinite Mind to create the universe through the Big Bang, a love that we can sense when we look up into the starry night sky and know that behind such magnificence there is a wonderful intent. It was a prayer for insights into the spiritual experiences reported by people all over the world, of a love that invades consciousness from outside and yet really from deep within, leaving them feeling that the usual ego boundaries between themselves and others are not real walls but just low fences that allow for a oneness. Secondly, it was a prayer that someday there might be a chair at Harvard Divinity School held by a great scholar and researcher who would focus on this topic, the profoundest of all spiritual themes.

Patience! Patience! These two miracles happened, five and sixteen years later, respectively! God always hears the right prayers, but they are fulfilled in divine time, and we first have to work really hard to inspire God's confidence in us, creating the conditions for divine action. Ultimately, though, all our efforts are just a tiny fraction of what God does to complete the equation. If it is a prayer consistent with the loving nature of God, it will be answered, although we know not when.

The first part of the prayer was answered in 1998, about eighteen months after it was prayed. That was when the boy received a call from Charles L. Harper, the visionary vice president of the John Templeton Foundation. Chuck invited him to organize a research symposium on *agape* in October of 1999 at MIT in Cambridge, Massachusetts, which the boy also co-chaired. The three-day conference was officially entitled *Altruism, Empathy and Agape: A Scientific Symposium,* and included outstanding practitioners of selfless love, twenty major researchers in the field (such as Antonio Damasio, Daniel Batson, and Jerome Kagan), and twenty leading religious and moral thinkers. The website remains available at www.altruisticlove.org.

Among the leading lights of love that spoke about their lives was the remarkable Templeton Laureate Dame Cicely Saunders, then eighty-three years of age, and known all over the world as the creator and founder of the hospice movement. Dame Cicely flew in from St. Christopher's Hospice in London and began her dinner plenary address by stating that her entire life work was guided by God and by her experience of divine love, however much the standard professional textbooks manage to leave this out. The boy and Dame Cicely were close friends and had talked over the years about hospice care and deeply forgetful people, who also need to die free of pain with no intrusive technologies attached.

At the end of her talk, which she entitled "Why I Can Never Retire," Dame Cicely said that God could never allow her to retire and that she still went to St. Christopher's Hospice to listen attentively to dying people as they spoke about their lives, and to change bedpans and carry out all the other small chores of hospice life with great love. When she herself died several years later, virtually every news organization across the globe printed long obituaries praising a modern saint who restored dignity and significance even to those who could no longer be rescued from death.

That night at MIT, Sir John Templeton and the boy sat side by side at dinner, with about 120 people seated at other tables around them. After Dame Cicely's talk, they all stood up and Sir John said forcefully, "No, never retire! Retirement kills!" as he clapped appreciatively.

"Retirement will kill you!!" he whispered in the boy's ear. "Don't ever do it! It's a death sentence!"

After the conference, Sir John began writing his book, *Pure Unlimited Love: An Eternal Creative Force and Blessing Taught by All Religions.* The boy liked the "pure love" idea because he had written articles on the "pure love" in Western and Eastern spiritual thought, especially on how human nature is incapable of this, and how we only connect with it through meditation and prayer. Many people experience such cherishing love as spiritually transforming, invading them from beyond themselves in the form of divinely sourced energy, a higher Love.

Sir John told the boy at dinner that night in Boston how he was not terribly interested in human love, because, while the cherishing love of a mother for a child is the highest form of human affection, human emotions are still unreliable, narrow, and small when compared to the spiritual Love that made humans, preceded the Big Bang, and underlies all of reality. He said that people like Dame Cicely had connected with something beyond themselves, and this was what he wanted people to research more than any other topic. "Pure love" comes from the soul, from the inner being, which is God within, not from the physical bodily substrate. Sir John and the boy were both pessimistic about human nature, which they considered much more disposed to arrogance than humility, hostility rather than kindness, and violence rather than peace. But they agreed that hope for the future comes when we can awaken awareness of the infinite Mind and spirit within us that is equally manifest in the orderly elegance of the universe. "Human love," said Sir John, "is somewhat interesting, but only as a very flawed and imperfect reflection of pure unlimited love, which is the ultimate reality. Humans did not invent love; it was there in the beginning before the universe with its time and space came into existence. Don't forget the difference."

They had actually first met ten years earlier at a conference on religion and health in Virginia where the boy was speaking. He introduced himself to Sir John, who was seated in a hotel lounge, at the suggestion of a mutual friend, David B. Larson, MD. Sir John asked him what he was most interested in, and the boy answered, "infinite Mind and divine love." They spent the next three hours talking, because Sir John was excited to discuss both of these things. At the end of the discussion, Sir John asked the boy if he thought that some of the Sufi Muslim mystics were right in seeing divine Love as a bluish energy, and the boy mentioned Chagall. As the boy proceeded to describe Chagall's blue angel experience, and his windows in the Union Church in Pocantico Hills and the United Nations, Sir John exclaimed with a huge smile that he also had stood awed before Chagall's *Good Samaritan Window* because, as an investor who worked with the Rockefellers, he had visited the church a few times years ago. The boy and Sir John agreed that if divine love energy had a color, Chagall got it right in that beautiful blue window.

Of course to the boy this was all an astonishing example of synchronicity, for how uncanny that Sir John and he would both be inspired by Chagall's great window of love. This was the basis of a trusting relationship. Sir John was not himself a blue angel dreamer, but he knew that the boy was one and accepted this warmly with his characteristic open-mindedness.

The boy told Sir John the story of the dream and going to Yale Divinity School for a day to speak about it, of Route 80 and the ledge, and of Kazuko's rice balls and many such things, including the Unity School of Christianity. Sir John smiled as he listened and laughed nonstop before mentioning that he had run off to Israel in his younger years, and that his mother too had had a frightening premonition that he was in big trouble one night when indeed he was, that he was. Sir John was a Christian who wanted to learn from all the different ways that people on earth seek God, and he was unwilling to believe that any one faith had all the answers. He had for a while attended the same Unity "One Mind" center on 58th Street that the boy had, and like the boy he never actually joined. Sir John valued the teachings of Charles Fillmore, the founder of the Unity School, as did the boy, and mentioned how much he had learned from Fillmore's "Mind before matter philosophy of Ultimate Reality," which led him to consider physics and math as windows into the divine. When the boy talked with Sir John, synchronicity was everywhere.

The Institute for Research on Unlimited Love

The boy was sitting in his office at Case Western Medical School in June of 2001 when he received a fax from Sir John asking him to start an institute to study spiritual love, and suggesting that it be called the Institute for Research on Unlimited Love. "Sir John," the boy faxed back, "how about the Institute for Research on Creative Altruism?" which sounded a little more scientific and might be easier for his colleagues to accept. But the boy knew that such conformity to the secular language around him was untrue to Chagall and the dream, and that he ought never to be diverted away from the spiritual core of this new research.

Sir John faxed back, rightly, "No, I think unlimited love," promising a considerable sum to support the institute. The boy quickly agreed, and faxed back "Sir John, I love the name. It jumps right off the page!" And Sir John was absolutely on target, because the rather bold name attracted immense media attention, and invited more open dialogue between science and spirituality. *Altruism* is a dry, secular term that does not come close to expressing the radiance and warmth of *Pure Unlimited Love.*

Later that month, the boy sat down with a lawyer in the old Caribou Coffee House on Coventry Road in Cleveland Heights, Ohio, to discuss founding such an institute, one that would nurture new scientific research and spiritual-philosophical reflection on the topic of love. Not any kind of love, mind you. Not giddy romantic love or love of chocolate or designer shoes, but the kind of love that holds the security, well-being, and happiness of others to be as meaningful and real to us as our own.

No modern academic starts an Institute for Research on Unlimited Love at a secular scientific university without getting tons of grief for it. But the boy was a Route 80 blue angel dreamer, a spiritual friend of Chagall's, and Sir John was worth the risk because he was so accepting of all those Route 80 adventures he heard about. In fact, he trusted the boy not because he was brilliant, which he was not, but because his thinking resonated with Sir John's ideas about infinite Mind, Ultimate Reality, and Pure Unlimited Love.

So by June of 2001 the boy had founded the Institute for Research on Unlimited Love as an independent 501(c)3 nonprofit located at Case

Western Reserve University and funded largely by Sir John Templeton.[24] The idea was to support excellent science through competitive requests for research proposals, to study how it is that love can sometimes reach beyond the ordinary limits of human emotion to include all of humanity without exception, and how spirituality might affect this expansion. He gathered a fabulous Board of Directors from Greater Cleveland. In 2001, the first call for proposals yielded 320 letters of intent from researchers around the country, about ninety of which were outstanding. The ninety full applications that resulted were carefully reviewed by a team of scientific consultants and experts, and twenty were funded at a total cost of several million dollars.

These, then, are the seven core questions that Sir John agreed to and that the institute would become known for worldwide:

1. Does the unselfish love of others contribute to the happiness, health, and resilience of those who give it?

2. How does such love prevent illness and contribute to healing?

3. How can parents and communities raise children who flourish in such love?

4. Can the spirituality and practices of Unlimited Love enhance the workplace and philanthropy?

5. What do people mean when they report a spiritual experience of Unlimited Love, how common is this, and is this experience objectively associated with emotional healing and expanded benevolence?

6. Do physics and mathematics point to an "Ultimate Reality" or "Ground of Being" that underlies reality (the laws and constants of the universe, as well as energy and matter), and if so, might this be described in terms of creative Mind and love, which mystics, philosophers, and theologians, along with some leading quantum theorists and cosmologists, suggest is at least plausible?

---

24 www.unlimitedloveinstitute.org.

7. How can the major spiritualities and religions of the world come to abide in their various conceptualizations of Unlimited Love and practice love for all humanity, rather than merely for those who adhere to a particular set of beliefs?

This is a broad list that rises from love in general to the spiritual experience of Unlimited Love. The boy thought that if the institute could make progress on these seven questions it would have served its purpose for humanity.

The definition of love the institute developed is this: w*hen the happiness, security, and well-being of another feels as meaningful and real to us as our own, or perhaps more so, we love that person.* This definition includes proper love of self as a standard for love of others. Unlimited Love includes, as well as extends beyond, our nearest and dearest to all humanity, based on our shared dignity and interdependence with one another and with nature. For those who are secular, this ideal can be rationally defended. For those who are spiritually or religiously inclined, Unlimited Love is deemed to be a Creative Presence or Ultimate Reality underlying the universe, the participation in which leads to inner peace and expanded benevolence. Whether we define ourselves as secular, religious, or spiritual, we can generally agree that such love constitutes the greatest imaginable leap forward in human consciousness and behavior.

With initial funding from the John Templeton Foundation (2001–2005), the institute moved quickly, beginning in 2001, to provide support for the study of the seven questions above—and ones like them—at more than fifty research universities across the United States, from Stanford to Harvard, from Chicago to Princeton. Based on significant results, the dialogue on Unlimited Love at the interface of science and spiritual thought has grown dramatically and achieved recognition, with major events that addressed the subject taking place not just in the United States, but in England, Germany, Japan, Australia, and Canada.

The institute has been covered on more than six hundred radio shows, such as *Talk of the Nation, Mehmet Oz,* BBC Radio, and *the Dennis Prager Show.* Television features include the *John Stossel Show, 20/20, The Daily Show,* and *Nightline.* More than four thousand print articles have appeared in venues such as *Parade,* the *New York Times, "O" Magazine, USA Today,* and *US News and World Report.* Blog coverage exceeds five hundred thousand sites, including BigThink.com, WebMD.com, BigQuestionsOnLine.com, and Beliefnet.com.

***

Just before Sir John died in 2008, he asked the boy to write the book that he would now never have time to write: *Is Ultimate Reality Unlimited Love?* Out of faithfulness to Sir John's request, the boy wrote it to reflect as closely as possible what Sir John would have wanted to express. But this was easy, because they were very much of one mind on the subject.

Plus, on Route 80, loyalty to the people God brings your way is all you really have to find your destiny.

The Harvard Watson Chair

Then, in answer to that same March 29, 1996, prayer, lo and behold, a highly philanthropic Cleveland friend of the boy's by the name of Richard T. Watson (1933–2011), a co-owner of the Cleveland Cavaliers, came along to endow the Richard T. Watson Chair of Science and Religion at Harvard Divinity School.

Who had ever heard of an endowed chair of science and religion? But the idea made a lot of sense to Dick, and the boy was to encourage him.

Dick had entered Harvard College in the 1960s as a sixteen-year-old scholarship student and math genius from the Cleveland suburb of Maple Heights, where he grew up working in the steel mills from age thirteen for extra money when he wasn't in school.[25] Dick was a mathematical mystic, who saw a creative Ground of Being underlying and sustaining the beauty of the equations, constants, and intelligent mathematical principles of the universe.

Whether in the complexities of calculus or in the simplicity of a geometric formula, Dick found fingerprints of a divine Intelligence. A rationalist through and through, he had had no single, astonishing spiritual experience, at least that the boy knew of. Instead, his window onto the divine was the elegant mathematical order that he saw underlying creation. For him, the underlying mathematical intelligence of this beautiful universe was a doorway to the perennial philosophy of a loving and intentional infinite Mind. In this sense he was a modern Platonist, a participant in Divine *logos*.

Dick Watson had been a friend for several years from their Episcopal Church St. Paul's in Cleveland Heights when he flew in to attend the boy's 1999 MIT conference on altruism, empathy, and *agape*—an event that perfectly ignited Dick's appetite for science and religion. It animated his interest in such themes as love, the Golden Rule, game theory, and altruism in dialogue with science. He started reading every book that had been published on religion and science, and two years later he joined the board of trustees of the Institute for Research on Unlimited Love. Then, late in 2003, Dick started talking about funding a Professorship of Science and Religion at Harvard Divinity School, which was also about the time he became a member of the Templeton Foundation. By now, his office and bedroom bookshelves were filled with the works of scientists and theologians interested in concepts such as cooperation, generosity, and altruistic love.

Dick died on July 20, 2011, while on a visit to New York City. Just weeks before, Ahmed Ragab, PhD, MD, had joined the Harvard Divinity School faculty as the young scholar selected by Harvard Divinity

---

25   www.cleveland.com/obituaries/index.ssf/2011/07/richard_t_watson_was_the_cavs.html

School to hold the Richard T. Watson Chair of Science and Religion. In the months before his passing, Dick and the boy had had several discussions regarding Dr. Ragab, and Dick seemed very hopeful about the young man, in whom he saw immense potential.

Dick's widow and beloved wife Judy invited the boy to join her at Harvard on March 29, 2012, to hear Professor Ragab's inaugural lecture, entitled "Disciplining and Persuading: Science, Religion, and the Making of Knowledge." On March 28, the boy took Amtrak up to Boston from Bridgeport, Connecticut, and when he arrived that afternoon, he went directly to Harvard Memorial Chapel and said a prayer of thanks. The next day, March 29—sixteen years to the day after the prayer he had offered in 1996—the boy joined Judy and the Watson family in a crowded lecture hall at the Divinity School, heard a fine inaugural lecture, and then, with a small group of other attendees, joined Dean Graham of the Divinity School for a dinner to mark the occasion. Judy spoke about Dick and what the Richard T. Watson Chair meant to him and was gracious in acknowledging the boy's role in the development of that vision, going back as far as the 1999 conference that Dick had attended at the boy's invitation, and all the intellectual exploration that followed through his association with the institute.

The boy felt at that moment that the infinite Mind had answered his long-ago prayer much more abundantly than expected. From his perspective as a Route 80 quester, this was all a wonderful synchronicity, inexplicable by the laws of even the most unlikely probabilities.

Sixteen years to the day, and there was the boy at Harvard Divinity School, being acknowledged for helping an extraordinary friend endow a Harvard professorship. His mind drifted back to sharing his blue angel dream with a class at Yale Divinity School years before because Rev. Welles saw something in it. Not many would. But now he was at Harvard, and now there was a professorship that he had helped to bring about, beginning with a bold prayer.

Sixteen years is *not* such a long time to wait for a prayer to be answered. A loving God is not going to test you. John 15:7 reads, "If you abide in me and my words abide in you, you shall ask what you will, and it shall be done." Divine time (*kairos*) and human time (*chronos*) are different. The Watson Chair was proof that in due time infinite Mind works miracles on divine schedule.

***

How little we know about divinity, but we can still experience God's love. Yet so often doctrines separate us from one another and deny the unifying spirit of divine love that is the essence of true spirituality. When religions have put doctrinal "truth" above love they have inspired massive evil, from conflict and coercion to terror and torture. Religious wars are manifestations of a human arrogance and tribalism that amplify the worst in us.

The world will know sustained peace when all religions live up to their inherent ideal of a divine love applied to all humankind without exception. Only by taking such love much more seriously than we do—even to the point of extending profound love to our ancient enemies—can we expect to avoid increasing destruction. To the degree that religions fall short of universal divine love, violence will overcome us all. To the extent that truly universal love can be captured in the ritual worlds that religions create, and expressed in spiritually inspired forgiveness and compassion, we will have a human future.

Interlude

Harvard Memorial Church

The prayer of a righteous man is powerful and effective.

—James 5:6

Unlimited Love has an origin divine
A blessing to be equally shared as yours and mine
Unlimited Love is uniquely profound
as an unfathomable invisible presence everywhere found

—Francisco Gomes de Matos, a peace linguist, Recife, Brazil

Why do we close our eyes when we pray, cry, kiss, or dream? Because
the most beautiful things in life are not seen but felt by the heart.

—Denzel Washington

How to Follow a Dream—Lesson Seven: Sometimes we may want to
pray for something big and bold that is really worthy of God's attention,
and if we do, we should then work very hard and patiently to nurture

the vision, knowing that dedicated effort can be a precondition for God to fulfill it. The infinite Mind is perfect, a reliable guide that **always** responds to wise, loving, prayerful requests when the time is right and when the effort is being made. This Mind that orders the universe also exists within each of us, and wants to see all loving purposes fulfilled, so the answers and the means will come.

And sometimes we will start whole new organizations with unusual names, like the Institute for Research on Unlimited Love, but that is just because Unlimited Love is another way of talking about infinite Mind and God, and a lot of people don't know God. So a boy has to be brave to start something like this, and he often needs a caring old mentor who stopped caring what the world thought many years ago. Pray and meditate to escape the petty clamor of the brash world and more clearly envision the path to noble goals and dreams and have confidence that, when we put forth one hundred percent effort, the infinite Mind will be eager to cooperate with us. There is a power for good in the universe greater than us that awaits us down Route 80, revealing itself at the right time and in the right place and way. Just stay on the road.

The boy with Sir John Templeton at Duke University

*Could unlimited love be described as a creative, sustaining energy?
When we embrace our creative energy, can we draw, from the
universal Source, a tremendous spiritual energy matrix into many
areas of our lives? Does a divine fountainhead of love exist in the
universe in which degrees of human participation are possible?*

—Sir John Marks Templeton

The Road to Milesburg and the Mystical Walking Stick: A Bus Ride on Route 80

The greatest gift that you can give another person is to gracefully receive whatever it is that they want to give us.

—Fred Rogersx

H ow do you tell what is synchronicity and what isn't? The boy did not speak much of synchronicity in his daily conversations with the many psychiatrists who were his colleagues or students at the nation's premier medical centers. He had to be circumspect, not wanting people to lose confidence in him and all the trust he had worked to achieve over the years. They were willing to talk about religion and mental health in seminars and grand rounds, but they did not appreciate a professor talking about boyhood dreams and synchronicity because this smacked of "magical thinking," or "apophenia"—meaning that you see a few too many meaningful connections, or remember or interpret information in a way that confirms beliefs that you already hold (also known as "confirmation bias").

In fact, most people who learn about the concept of synchronicity think that it is real and cannot be explained away by probabilities. They are not materialists, they are open to the concept of a nonmaterial soul of some kind, and they refuse to be diagnosed by any biased secular psychiatrist who insists that we should not dream in ways that open the door to infinite Mind. The disenchanted, materialistic view of the universe and of human experience has resulted in so many people suffering from meaninglessness, anxiety, depression, addiction, and even contemplating suicide, like Harry on the ledge or the kid at Hanna Pavilion. But the boy could never succumb to materialism. He had met the youth on the ledge, his mom knew he was almost killed on that motorcycle, and he had experienced such powerful synchronicity whispers, as well.

True, the line between authentic synchronicity and just "magical thinking" is not always clear, and extreme "magical thinking" that amounts to delusion is obviously dysfunctional. So the boy was careful to ask himself if his experience on the road to Milesburg, Pennsylvania was set up by God or just totally random. Sorting things out requires attentive listening for the echoes of synchronicity and noticing things that happen.

So herein follow two true stories. The first—the one that occurred in a bus en route to Milesburg—is probably not a story of synchronicity, but it could be. It was a tad uncanny, and maybe the script was more God's educational curriculum than the boy knew. There is room for doubt. Yet the boy had no doubt at all that his encounter with an old African-American man, guided to him by a shaman dream in the Cleveland ghetto to deliver a special walking stick at a time of desperate need, clearly involved synchronicity, and the Mind of God.

The Road to Milesburg

In August of 2004 the boy was at a meeting in New York City with some philanthropists, raising funds for the Institute for Research on Unlimited Love, but knowing that it was a little over the top for their tastes and that it might take a few decades to expand the work of the institute to the global level. The meeting was going no place, but voting with his feet was not an option because that would have insulted some very influential people.

As a result, nine thirty rolled around, and he had missed the last flight home from Newark to Cleveland. The boy had to deliver an eight o'clock lecture the next morning at Case Western University School of Medicine, where he was a professor, on the health benefits of giving. With no more flights available, he quickly jogged over to the Port Authority building on Eighth Avenue in the humid ninety-five-degree heat and boarded a crowded ten o'clock bus bound for Ohio.

They were all set to pull out of the terminal when the driver turned around and shouted, "Sorry, folks, air conditioner is busted. Do you really wanna go to Cleveland?" Voices rang out from a sea of sweat,

"Yes, let's roll! Clap for the driver!" And everyone clapped and smiled like they were all heat-resistant.

About five minutes into the trip, they were already through the Lincoln Tunnel, into New Jersey, and about to hit Route 80 heading west to the Delaware Water Gap and beyond when the boy felt a light tap on his right shoulder. He turned around and saw a young man, perhaps eighteen or so, with the facial features of an individual with Down syndrome, who asked him in a remarkably gentle and loving voice, "Sir, are we in Cleveland yet?" This was definitely an odd question, since they were only a few minutes out of Manhattan.

The boy answered, "No, but I will be sure to let you know when we are, okay?" Every five minutes across New Jersey and Pennsylvania along the boy's beloved Route 80, the young man asked him the same question and he gave him the same answer. During the nine hours on that hot, crowded bus, they became Route 80 friends.

The boy always felt that divinity wanted him to learn something from the really crazy, unforeseen Route 80 situations he kept encountering, and this night was no exception. In the seat in front of the boy sat a man maybe thirty years old or so with two little boys who might have been age five or six. About every half-hour, this big, tough-looking guy jumped up and, seething with hostility, screamed an expletive and slammed his fist into the metal roof of the bus, producing a loud, echoing boom and scaring everyone on board, including his poor sons.

The sharp contrast between the terribly destructive emotions on display in front of the boy as the dad pounded away at the ceiling, and the positive ones he saw behind him, in the smile of the young man with Down syndrome, continued to play out over almost three hundred miles. The dad was rough, overbearing, and never smiled once, while the young man was always peaceful and serene.

The bus made Milesburg, Pennsylvania (exit 158) at about four in the morning, hotter and sweatier than ever, air conditioner still busted. Milesburg is a stopover exit for buses, where the passengers all got out, bought snacks, stretched their legs, and about twenty minutes later headed back to the refueled bus. As they were filing back on, the boy noticed that the security officer wouldn't allow the hostile fellow who'd been seated in front of him, or his two boys, to board.

The boy's last, sad view as the bus pulled out was of the man continuing to kick the side of the building, screaming, with his two boys in tears. Then the bus headed west again on 80 and almost immediately, from the seat behind him, the boy's new acquaintance asked, with a hint of hilarity, "Sir, are we in Cleveland yet?"

They arrived at the Cleveland Greyhound station on Chester Avenue at about seven in the morning and the boy helped his new friend off the bus, gave him a pat on the back, met his mom, and they all laughed and talked for a few minutes. Then the boy hopped in a cab and made it to his lecture at the med school with exactly one minute to spare.

What is the lesson of this story? Simple. If you want to go to Cleveland, hostility won't get you there. A little light-heartedness and love will. Hostility will get you marooned in Milesburg, regardless of how much you think you deserve to be angry at the world. The bottom line is that, if you allow yourself to become caught up in destructive emotions, it will only make things a whole lot worse for you—and for everyone around you. If you opt for mirth and warmth, you have a better probability of making it all the way to Cleveland—even if you are challenged by a cognitive disability—than some really irate guy who pisses everyone off.

Now whenever the boy drives across Pennsylvania—a slightly too-long state—he always stops at the Milesburg exit, grabs a coffee, and takes a look at the spot where he last saw his hostile fellow traveler and two young sons.

Recalling that encounter reminds the boy to abide by the Christian and Buddhist admonitions to give up on anger altogether. For the most part anger just gets us in trouble, because we do and say things that we regret later. Never respond to anger with anger, and your life will be better.

The most destructive thing about anger is that is really blocks your ability to serve as a channel for the flow of love energies; the two just can't coexist in the body and soul simultaneously.

Sometimes a controlled expression of anger is necessary to draw some boundaries, especially when someone has hurt you badly and no reconciliation can happen without a real meeting of the minds based on acknowledgement of the wrong and an apology on their part. But out-of-control anger is always bad for your own emotional, mental, and physical health. The best way to deal with it is just to meditate a bit on how hurt people are the ones who hurt people, which usually is true.

Maybe synchronicity was operating there on the road to Milesburg. The boy doubted it. But he was certain it was responsible for the shaman's dream late one night in his Cleveland neighborhood.

A Walking Stick That Appeared One Night via an Old Man's Dream

Cleveland had been the boy's home for two decades. So when he and his family had to move to Suffolk County on remote eastern Long Island, the boy almost felt that the power of dream was lost and that God had left him.

Refugees are people who have to leave a place because they are pushed rather than pulled, and it is the feeling of being pushed out that really stings. When that happens, the road before you is not the free and joyful one celebrated in Whitman's "Song of the Open Road." Even if the place it leads you to does have redeeming qualities, because there are good people doing good things everywhere, your heart is closed. The boy had to remind himself that life, anyway, is more a journey than a place, and "The Lord is close to the brokenhearted."[26]

So moving was hard because the boy and his family had really found a home, and for the boy home had always been a hard thing to find. But maybe he had become just too attached to Cleveland, and the infinite Mind wanted him to experience some dislocation for the sake of an unspecified future vision, or perhaps to indemnify past mistakes, or to learn more deeply than ever that one of the passages he burned into a plank as a boy with Mr. Muller was true: "The Lord is with you wherever you go."[27]

In any case, it was about eleven at night on July 28, 2008, the night before the boy and his family were moving on from Cleveland to Stony Brook, New York. They had sold their Shaker Heights home and were spending the night at the good old Glidden House hotel in University Circle, a favorite spot across from the Cleveland Museum of Art. The boy was sitting on a bench with his old friend Tom, behind the Arabica café right next to the hotel, drinking coffee. They were talking about Cleveland and why he was leaving after twenty good years. Tom thought that leaving made no sense and that the boy should have made more of an effort to stay.

As Tom and the boy sipped their coffees, the night was lit only by the streetlights in the distance. Arabica had closed, and the two of them were completely alone in the empty darkness.

Suddenly an old man wandered toward them out of the shadows. He was wearing a handsomely aged red leather jacket with beautiful blue leather tassels and little bells dangling here and there. He stood in front of Tom and the boy, smiled, and said, "Young man, you will need a walking stick before you leave, and I know you are starting a journey

---

26   Psalms 34:18.
27   Joshua 1:9.

because I dreamed about it and awoke. The Lord, He came to me in a dream. What the world needs now is love!"

The boy, being open-minded about dreamers, said, "Whoa, that was a great dream. Fabulous." Then he looked at the walking stick the old man was carrying and asked, "How much?"

"Forty dollars. I carved it myself and it took three whole days."

"Okay, but I don't have any cash with me," the boy said.

Instead, Tom offered to pay for the stick with the little carved face on it, and he handed the old man two twenty-dollar bills, saying, "He can use this because you are right, he's about to head off on a journey, and maybe this stick has at least a little more in the way of brains than he does."

The boy laughed. "Probably."

"It does," the old man responded. "Take this one, and just follow it wherever you go. It will lead you. I knew you would be here waiting for it, so that's why I wandered out so late at night. It sounds strange, but you, young man, cannot choose your own walking stick. The stick chooses you, and then it finds its way to you."

Then the old man handed the boy the hand-carved, mystical walking stick. It was about five feet long and an inch thick, hand-finished in a brown varnish, and laced with elegant, leaf-like motifs. Its central carving was a male African-American face with a look that expressed strength and wisdom. Various other spiritual symbols were carved on it as well.

The old man said, "When you feel lost, tap the stick on the ground three times and empty your mind. The Lord will show you the way."

"Okay, sounds good. Thanks."

Tom added, "Yup, he's gonna need to do that."

Nodding, the old man, in his red leather vest with its blue leather tassels, wandered off the way he had come. But as he ambled slowly away down the sidewalk, he suddenly turned and said, "Don't forget to tap and pray."

Tom, an analogically minded mystic who once ran a big law firm, remarked, "That stick probably makes better decisions than you do. Maybe it will lead you back to Cleveland when the day comes, and hopefully soon."

The old man with his stick and his feeling that on this night he must find the boy, Tom with his forty dollars, and the open road that awaited the next morning—this was pure graceful synchronicity for sure. The boy did not choose the sick, the stick chose him. The boy had never even imagined that he needed such a stick, much less that he would encounter one. It was like a scene from a Harry Potter film, when Harry goes into a store to buy a wand and the right one jumps into his hand. Like the boy and the walking stick, Harry possessed that wand, but in a deeper sense the wand possessed him.

That stick became part of the boy's Route 80 journey for good. Every once in a while, the boy still walks with it, and when he does his creative intuition kicks in, because as it taps the ground the clamor and clutter and concerns that tend to fill the mind recede. And in the mental space that opens up, he gets closer to the divine Mind.

The boy and family left early the next morning and drove east. Six hours later, they stopped at the Appalachian Trail where it crosses Route 80 at the Delaware Water Gap National Recreation Area, at the point where western New Jersey and eastern Pennsylvania meet. This is one of the most beautiful places in the entire country, with magnificent mountains, sparkling streams flowing over rocks and knee-high dams, exhilarating paths through miles of green-brown forests, and the Route 80 Bridge over the glistening Delaware River, full of canoes and fishermen as far as the eye can see.

The boy pulled over and stopped along the Appalachian Trail for a few minutes so they could get out and stretch a bit. Whenever the boy drives through the Gap, he takes a deep breath and tries to inspire anyone who is in the car with a big "Awesome!" If time permits, he gets off Route 80 at the Recreation Area exit, imbibes all the sheer beauty that is so abundant there, and recalls a phrase from the Roman philosopher Marcus Aurelius: "Remember that very little is needed to make a life happy." Thankful simplicity is what he feels, mixed with wonder. In today's materialistic and device-filled culture, it's simple to be happy but difficult to be simple!

When he got out of the car, the boy carried his new stick with him. The mystical walking stick, however ornate, took him back to a simpler time, and it was something to lean on. In the end, a beautiful walking stick is something stable in an unsteady world.

Among the American Puritans, a walking stick was a popular item, signifying the dignity of the common man of faith. Going back further, walking sticks were widely used on pilgrimages and spiritual journeys. Moses got into trouble because he hit the rock with his stick when he was not supposed to, but it is human nature to tap your walking stick along the ground, especially on rocky paths. Shamans the world over have staffs that they use in their rituals or to find lost objects, and Native American medicine men carry a spirit stick to evoke powerful, healing spirits.

It could be that the old man in Cleveland who carved the boy's stick was inspired by what such sticks meant in African tribes, where chiefs wielded them as signs of real and ritual power. Judging from his words and expression that night, though, it seemed that he viewed the stick more mystically, as something to be trusted. It was an object that could help intuitively with big decisions in life.

We make many choices in life because our consciousness is riddled with past misunderstandings, miscommunications, misinterpretations, and miscalculations. We may only know if our choice was a good one when we can look back on it after a few years and see where it led and how it worked out. But then again, circumstances might change a little later and the situation could fall apart. Then forgiveness is key to love because bitterness blocks the flow of the Supreme, and so we disconnect from the inner essence of peace that is our original spiritual nature.

Hope lies mainly in responding with faith and love to what finds us on our journeys, even difficult possibilities that we never have imagined. They find us more than we find them. But they make a certain amount of sense, because no spiritual journey should be too easy or smooth. Complacency is not what makes us grow. By the time he received the walking stick late that night, the boy had begun to realize more deeply that the next leg of the Route 80 journey would be a challenge.

A Storm at the Three Village Inn

As soon as the boy and his family hit Long Island, a big storm struck, literally, and all hell broke loose that very night.

They had just exited off Route 80, drove over the George Washington Bridge, and arrived at the Three Village Inn in Stony Brook Village, on the Long Island Sound about an hour east of Greater New York. Their little cottage felt old and cold. It had two beds, a few pieces of furniture, and the bathroom had black mildew on the walls. Now thunderstorms made the skies darker than they had ever seen before. The lightning lit up everything; thunder shook the cabin; the rain was torrential.

For the boy's wife and son, the reality of this move from a place they all liked to a place that was so different began to sink in at a very deep level. His son was getting texts from his buddies in Shaker Heights who were starting the new soccer season, and he missed his team already. Mom was realizing how remote Stony Brook is from New York City. "I can't believe this! There's nothing out here and we don't know anyone."

Things got worse in that cabin as the thunder boomed and the lightning zapped down from on high. The boy listened to them both for about half an hour and tried to calm things with a few pointless words, but it was hard. This was the worst night of his adult life and there was no going back.

So the boy did the only thing he knew how to do. "Listen, I'm going out to get some pizza. I'll be back soon." He would take a drive and come back a little later, the worst husband and father on the face of the earth.

He got behind the wheel in the red Toyota Highlander and drove out to Route 25A, the main street from Stony Brook to Setauket to Port Jefferson. In Setauket he came across Little Joe's Pizzeria and pulled in. Little Joe's is a plain, everyday kind of pizza place, but as the boy walked in, he glanced down and saw a magazine rack, and there on the rack was a local newspaper called the *Village Times Herald*, which he had never heard of. An article on the front page, with a two-inch headline, caught his eye: "Unlimited Love Arrives at Stony Brook University."

He wasn't prepared for this kind of attention and did not desire it. It was not the ideal way for him to be introduced to the highly secular scientific medical community of a state university, and it only added to his overall sense that Long Island would not be easy. The task before him was to establish and build a new Center for Medical Humanities, Compassionate Care, and Bioethics at Stony Brook, and to save institute work for weekends away from the university. Actually, when he read the whole article, it was not that bad. The reporter had interviewed the medical school dean and a few others, who made it clear that the boy had been recruited to teach medical humanism and empathic interactions, and not for other more metaphysical reasons. That was a fair statement.

Yet that first day of work at least a few people looked at the boy skeptically, and one asked, "Are you the Unlimited Love guy? Are you okay? How will you save us?"

"Well, I hope to contribute to a positive culture, and try a little kindness," the boy responded with a smile.

"Well, that shouldn't be that bad. I am okay with kindness. But Unlimited Love is a little over the top around here."

"Thanks for the wisdom. I keep my spiritual writings completely separate from my day job involving medical school life. The boundaries are clear, but it is okay to study and work on empathy and compassionate care, which is what we all want here," said the boy.

A few days later the boy called the president of the university. "Shirley, did you see that article in the *Village Times Herald*?"

"Yes, I did see it. It was hard to miss."

"Did you get any responses to it?"

"Why, yes, I did. I got a few calls from male emeritus professors."

"What did they say?"

"They wanted to know what kind of love we're talking about!"

They laughed. She was nice.

***

The president was slightly surprised by the article, but the boy was not feeling too badly about this because, after all, she had suggested to him that Governor Elliot Spitzer planned to be very helpful to the program he was building, which was perfectly true. But just about the same day the boy arrived, the governor was on the front cover of the *New York Post*, having been photographed with the hooker he had the New York State taxpayers pay for. A hooker was a problem, but having the citizens cover the bill is really over the top. So he was out, and the new governor, David Paterson, was in. Now, with Spitzer out of the picture, the boy looked back and thought again about his decision to leave Cleveland.

You never know about decisions in life, because there is so little that we control. Things happen for better or for worse, and maybe they work out and maybe they don't. How do you know?

Between the *Three Village Herald* and Governor Spitzer's hooker escapades, the boy's arrival at Stony Brook began to feel like one of the Jackson Pollock paintings he used to describe to undergrads years back, the ones that start with a motley black splash at the center but, as the colors expand outward, end up looking beautiful. Leaving a nice home in a good neighborhood like Shaker Heights, Ohio, surrounded by friends, with a nice church like St. Paul's Episcopal down the road, and a lot of literary supporters—this was the splash of paint that the boy could only hope would lead to an expansion of beauty. But things happen for a reason.

Sometimes there is great value when your world and support structures crash, because then you are spiritually naked before the universe and can refocus without ego or arrogance. Maybe the boy had become too successful in Cleveland and now that had to end for longer-term growth. As they say, "What doesn't kill you makes you stronger." Things do work out, but you need a belief in Infinite Mind and a lot of prayer, like the old African-American man said the night they left Cleveland. It was a time in life for the boy to go through something hard, and over the years this all deepened his commitment to living out the blue angel dream no matter what, and probably to writing this book. He had emailed out little snippets of *God and Love on Route 80* from the institute as early as 2000, but then stopped. Now somehow he knew that the book wanted to be written and that the dream had a life of its own.

***

The canvas is always expanding. Hope is having faith that difficult moments are good moments in disguise. But that hope comes from a feeling that the infinite Mind can reshape mishaps to create magnificent new realities. There is a passage in the New Testament from St. Paul: "We know that all things work together for good for those who love God, who are called according to his purposes."[28] This idea that "things work together for good" means that beauty emerges with the passage of time, as we gain perspective. In the meantime, tap that walking stick and be patient.

The Daily Show Comes to Stony Brook Med

Anyway, maybe any decision is a good one when you end up on the *Daily Show* for a special with John Oliver.

Even the "brutalist" style architecture of Stony Brook Med was an opportunity. In 2011 John called, hoping to do a show with the boy on "cooperation" in a scientific environment. He brought his team—four cameras and a writer—out to Stony Brook, although they were slightly delayed because they stopped by the Gap store in Port Jefferson Village to buy two sets of identical clothing, one for John Oliver and one for the boy.

John loved the med school architecture, which he thought was completely futuristic, apocalyptic, and Space Age all the way. His camera team captured the bottoms of the two huge, brownish cubes sticking up on their rusted metal stilts into the sky for a hundred yards on each side. They especially loved the collection of dinosaurs that stood in the main lobby, in front of the Starbucks, and Oliver himself thought that the Health Sciences Tower was out of *The Lord of the Rings*. Oliver then proceeded to select the most beat-up, dilapidated, disgusting, pathology research lab on the tenth floor of the bigger, brownish cube, filled with broken test tubes and cobwebs, as the setting for our interview.

---

28 Romans 8:28.

The camera teams set up and the interview began.

Oliver started out easy on the boy, asking him factual questions about the evolution of cooperation and how we go about studying it. He was interested in the science of imitation, and fairly soon, began to parrot the boy's tone and mannerisms. Then they took a break, after which John walked in wearing the same set of clothes that they had asked the boy to wear.

About an hour into the filming, John started yelling, "You know what I think of you? I think you are f—ng full of it, full of SH—!!! There is no cooperation. This is all f—ng BS! You suck, dude!"

All the camera operators started mimicking him and shouting at the boy too.

Then John put on a white plastic face mask, the kind hockey goalies wear, and started spitting out of the mouth of the mask—large gobs of white froth—and screaming curses at the boy, trying to get him angry.

The boy just breathed deeply and smiled. After more than ten minutes of mockery, he said, "I love you guys!"

And they all quieted down.

They did a little more filming in the hallways and then they took off for the Port Jefferson ferry to Bridgeport, where they spent the next day with two candidates for the US Senate seat, one a Republican and the other a gay Democrat, who were making the news because they were campaigning together—cooperatively—in the hope of creating more civil political discourse. The show turned out well, including an E.T.-like ending as people chased the politicians into the sky on bikes with big baskets.

Suddenly, for a few days, the boy was the most famous person in Stony Brook. Students from all over were emailing or wanting an autograph, and he was hearing from people he hadn't seen for years. He began to feel that his Route 80 journey was still all there before him, at least maybe, but he had a lot to process.

It turned out that the canvas did expand, and the boy came to realize that Stony Brook was the best medical school he had ever encountered because of the deep empathic quality of its community and culture, its emphasis on communicating compassionately with patients, and the traditions of medical humanities that had long been a part of the place. His years there were good ones, and people came to trust him. Out of respect for boundaries, he wrote this book entirely at home on the weekends over five years and was in his office at school most days from seven in the morning until seven at night.

Interlude

Getting to Cleveland

What am I seeking? I am the same as He. His essence speaks through me. I have been looking for myself.

—Rumi

Hardship often prepares ordinary people for an extraordinary destiny.

—C. S. Lewis

My soul is from elsewhere, and I intend to end up there.

—Rumi

How to Follow a Dream—Lesson Eight: Love can get us to where we want to go, but hostility only gets us marooned. Love works, it will make us welcome on the bus all the way to Cleveland or wherever. If we want to succeed at anything really well, we can do so only with love. We might otherwise have partial successes, but nothing great or lasting.

Boys build their stone temples in life, and sometimes they are torn down as a spiritual test of character. They build their careers, their families, their communities of worship and their friendships. They buy houses and build new walls and plant trees that will last forever. They invest all their time and energy and heart. But sometimes these things get thrown down, and the stones fall and break. Things meant to last go away, and the monuments of meaning we build sadly perish. Leaving some place we love because we don't see a choice can feel very bad, but the Buddhist will say that no one should be overly attached to place, and anyway life is a journey, so we are pilgrims by necessity. All a boy can do is press ahead and learn resilience.

The lesson here is that no one ever said that following a dream would be easy, that there would not be hard and painful tests to endure. Buildings can be thrown down, but these are necessary tests, mainly because we get too comfortable and we start resting on our local laurels so we cannot see that we still have miles and miles to go. Boys need to be disrupted at times. So God has to wipe the slate clean, often by sending along someone to make things difficult. Someday we may return to the place where we started, but way usually leads on to way, and the place we knew and loved so much begins to look a little strange and unfamiliar as the years pass by.

One thing that infinite Mind can do to make difficult moves a little easier is to cause a dream in the perfect old man who will feel called to meet us late at night with the perfect walking stick, the one that we desperately need for assurance that the infinite Mind is at work out in front of us even before we leave town. Those who make no mistakes make nothing. We can only drive forward. Self-forgiveness really matters, but it can be hard to do.

The old man's mystical walking stick for the boy

Humor is the fastest, fleetest way of giving—it can change pain to joy in a mere millisecond.

—Anonymous

The Limo Driver and the Cross in the Sky: A Highway Revelation

(For Kenny Smith, 1937–2014)

If you judge people you will not have time to love them.

—Mother Teresa

Kenny was the kindest limo driver imaginable. He never judged anyone. He only said good things about people.

The boy needed to find someone he could talk with about his unexpected life back on Long Island, which had removed him from the mainland and from Route 80 and put him back in a place he thought he had left for good in his youth. In the quiet of Kenny's limo, he found a generous listener, who humbly offered his own perspectives and a bit of inner peace. Kenny was a Main Street mystic who had experienced a deep spiritual transformation through a vision on the road and now saw divine dignity in everyone, which is what allowed him to be as kind as he was.

The Driver's Vision

One definition of hope is being open to good surprises. Early one afternoon in September of 2008, two months after he and his family arrived on Long Island, the boy had called Spartan Limo in Port Jefferson, New York to see if they could send a driver over to Stony Brook for a trip to the airport, and Kenny showed up. He was a slim, elderly guy who "tawked" Long Island. He didn't impress at first glance, and his old limo was nothing to write home about.

But first impressions are often wrong.

Kenny settled the boy down. When the boy and his family landed on Long Island, fresh from twenty years around University Circle, it was quite a change. Back in Cleveland, the concept of the neighbor was real, people always took the time to greet one another, and community meant much. People also identified deeply with their great cultural institutions—the Cleveland Museum of Art, the Orchestra, the Clinic, the awesome churches and synagogues, and other hallmarks of spiritual and philanthropic creativity. By the time they made the drive to LaGuardia for the third time, Kenny and the boy had talked about life and the move, and Kenny turned out to have a lot more to offer than just a reliable ride to the airport. He was a limo pastor with a mission.

Driving down the Long Island Expressway, Kenny told the boy about an experience he'd had some years earlier. In a tone of awe and wonder, and with his heavy Long Island accent, Kenny described what had happened to him: "I looked into the sky in front of me as I was heading down this same Long Island Expressway going west—right about here. I looked up and a little to the left, over there in the sky."

He pointed to the left and upwards. "I saw a bright light in a cloudy sky, and it was in the shape of a perfect cross. It just radiated there for a few minutes, and I knew that the Lord was watching over me—and the Lord is watching over you, too."

"Sounds like it was quite a moment for you," the boy responded.

"Oh, it was," he declared. "I was overwhelmed by it, and for a few minutes I lost my sense of time and place completely. It was like I was driving in heaven! I felt completely surrounded by a warm love that was anything but human. It was like everything became clear in terms of what really matters. I was totally at one with the universe, and with the doctor I was driving that day. He was a Hindu, and when I asked him if he saw the cross, he said not a cross but that wiggly *Om* symbol, like those folks chant, you know. We both felt invaded by a warm energy. There were no boundaries between me and the other people on the road. I mean, if someone had hit my limo I would have gotten out and hugged them. I felt so at one with God. It was perfect, and I felt fully healed in every way, because life can be an ordeal and resentments snowball in your soul."

"Whoa!" said the boy. "That is an awesome experience. You should write a book about it, Kenny."

"Nope, I don't write, but you can write about me some day."

Kenny, always an excellent driver, didn't drink or take drugs of any kind. He simply had a vision that the boy, being a dreamer, took at face value.

Kenny continued, "That's why I know that I'm supposed to be a limo driver. This is what the universe wants me to be doing. I think that you being here with me is the universe at work, and I believe that Cleveland's loss is New York's gain."

"Really?" responded the boy. "Well, if you say so, Kenny. Did you ever have that experience again?"

"No, I didn't need to. Once was enough. Someday it might happen again, but you shouldn't need booster shots when it comes to experiences like that."

"Okay, I get it. You should have told that to Mother Teresa, because she got so sad and even depressed when her spiritual experiences never repeated."

"You can't expect that, no need for repeats," said Kenny. "So, what do you think, is something like that real? Like what I experienced?"

"Kenny, that was such a great experience. Our minds have an eternal side to them, and a connection with spiritual things. So it's all good."

"See, there is so much hope when you really experience the Spirit," said Kenny. "If there is no love from above, we are really cooked when it comes to figuring out why we should stick around."

"So, Kenny, if your vision experience makes you the awesome limo driver that you are, I'm all right with it," the boy told him. "Just drive carefully if that ever happens again!"

"Oh, I will, I will. Always carefully! Don't worry about it." And Kenny laughed with the boy.

Then the boy asked Kenny if he knew Route 80 very well. He said he did, because he had once owned a cabin in the Poconos, so he used to drive west through part of the Delaware Water Gap back in the day. But he'd sold the cabin.

"Well, Kenny, I can tell you a story about Route 80 and my dream and my dad's car," the boy said, and he proceeded to give Kenny a ten-minute recap of his dream and his trip west. Kenny listened attentively.

"You are pretty unusual for a Stony Brook professor."

"Yeah, but I only talk about these kinds of things with everyday folks like you, Kenny, and not around work, you know. The psychiatrists don't get these things. There are a lot of very spiritual physicians around, though, who are open-minded about spirituality…who are Mind-before-matter types."

Kenny and the boy understood each other. Next to the African American dreamer who had sold the boy his walking stick the night before he left Cleveland six months earlier, Kenny at that time was the best living proof of synchronicity in the boy's life.

***

Kenny just liked people. He'd owned several delicatessens on Long Island over the years, including the Se-port Deli in the village of Setauket, and had made out pretty well. He told the boy he'd saved over a million dollars but had spent it down helping people over the years, including members of his family.

"Your kids get older and their problems become more expensive," he said.

Working at the Se-port got overwhelming, so he sold it. His son, Kenny Jr., still worked there, making sandwiches with names like the "Ward Melville," after the local high school that serves Stony Brook and the surrounding villages. As the minister said at Kenny's memorial service,

"You really have to like people to be successful with a deli, and they have to like you."

Kenny believed that his big spiritual vision on the expressway made him a more loving individual, but he just may have been born that way, or learned to be like that in the deli business, or suffered enough in life to have figured out that kindness is the only sustainable response to hard times. The boy admired Kenny because there was a wonderful inner freedom and joy about him. Kenny was so far beyond relating to people in terms of how they might contribute to his little agendas. He practiced the love of neighbor as well as anyone, and the neighbor was anyone he encountered, especially in his limo, which was a sacred space. He had no need to manipulate anyone on the face of the earth. He was about as unselfish and caring a person as the boy had ever known, and he never said a bad thing about anyone. Kenny had conquered the "will to power," and there was no hubris anywhere in his soul. He was a free soul and his own boss, doing good and enjoying it. As Dostoyevsky described old Makar Dolgoruky in *The Adolescent,* "There was a gaiety in his heart and that was the beauty in him."

***

Kenny drove the boy to the airport about twice a month. He only allowed himself a couple of trips monthly and spent no more than two days away at a time, because he said he had teaching to do. During these drives the boy would talk with Kenny about what was on his mind, including how impossible it is in the State of New York to get ahead financially on a house because the taxes are so high. Kenny knew that the boy had bought his when prices were inflated, just before the economic bust of October 2008, and that the house was pretty expensive, so with depreciation and taxes the boy had lost money.

"But, Kenny, this whole place has lost value. There's no certainty that the market will ever get back to where it was, and even if it does, it still won't make up for the taxes. So what can we do?" the boy asked.

"Don't worry, the perfect buyer will come along!" Kenny replied.

And she did!

Her name was Maria. She came along in September of 2013 and gave the boy something close to what he had invested, so they were out of the "house trap" of New York and started renting a nice little townhouse that gave them so much less to worry about and a lot of freedom going forward.

"See, I told you that you were going to be okay on that house," said Kenny, when he picked the boy up one evening at the new address. "You lost a little, but you'll get it back in a couple of years."

"Mousetraps and house traps, Kenny," said the boy. "You were right. It just took one person. It is a nice house, and it's well located for their kids to go to school. But we don't need that anymore."

***

Kenny was there to pick the boy up at JFK the day in late October 2012 when he came in on the last flight before the whole area closed down due to "Super Storm Sandy." The boy was heading home from a weekend in the Great Hall in Heidelberg, Germany, where he had attended a celebration of Sir John Templeton's (1912–2008) one hundredth birthday and delivered the plenary speech on Sir John's ideas about Ultimate Reality, God, and Unlimited Love. The Great Hall is among the most famous halls in Europe and was the epicenter of the Protestant Revolution. The boy was so excited to be going there, and so grateful to be presenting Sir John's core thoughts. But three days ended quickly, and it was time to fly home.

When the boy landed at nine that evening, the winds were howling at seventy miles per hour, most of the power and lights were already out, and just a minute or so later the whole airport shut down.

They drove through a lot of bad weather that night, and Kenny did a great job of getting them back safely, especially for a guy who was seventy-six. He dropped the boy off at the house just as a huge willow tree blew down in the backyard. The boy was glad to be home to deal with the wreckage, and there wasn't another limo driver out working that night, anywhere. Mitsuko was relieved that the boy had made it back and thanked Kenny profusely. Then Kenny went driving off through the storm to get home himself. That was the kind of guy he was—trustworthy and loyal. He put God first, neighbor second, and himself third.

***

The boy's last ride with Kenny was on a Tuesday—November 12, 2013. Kenny picked him up at eleven in the morning at the entrance to Stony Brook Hospital and they were off to LaGuardia. He looked pretty good, and said he felt that he might be driving for another ten years, God willing.

"Kenny," the boy said, "You've got a lot of miles in front of you, and a lot of people are your beneficiaries, especially my wife's husband."

"That's you, my young friend," he laughed.

"Yup, that's me, Kenny, a Route 80 friend."

Kenny wasn't able to pick the boy up the next Saturday night, when he was coming back late from Houston, so he sent his friend Gregory instead. Gregory was a Greek Orthodox guy and less spiritual than Kenny, but he loved to talk European politics, so the ride went quickly.

The boy called Kenny every few weeks in December and January, and then just a week before he died. By then Kenny was an inpatient at Sloan Kettering, but he still kept his cell phone turned on.

"I hope to be driving again, but it won't be in this world. I think the Lord is telling me now that this is it. And I'm ready. And, thank you for being who you are and for sticking with the things that matter. And don't worry about a thing."

Those were his last words to the boy: "And don't worry about a thing."

"Thanks, Kenny, hang in there and be open to surprises. You're the best limo driver I ever had. I'll call again in a day or so."

Kenny and the Spring Flowers

Kenny died on February 9, 2014, age seventy-seven, after a battle with cancer that had him going back and forth to Sloan Kettering for quite a while. The boy heard from Kenny's wife that Kenny had all of his family around him on the day after our phone call and was lucid enough to say goodbye to them meaningfully. He was well prepared for that last drive to glory, since he already had one foot on the gas.

***

On Saturday, February 15, 2014, the boy attended Kenny's memorial service at Maloney's Funeral Home in Lake Ronkonkoma—a small town in Suffolk County south of Stony Brook. At the end of the service, the minister invited folks to stand up and say something about Kenny.

The boy choked up. "Hello, folks. Kenny Smith was the best limo driver I ever had. When we came here from Cleveland it was a little challenging for my family, as moves go, but Kenny settled me down and that made all the difference." It was all the boy could manage before he sat down.

Then he stood up again and added, "He was to me like an angel in the night. He loved everyone. He was a dreamer, and the world needs dreamers."

***

The grass will grow again this spring after a long, hard, cold winter. People will begin to forget Kenny with time. But the boy believes that Kenny may go on loving folks from his cremation urn, wherever it is now, because he always said that when it comes to love, death doesn't make a difference. The first spring flower the boy saw a month later moved him to pause and listen to the spring breeze calling out, and what he heard was "Hey, it's Kenny. And don't worry about a thing."

Interlude

A cross like Kenny's in the cloudy sky

Not I, not anyone else, can travel that road for you. You must travel it yourself.

—Walt Whitman

You are not stuck where you are unless you decide to be.

—Wayne W. Dyer

The Lord is with you wherever you go.

—Joshua 1:9

How to Follow a Dream—Lesson Nine: God will provide the perfect driver as needed to help along the rough spots on the journey. A driver may have suffered all kinds of hardships, and emptiness, and never encountered a luminous soul. But after they have one breakthrough spiritual vision—maybe of a bright light in a cloudy sky in the shape of a perfect cross—they can radiate joy and love to everyone they meet, because now they know that God is watching over them, and they can perceive the infinite Mind within every soul. And if they drive a limo, they do it mainly to reveal to every passenger his or her own divine dignity and beauty and awaken them to the Oneness within each peaceful soul. Then they become the right driver that God provides for us at the right time and works through to bring tranquility to our life when we feel dazed and a little lost. Such encounters are pure synchronicity made possible by a cherishing God.

The Great Hall at the University of Heidelberg

Thou hast made us for thyself, O Lord, and our heart is restless until it finds its rest in thee.

–Augustine of Hippo

The Golden Rule and the Cheerful Giver: A New Jersey Trip

Be curious, not judgmental.

–Walt Whitman

G̲ive expecting absolutely nothing anything in return, but the spiritual odds are that kindness will be reflected back by others, and at the right time and place God will bring more blessings into our lives. "Give and you will receive"[29] is not a law of human calculating reciprocity at all. Just pay it forward with a smile. Another passage the boy learned from Mr. Muller, one that truly hit home, is this: "God loves a cheerful giver." The two of them nailed that one to a tree. But the whole passage of the Cheerful Giver[30] was too long to burn in the pine, so Mr. Muller still had the boy learn it by heart:

"The point is this: whoever sows sparingly will also reap sparingly; and whoever sows bountifully will also reap bountifully. Each one must give as he has decided in his heart, not reluctantly or under compulsion, for God loves a cheerful giver." Be a cheerful, free giver and at some point, when you are in need, there will come a synchronicity whisper out of the blue, so perfectly timed as to be a miracle.

The boy believed that if he was a cheerful giver following the Golden Rule, he might as an unintended by-product experience more flourishing and synchronicity than would otherwise be the case. Like the Hindus and Buddhists teach, good *dharma* (helping others rather than harming them) leads to good *karma* (good things come your way). Of course bad things happen to good people like they do to everyone, we have to persevere and grow through tests, and no one gets out of life alive. Still, on the whole, good things certainly tend to happen to good people. What we radiate outwards in thought, word, emotion, and action radiate back to us, like light reflecting off a mirror.[31]

When we follow the Golden Rule and go out of our way to help someone on their particular ledge, spiritual thinkers through the ages have maintained that things will trend in our favor even though this is not our motivation. We help others with absolutely no expectation of

---

29   Luke 6:38.
30   2 Corinthians 9:6–7.
31   www.whygoodthingshappen.com.

benefit to self, but in the giving of self lies the unsought discovery of a deeper self, and this self tends to flourish. This is a classic spiritual law. In the words of the apostle Paul that Mr. Muller taught the boy as a child on lonely Oak Neck Lane, "Be not deceived; God is not mocked: for whatsoever a person soweth, that shall they also reap."[32]

The boy's hypothesis: While synchronicity exists and operates unconditionally because God cherishes us despite our imperfections, when we abide in kindness (good dharma) we tend to see more good things flow our way.

His method for testing the hypothesis: Do something completely inconvenient to help a total stranger, make the sacrifice, and see what unfolds. The opportunity arose.

When we harm others, we harm ourselves; when we help others, we help ourselves. Things happen for a reason. There is more Oneness than we know.

The Bonefish Grill

One day in the middle of January 2012, the boy got a chance to carry out just such an experiment. He received a call from Secaucus, New Jersey, from someone by the name of Toni Ann Collins. He was sitting in his med school office and had a hard time understanding her, because the connection was bad. But he gathered that she was the director of Animal Life Savers, Inc., a new startup nonprofit, had read about his book in the magazine *Natural Awakenings,* and wanted him to give a speech at the organization's annual fundraising luncheon.

Toni said she believed that helping others was saving her life as well as the lives of the animals rescued by her organization, by helping her deal with the loss of a beloved family member. The boy was silent

---

32   Galatians 6:7.

and listened. It was hard to understand the details of her request, and he couldn't tell if she was serious or what her motives were. The boy wished her well but turned down the invite. She was still insistent about wanting him to speak when she called him back several weeks later to tell him that her organization offered no honorarium and could not cover his expenses. This was getting slightly annoying because the boy was so busy in the medical school and time was scarce.

In the end, the boy felt moved by what he felt was Toni's sincerity and decided he would make this into an experiment. So he agreed to drive to Secaucus on a Saturday, February 25, 2012, to give a noon lunch talk at the Bonefish Grill, not far from the Giants football stadium in the Meadowlands. Still somewhat hesitant, he left home about ten and headed west on the Northern State to exit 21, onto 295 North to get over the Throgs Neck Bridge and then across the George Washington Bridge and down a few miles off Route 95 South to Exit 17. Somehow he made it to the Bonefish on time and walked in to absolutely no fanfare.

A video playing on the restaurant wall was all about sick cats and dogs that needed to be adopted by a loving family. The film explained that abusive owners were the cause of most of the animals' illnesses, including dog diabetes, cat cancer, and behavioral issues. Over a hundred people had gathered in the dining hall to raise money through a raffle of various items, including the boy's books. The group included men and women of every age, and each and every one of them was a real New Jerseyite: they talked Jersey, looked Jersey, and dressed Jersey, and they were busy eating fish, buying raffle tickets, and talking at the top of their lungs.

What a long drive, the boy thought…and for this? He could be home instead, writing and getting things done.

***

A woman approached the boy and said, "Hey, you must be da professor! You look like dat picture I saw. I'm Toni's mama!"

"Yup," he said, "it's me, ma'am. Toni around?"

A few minutes later, Toni approached him from the far corner of the restaurant, where she was selling raffle tickets. He could see that she was putting her heart and soul into this event. A tall woman, perhaps in her early forties, with black hair and wearing a black dress, she leaned over immediately and gave him a big kiss.

"We are touchy-feely around here, ya know," she said.

"Okay, got it."

"I am so excited you came here, Professor, it means so much to me."

"Why?"

"Three years ago my grandmother died, and I was really close to her. I was so sad, I couldn't get over it; I just got sadder and sadder and sadder. And that's when I decided to build this Animal Life Savers group because it made me feel so much better to be helping these dogs and cats get adopted, ya know! And bringing these people together and seeing them helping the animals too makes me happy again. So I really loved that article about you, because I know you're right about that—I mean, that helping is a good way to cope with loss."

A little later, Toni introduced the boy and he spoke for twenty minutes or so about how helping and volunteering is good medicine. But honestly, people seemed not able to hear all that well, and he seemed to be not quite what they expected. He told them that it was good to be good, and that includes being good to animals, and that dogs are great symbols of perfect unconditional love because it doesn't matter how many bad things you might have thought, said, or done over the course of a day, that dog is there wagging its tail and happy to see you when you open the door. And he added that people who are nasty to animals tend to be more nasty to people, and that's a fact. He mentioned that the theologian C. S. Lewis had thought that dogs go to heaven! They clapped politely, and then the boy said goodbye to them and to Toni.

It was about one thirty when he left the Bonefish Grill and headed home.

The boy had done something for someone else at considerable inconvenience to himself and for no material reward whatsoever. He even had to pay for his own gas. So this was definitely a selfless act. Would the infinite Mind respond by injecting a little extra synchronicity into his life? Possibly not, because they say it is not good to test God. But maybe.

The Se-Port Deli

Two months later the boy was at home on a Saturday morning, sitting at his desk and writing a description of this little Route 80 memory. But at that moment he just couldn't remember the song that was playing at the Bonefish as the video flashed pictures of cats and dogs across the screen on the restaurant wall. About ten, his then seventeen-year-old son Drew woke up and asked the boy to go down the street to the Se-port Deli and get him a Se-port Bomber Bacon, Egg, and Cheese for breakfast. So the boy interrupted his writing, headed down to the deli, and placed the order "to go."

As he walked in the door of the deli, he realized that the music playing over the speaker system was the same music he had heard accompanying the video at the Bonefish. He asked the Hispanic guys who worked at the Se-port if they knew the name of the song, and one of them, a tall, slender guy, placed his iPhone by the speaker and claimed that it would identify it. Lo and behold, up popped the message "Angel by Sarah McLachlan."

Such moments can be attributed to pure coincidence, and this one could have been—because it was not dramatic, like connecting with the youth on the ledge back in San Francisco. But it felt very spiritual, because the boy believed it was all about the Golden Rule and how synchronicity whispers flow better when you try to be kind.

These sorts of minor events may be just coincidental, and the cognitive psychologists say we like to think of them as more significant than they are. But a lot of people are astonished when they need some little thing and it suddenly jumps out at them from some unknown cranny of the universe, like searching for a book that just happens to fall off the library shelf, or perhaps the dollar that's right there on the sidewalk in front of you just when you need it most.

But you don't know for sure. This sort of thing does not rise to the level of a blue angel dream. Yet the boy assumed that when we go out of our way to help someone, without any calculation or anticipation, things just flow our way a bit more. No one has been able to prove this empirically, but again, most spiritual traditions teach it.

Here's the lesson: When someone reads about you and is inspired to call, even if the request is not exactly one you would ordinarily accept, you might want to take the risk. It turns out that, in addition to helping a lot of animals and animal advocates, Toni was helping herself get through a painful loss. If you're going to study how Unlimited Love operates, you have to make room in your heart for a Toni. And so the boy had his day at the Bonefish with all the members of Animal Life Savers, Inc.[33] He sold no books but gave one signed copy to Toni with a personal note of appreciation for her good works, in addition to the copies he had contributed for the raffle. She was thrilled.

---

33   www.animallifesavers.org.

The painter Norman Rockwell conveyed this lesson better than anyone else. Just stay focused on helping others and let the rest take care of itself.

Rockwell's Golden Rule

Rockwell said all he had to say about this with his image of *The Golden Rule.* Painted in Stockbridge, Massachusetts, his masterpiece appeared on the cover of the April 1, 1961 issue of the *Saturday Evening Post* and injected his vision of love into American culture. He shows a host of people thoughtfully reflecting on the positive version of the Rule, inscribed in gold letters across the center of the painting: "DO UNTO OTHERS AS YOU WOULD HAVE THEM DO UNTO YOU."

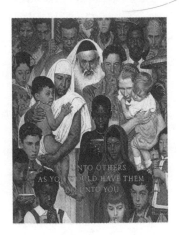

Now, this is not the minimalist version of the Golden Rule, namely, *not* doing to others what you would *not* have them do unto you. The minimalist version only requires that you not jab an elbow into the back of an innocent bystander—and of course, if you do you may also end up being charged with an assault misdemeanor. Rockwell decided to focus on the more elevating version of the Rule, the one that requires us to use our moral and spiritual imagination to determine what we can do to benefit others, not just to avoid harming them. And there they are, men and women, young and old, representing every conceivable religious and spiritual tradition, each asking themselves in the voice of inward conscience if they are benefiting others as they themselves would wish to be benefited.

***

When he was away at school in New Hampshire, the boy had heard Rockwell give a wonderful talk on this image at a church in downtown Concord. The painter said that he was not a religious man, but that there was a spiritual energy one encounters in abiding by the positive Golden Rule. He pointed with a stick to the white halo in the center of his painting, drawing a circle from the rabbi's white beard around to the right through the little child's shirt and continuing below and to the left, ending at the woman's white robes. He called this the *Golden Rule Halo*, and then asked if any of us surfed.

"Yes, I surfed at Gilgo Beach sometimes," the boy offered.

"Well," Rockwell said, describing the spiritual energy he'd mentioned, "this is kind of like surfing. You paddle real hard to catch the wave, but once you catch it the wave has its own powerful energy and it just carries you forward…. All you need to do is stay balanced, so you don't fall off."

***

When we follow the Golden Rule, we set up the conditions for more synchronicity to flow a little more easily into our lives. It is still "graceful" and freely given because we are none of us good enough to deserve it, but we can make synchronicity a little more likely by doing good…and not inflicting harm.

Notice too that every face in Rockwell's image looks tranquil and free of bitterness, fear, and other destructive emotions. That is because showing kindness to people—or even just thinking about how you might be a little kinder to someone—shuts down the neural circuits associated with hostility and rumination, responses that are very destructive to the body over time. So in this sense "Perfect love drives out fear,"[34] it is always "more blessed to give than to receive,"[35] and "God loves a cheerful giver."[36]

---

34 I John 4:18.

35 Acts 20:35.

36 2 Corinthians 9:7.

Interlude

The boy with a book

Why make much of a miracle? As to me, I know of nothing else but miracles.

—Walt Whitman

Him to whom you pray is nearer to you than the neck of your camel.

—Muhammad

This is the day that the Lord has made. We shall rejoice and be glad in it.

—Psalm 118

How to Follow a Dream—Lesson Ten: The whole point of life is to be a cheerful giver. When we follow the Golden Rule, we may well be surprised by some beautiful moment of graceful synchronicity that just seems to be a little miracle on Route 80. After all, God is the great Cheerful Giver, and we are made in that divine image. Help others and we allow infinite Mind to work more freely in our lives. In this sense we do reap what we sow, although pure unmerited grace is also real because none of us is all that great or deserving. And whenever we have a big decision to make, try to meditate and pray first with an image of Rockwell's Golden Rule in mind, and be guided by whatever insights flow from it. Hold that image up in your mind in all its fine detail as if before a mirror, as if we are holding it up for God to see. Then trust the infinite Mind to let it be. But keep up your part of the bargain by contributing to the lives of others actively and humbly.

Friend Bob Votubra (like Chagall on a blue bus) stops by Stony Brook from Cleveland via Route 80 with his One Million Acts of Kindness Bus Tour

God loves a cheerful giver.

—St. Paul

The Blue Angel and the ISIS Web Attack: Things Happen for a Reason

The journey of a thousand miles must begin with a single step. The softest things in the world overcome the hardest things in the world.

—Lao Tzu

I n those earlier Tarrytown years, the boy had read everything he
could about Chagall and even taught the college kids about him.
He learned that Chagall believed that blue is the color of love, and he
became something of a very minor authority on Chagall's angel images.

Twenty-six years after heading west to Cleveland, and six years after
arriving at Stony Brook, he was back in good old Pocantico Hills, next
door to Tarrytown, to speak about Chagall—the consummate artist of
infinite Mind and Love—at the Rockefeller estates. He had been invited
by the artist's personal friend and biographer Vivian R. Jacobson,
who was the featured plenary speaker on that evening of November
8, 2014, whereas the boy was only there to provide a response. He
spent the night in the Tarrytown Hilton, right across the street from
what had once been the HoJo's parking lot where years before he and
Mitsuko had prayed for a hundred-dollar bill that arrived in perfect
graceful synchronicity. Now it was a Honda place. His friend Tom from
Cleveland had come out to Tarrytown for a couple of days by Amtrak
because he loved that Union Church too, and they talked about their
days in Ohio, including the forty dollars Tom came up with to buy that
walking stick the night before the boy headed east. Tom considered
the Union Church with its Chagall windows to be the most sacred and
spiritual place in the Protestant universe.

Things went well that evening, with an audience of about fifty Hudson River Valley folks who listened attentively to the presentations about Chagall.

The boy drove home late the next day through the rain and went to bed but woke up around three in the morning and checked email. There he found a message from a close advisor in Pakistan—let's call her "Dr. A" to maintain her safety. She was writing to notify him that the website of the Institute for Research on Unlimited Love had been completely taken down and replaced with the dreaded black flag of ISIS, or the Islamic State of Iraq and Syria—by ISIS's "Team DZ" (the ISIS hacking team located in Iraq at the time), he soon discovered.

The sharp contrast between Chagall and ISIS became so striking that night in just the two short hours it took the boy to drive from Tarrytown to Stony Brook over the Throgs Neck Bridge. It all felt so uncanny, so "set up" in graceful synchronicity. This was God at work. Sometimes what does not look like divine synchronicity as first glance really is, once you respond rightly and connect the dots, so you have to be creative and open to surprises. Getting hacked by ISIS on November 10, 2014, thirteen years after the institute was founded, was also, he realized, a sure sign of worldwide success. Real results are sometimes demonstrated from the enemies one makes, which means that at some point in your life your actually stood up for something. Thus began a lesson in using a hideous act for a redemptive purpose.

Human beings have a desire for oneness. They can approach this oneness through a love for all human beings without exception, encompassing all differences in religion, race, color, class, cognitive condition, and so forth. This is the sublime oneness that Chagall and Rockwell tried to portray in their art. But human nature is a mixed bag, and with depressing regularity across history we find people seeking this oneness instead by eliminating those "outsiders" who are a little different than they are. The eliminators like ISIS choose reduction—often through genocide and other forms of brutality—over openness and acceptance. Those who prefer to eliminate can only love some small fragment of humanity and lash out even to the point of assassinating those who love humanity as such (Lincoln, Gandhi, Rabin, King, Bhutto). The children of spiritual light want to achieve oneness by overcoming boundaries and affirming our shared dignity and humanity, while the children of spiritual darkness seek the oneness that comes from the extermination of whole communities, cultures, and even the artifacts of history. They are unable to acknowledge all humans as equals, and human life as sacred and of infinite dignity despite our superficial differences.

Chagall had escaped the Nazis in 1941, as did the more fortunate European Jews, while others were subjected to mass murder. Chagall was one of the children of light, and spiritual in a very open-minded, joyous, and humble way. In seeking the oneness consistent with life, liberty, dignity, and love, the children of light, like Chagall, understand that it must be grounded in a source higher than unreliable human nature, or from reason alone, with its problematic rationalizations. Rather, it must spring from the universal spiritual vision that we all participate in, and are all equally loved by, a Supreme Being, an infinite Mind. In other words, hope lies in the higher love that Hindus, Christians, Jews, Muslims, Buddhists, and all other great spiritual traditions identify with God—existing before the Big Bang, beyond time and space, sustaining the universe, and creating us, so that we in turn might freely express our own loving creativity.

Chagall died in 1985 at age ninety-seven. On that very day, he was working in his studio, just back from an exhibition of his work in Russia, and painting a blue angel.

Chagall wrote:

"In our life there is a single color, as on an artist's palette, which provides the meaning of life and art. It is the color of love."

"Only love interests me, and I am only in contact with things I love."

"In the arts, as in life, everything is possible provided it is based on love."

As Jung suggested, maybe the theologians need to reinstate the study of angelology that medieval scholars had pursued, but with modern science to help them.

The Institute Encounters ISIS Team DZ

The boy had been feeling inspired that November 9 night while driving across the bridge to Long Island over the Sound. It was raining hard, and he was thinking about the all-embracing spirituality of the *Good Samaritan Window* as he watched the glow of the streetlights and their shimmering reflections rush by around him.

The boy arrived home. He had always been a light sleeper and, when he woke up four hours after getting to bed that night, saw a new email from his institute advisor in Pakistan, notifying him that the entire institute website had been taken down and replaced with the notorious black and white ISIS flag, he was horrified.

But the boy felt almost at once that somehow the Institute and Chagall and the blue angels were connected, and that being hacked by ISIS could give rise to something good. Things happen for a reason.

As he thought about how to turn this negative into a positive, the idea of a youth essay contest came to the boy, because his old friend Sir John had initiated essay contests for teens on what he called "the laws of life," basic virtues that he described in his book *The Essential Worldwide*

Laws of Life. Sir John really believed in the idea, and throughout the 1990s he had sponsored these competitions all over the world. So the boy followed Sir John's lead in response to the ISIS hacking, and decided to organize an essay competition for young people that would get them to reflect on how they had resisted when pushed to hate those whose beliefs were different from their own.

Nonetheless, it took the boy some time to get over the rude surprise of the ISIS hack, especially after spending such a marvelous Chagall-filled day in Pocantico Hills. Many months later, in June of 2016, to establish a clear picture of those events for the historical record, he asked that same Pakistani friend to send him another email with her reflections on what had happened.

Here is her email:

> *From: Dr. A, Jun 9, 2016 at 12:47 a.m.*
>
> *Subject: IRUL at the UN*
>
> *Recalling how I discovered that the IRUL website had been hacked: I had been searching for Ursula's email address unsuccessfully. Then I recalled she was on the IRUL Board of Advisors and thought I might find it on the website. Initially, I just saw this jet-black page, which completely filled my screen. As you know, when we recall an intense experience, we try to give it a serial order but actually the emotions and thoughts came tumbling rapid fire, almost simultaneously. So, my mind moved all over the place: confusion, the black really felt sinister. I was not sure if it was my computer that had been infected/hacked, or the website. ISIS came to my mind for an instant, but more importantly, I must confess I felt scared—that black screen was seriously sinister. I was totally spooked! And just wanted to get the hell OUT of the site ASAP! Perhaps they were tracking me!!*

*Must have been less than thirty seconds and I exited hastily to
send you the mail.*

*It was only after I had informed you that I tried to make sense
of it; that, yes, indeed it was 'them.' Obvious question was why
IRUL? Who would possibly gain by hacking a small nonprofit in
the USA? Till then, I had thought that ISIS's main targets, real or
virtual, were Western geopolitical policies and, of course, Muslims
who were critical of them, including Muslim minorities such as
Shia and other communities seen as 'heretics.' So, I had thought
that on the Internet they would be targeting sites representing
such perspectives and policies that were openly opposed to
ISIS. But IRUL simply did not fit into any of this politico-
religious spectrum of (perceived) opponents. So what did that
blackness mean?*

*Then the realization set in: That this "war" encompasses much
more than geopolitics and religious differences. I kid you not when
I say I felt the proverbial "chill" in the body when I realized that it
was an attack on **anyone** promoting a notion of God as Love and
Compassion. As such, IRUL and its work becomes high on the
hit list of those who claim to speak or act on behalf of a God who
is primarily violent, horribly unkind, and utterly unloving and
cruel. As a Muslim woman, it is a frightening thought that these
people have imagined such a grotesque idea of the Divine. Even
scarier is that they ACT IT OUT. And I confess, for a moment
I felt scared because being on IRUL's advisory board perhaps
I would personally become a target. In short, discovering the
hacking was NOT a nice experience.*

*What was VERY nice, in fact quite wonderful, was your prompt
response and your next idea of the essay contest, which, of course,
I fully supported. The Muslim mystic Rumi said, "Let the beauty
of what you love be what you do." IRUL 'did' it beautifully; it was
in keeping with IRUL's ethos and what **all** religions urge humans*

to aspire toward, namely the ideals of love: "Love is patient, love is kind. It does not envy, it does not boast, it is not proud. It does not dishonor others, it is not self-seeking, it is not easily angered, it keeps no record of wrongs. Love does not delight in evil but rejoices with the truth. It always protects, always trusts, always hopes, always perseveres."[37]

*In response to the ugly hacking, IRUL's invitation for youngsters to write an essay on tolerance and God's Unlimited Love exemplifies a **universal religious ideal** expressed so beautifully in the Bible. Personally, I think this should be an annual affair and IRUL and the UN should steadily increase its outreach to young—and old—globally.*

The UN has an important duty to strongly support IRUL and such initiatives. Today, that black page I saw two years ago has become, for me, a symbol of a general darkness steadily engulfing the world. Last year in Mumbai, at the launch of a book by a former Pakistani foreign minister, Hindu extremists threw black ink (or tar) at the face of the Indian politician/journalist who was presiding over the event.

*In Europe and the US, it is becoming increasingly kosher to be derogatory and insulting about religious and ethnic minorities. Almost everywhere, xenophobia is on the rise. There seems no end in sight to this growing darkness in which it is increasingly difficult to discern the presence of love as patience, humility, tolerance, respect. Given the dark presence of fear and hate, the UN absolutely must spread and expand IRUL's small ray of light in which love shines as hope and perseverance. **Dr. A***

In June of 2016 the boy also asked Ned Barrett, former institute webmaster and nephew of his recently deceased and much beloved book agent Loretta Barrett, to offer his response to the hacking. After Dr. A

---

37 | Corinthians 13:4–7.

had written on November 10, 2014, the boy had immediately made a point of emailing Ned—and then calling him—early that morning.

Here is what Ned remembered:

> *On November 10, 2014, I woke up to find that the website for the Unlimited Love Institute website had been hacked. I learned about it through an email from you, after you were informed overnight by one of your colleagues in Pakistan. At first I couldn't believe it. I knew we had security protocols in place to protect all of the sites we manage and, besides, who would want to attack a site like IRUL, which exists only to serve as a beacon of light to the world? When I finally reached my computer and pulled up the site, I found that the site indeed had been hacked by an ISIS affiliate called Team System DZ. This was at a time when ISIS was steamrolling across Syria and Iraq, and visions of a cyber 9/11 were foremost in my mind. Our programmers started looking at the problem. Team System DZ had thoroughly compromised the site and it took months to repair. What really struck me was the extent to which global terrorist networks would go to stifle voices of love and reason. The IRUL site was a threat to their narrow message because it was sending a message of hope to young people around the world. What also hit me was the primitive and ugly nature of what they had put up on the site. The creativity of the IRUL site at the time featured blue skies, rays of light, and vistas that welcomed the enlightened imaginations of mankind. It invited people of good will from every faith to participate in a celebration of love. The ISIS message was dark and unimaginative, but it was easily erased. The lesson for me was that light will always overcome the darkness.*
>
> *Best Wishes at the UN,* **Ned**

It did not shock the boy that promoting the ideal of "Pure Unlimited Love" across the Middle East would elicit the wrath of a group like

ISIS—what an honor to have such adversaries. He was in no way fearful over the hacking, but for a while was more cautious because he learned from authorities that he had made some early ISIS target lists. Yet this only strengthened his belief that Unlimited Love was the correct terminology to use, precisely because it stuck in the craw of what was seen by many as the most evil and brutal organization on earth. So, through the attack, he experienced a renewed devotion to the institute and its activities. How could he overcome evil with good?

There is such a thing as synchronicity, even in unpleasant events like the ISIS takedown of the website, because how else would we have filled the United Nations eighteen months later?

Interlude

The institute website homepage after being taken down by ISIS Team DZ

Every person's concept of God is too small. Through humility we can begin to get into true perspective the infinity of God. This is the humble approach.

—John Marks Templeton

Remember love is ever present, here, now, and always.
Identify with love, and you are safe.
Identify with love, and you are home.
Identify with love, and find yourself.

—Marianne Williamson

I believe that unarmed truth and unconditional love will have the final word in reality.

—Rev. Dr. Martin Luther King, Jr.

How to Follow a Dream—Lesson Eleven: Religions are not going away, and so the only real hope for human beings lies in calling each and every religion to oppose abuse by emphasizing its true roots in Pure Unlimited Love. This is not human love. Human love is what screws religions up by tying them to ego, selfishness, and tribalism, by making them turn in on themselves in arrogance and then demonize nonbelievers. All hope for religions lies, not in flawed human love, but in the pure spiritual love that made humans, that existed before the Big Bang, beyond time, and that dwells within us each in the form of an eternal soul. God is not about buildings, wealth, power, and human ambition. God throws down the stones of the temples we create because they can become so empty. God is not about religion, other than that people benefit by coming together for worship to support their spirituality. Love for all humanity without exception is the only hope for humanity, and the best way to accomplish this is by realizing that we are all equally one with the infinite Mind. We can honor the divine nature of every soul and, through understanding our interconnectedness, see the value and beauty in everyone. But those who, in their arrogance, love only some small fragment of humanity hate the others, and thus present the most dangerous problem of our age or of any age. Maybe an Age of Pure Unlimited Love will finally arrive if people come to see that it is the only real option.

The Union Church in Pocantico Hills, New York

As long as you have peace of mind and some sense of the Presence of God you are on the beam, and you are safe, even if outer things seem confused or even very dark; but as soon as you get off the beam you are in danger.

—Emmet Fox

The Young Writers and The United Nations: Expanding Route 80 Worldwide

It is good to have an end to the journey forward; but it is the journey that matters most in the end.

—Ernest Hemingway

Y ou always want to see life as an expanding canvas. It is like a Jackson Pollock painting: he usually started with a big splotch of dirty-looking paint in the middle of the canvas, but as he expanded out and injected all sorts of wonderful colors and lines, it turned into something beautiful. You can take any minus sign and make it into a plus sign by adding that one vertical line.

The ISIS web takedown was most likely a response to an August 10, 2014 newsletter that the institute emailed to more than two hundred thousand recipients and that went viral in the Middle East. It was titled "An Open Letter to Young Members of ISIS" and highlighted Sayed Hossein Nasr and other fabulous contemporary Islamic writers on divine love who are able to interpret Islam beautifully. Three months later, on Monday November 10, 2014, the website of the institute was totally wiped out. It was probably the third website in the world to be taken down by ISIS.

The boy saw this as a good thing, in a strange kind of way—it showed that their newsletter was actually reaching a wide audience and causing a stir. He saw this as another opportunity to expand the canvas from an ugly splotch to a work of beauty a la Jackson Pollock. After considering the options for a while, he got in touch with his board back in Cleveland and shared his solution with them. "You know what we will do? We will have an international essay contest for young people from all around the world and ask them to write from personal experience about how they were able to push back against their peers who were encouraging them to hate other people just because they didn't believe the same things." There would be three nice cash prizes for each of three age groups: eleven to fourteen, fifteen to eighteen, and nineteen to twenty-one.

***

What really bothered the boy was that so many good young people get caught up in ISIS and other ultraviolent extremisms, killing in the name of a God of Love.

Here is the announcement of the first essay contest, distributed as a press release and published on the internet in June of 2015:

ANNOUNCEMENT

We are pleased to announce a new essay competition for young people ages twelve to twenty-one, to support the principles of religious freedom, tolerance, and love for all humanity, without exception, regardless of belief. A nonprofit public charity founded in 2001 in Cleveland, Ohio, and currently based in New York, the institute increases its worldwide outreach to youth.[38]

An international panel of institute advisors will choose the winning essays, which will be published on the institute's website and included in a forthcoming book. Essays can vary in length but should be no longer than 1,500 words, double-spaced, and written in English. Three competition cycles are planned with up to two prizes in each cycle (First Prize US $1,000, Second Prize US $500). The due date for the first cycle is October 30, 2015.

We define love as follows: "When the happiness, well-being, and security of another is as meaningful to you as your own, you love that person. Unlimited Love, often associated with spirituality and religions at their best, extends this love beyond our nearest and dearest, and beyond only those who believe as we do, to all humanity based on our shared dignity and interdependence."

Human progress requires a peaceful coexistence among religions, freedom of religion, and a respectful tolerance of individuals and groups with widely different beliefs, but recent world events demonstrate that these values cannot be taken for granted. Unfortunately, in some places around the world religious hatred

---

38   www.unlimitedloveinstitute.org.

is found in children as young as four years of age, and intolerance leading to religious persecution and violence is on the rise. We want to encourage youth to help us find a path to a future where Unlimited Love for all humanity replaces religious hatred, brutality, and violence.

The essay competition draws from one of the Guiding Questions which drive the Institute's research strategy and collaborations, namely, "How can the major religions of the world come to abide in their various concepts of universal love, and practice love for all humanity rather than merely for those who adhere to a particular set of beliefs?"

The institute invites youth to write essays that encourage all people and religions to abide by the principles of religious freedom, tolerance, and love for all humanity. Stories and reflections from personal experience can be a valuable part of the essay, including the motivations for speaking out through essay writing. The institute offers a series of questions to spark imaginations, including:

- *If you were able to speak to a fellow young person in your own religion who advocated religious hatred, how would you engage him or her? What would motivate you to do so? What would you say, and how would you steer him or her to Unlimited Love?*

- *If you were confronted with religious hatred from a fellow young person in a different religion how would you respond, and why?*

- *Can religious arrogance and hatred be replaced by a spirituality of tolerance, equal respect, freedom, mutual appreciation, and love?*

- *How might the spiritual principle of Unlimited Love be lived out and achieved in practice? Can it be shared and promoted within religious communities or even between different religious communities?*

- *Could a religious toleration youth movement be developed across all religions worldwide? What tools might make this possible that were not available in the past?*

- *What beliefs and practices in your own religious tradition (if you have one) can point youth in the direction of freedom, tolerance, and Unlimited Love? What positive role models exemplify the power of love in your tradition today, and what can we learn from them?*

With the help of Don Lehr, the institute's public relations advisor and one of New York's leading publicists, the press release was sent to hundreds of new writers worldwide. When Webmaster Ned posted the essay contest announcement to Facebook on June 30, 2015, it reached seventy thousand people and garnered more than thirty thousand "Likes" within ten days.

And the essays poured in, many hundreds of them.

A few months later, the boy was invited by the United Nations Population Fund to serve on a panel of twenty-five people from around the world that would reflect on spirituality and a global, sustainable future. The program was titled "Enhancing Human Flourishing Within the 2030 Development Agenda: The Role of Spirituality in Building Transformation and Resilience." The boy spoke that day about the spiritual heritage of the UN founders like John D. Rockefeller, Jr., who provided the land, and of Dag Hammarskjold, its great and spiritually oriented Secretary General. But he mostly spoke about Chagall, who created the blue angel UN *Peace Window* to commemorate Hammarskjold after his death in a plane crash over the Congo. And he noted that for Chagall, blue was the color of divine Love. Then he mentioned getting hacked by ISIS and the institute essay contest, and you could have heard a pin drop.

When they heard about the essay contest and the ISIS hacking that had inspired it, people at the UN liked the boy's response, and the institute was invited to be the featured event for the UN's World Youth Day on August 12, 2016. The entire UN Headquarters was filled with young people from around the world who were invited to hear the institute contest winners present their essays about love for a common humanity and how to push back against hatred. It was absolutely awesome, especially because the event was broadcast to eighty million young people worldwide via the UN webcast.

Life really is an expanding canvas. Take something negative and turn it into a huge positive. If you take a negative sign (-) and add a line across the middle (|) it becomes a plus sign (+). Nothing negative is ever final.

Filling the UN Headquarters

It is 2:14 p.m. on Wednesday, August 10, 2016. The boy is on the ferry from Port Jefferson to Bridgeport, and after arriving he'll get on Route 95 headed for New Bedford, Massachusetts. The drive across

Connecticut from Bridgeport takes about three hours. He's picking up his old Cleveland friend and mentor as well as Oprah's: the Rev. Dr. Otis Moss, Jr., and his wife, Edwina. They're arriving on the Fast Ferry from Oak Bluffs on Martha's Vineyard tomorrow morning, and after he meets them at the ferry dock at eleven, they will drive to Manhattan and to the UN One Hotel on 44th Street right near First Avenue, across the street from the United Nations. Pastor Moss is the lead keynote speaker at the Institute's UN International Youth Day conference Friday morning at the UN Headquarters building.

It has been nineteen months since that November 2014 hacking, and everything has been fine. Still, the boy had taken a close look at the UN Plaza a year later to be sure that it was secure. And as a precaution, he did not publicize the institute event, or send out an email announcement. He asked people he knew well to invite friends, and everyone had to RSVP by July 30 to allow time for UN security vetting.

It is 10:00 p.m. on Wednesday, August 10. The boy is at the Fairfield Marriot Inn in the historic whaling section of New Bedford, after a drive of about three hours from Bridgeport. He had made a point of talking to a lot of old friends en route via Bluetooth, including the Islamic feminist Irshad Manji. And he spoke with his old friend Tom in Cleveland, who was there with him behind Glidden House when the African-American shaman came out of the darkness so his mystical walking stick could find the boy. Tom was going to make a special trip to New York to be at the Friday event. The boy also spoke with Dr. Bob Haynie, his trusted friend from Case Western Medical School, via Bluetooth, and with Joanna Kaczorowska, the great violinist, who would be performing a meditational piece at the close of the event on Friday. Joanna was enthused about her upcoming UN performance and was inspired to wear a blue dress.

The boy is looking forward to reconnecting with the renowned Pastor Moss and his wife Edwina at the ferry dock at eleven in the morning tomorrow, August 11. So now a prayer and to bed, after answering some emails from last-minute invitees who had failed to RSVP by June 30, and thus had fallen off the UN ticket list.

It is 7:30 a.m. on Thursday, August 11. All is well as the boy looks out over the New Bedford docks across from the hotel, thinking about the drive to Manhattan, which is going to be a little tight. If Pastor Moss lands there at 11:15, it will take at least five hours, so they are looking at a five o'clock arrival, with luck. Dinner is at six. This will be a fairly intense drive, but it will work. There are really no other options, and driving is easier than navigating little airports.

It is 9:00 p.m. on Thursday, August 11. The boy has had a long day driving, because Pastor Moss and Edwina missed that ferry and did not reach New Bedford until 1:45. But it was such a joy to see them at the New Bedford docks when they did arrive, because Pastor Moss is a fabulous mentor. The boy piled their bags into the Jeep Patriot, which was already packed with things for the UN event, and they quickly headed off toward Providence and then onto 95 South across Rhode Island, Connecticut, and into Manhattan. They made 44th Street by 6:45, which was great time given the traffic and other challenges and were only an hour or so late for the six o'clock dinner. Meanwhile, Leyla Sharafi of the UN Population Fund had asked the twenty-five dinner guests to introduce themselves and run through some basics for the next morning's event.

Pastor Moss and the boy had spoken deeply for those four hours on the road. The boy asked him about getting married fifty years earlier on the Morehouse College campus in a ceremony conducted by Rev. Dr. Martin Luther King, Jr. They talked about his being co-pastor with King's father at the Ebenezer Baptist Church in Atlanta. They discussed his relationship with Morehouse president Rev. Dr. Benjamin Elijah Mays. They talked about Pastor Moss's great African-American friend, the preacher Howard Thurman, and his idea of infinite Mind.

In short, it was the ride of a lifetime.

Their arrival at One UN Hotel was interesting. As they pulled up and the boy got everything out of the car, he noticed that there were lots of security people around, as well as a bomb-sniffing dog that checked all their baggage. He was happy to see this level of diligence and awareness at the hotel, which is across First Avenue from the UN and an easy target.

Six months earlier, the boy had checked out this UN security system. He also saw the sturdy, waist-high steel pilings lining the sidewalks along First Avenue and knew that no vehicle could plow through them. He had worried about that very kind of terrorist attack months before a driver in Nice, on the French Riviera, slammed his truck into the crowd that had gathered to watch a parade. It could just as easily happen in New York, he thought. But the next morning, as they got ready for the International Youth Day event at UN Headquarters, he was relieved to see heavily armed guards at the top of the stairs leading to the entrance gate on 46th Street, where the staff had placed a big Youth Essays sign on a wooden easel.

The boy made security a priority while he was planning the event and had been careful to only invite folks who were well known to him, or to the ten young speakers, although anyone already affiliated with the UN could also attend. He had fully cooperated with UN security in providing invitees' names, affiliations, and emails, all listed with a clear RSVP. Institute invitees had to arrive at the entrance steps between eight thirty and ten thirty on Friday morning, August 12, and show their photo ID to the boy's wife, Mitsuko, and a couple of others on the team, who would check each one against the carefully compiled guest lists before handing them a ticket. Guests then would walk up the steps past the guards and through the airport-style X-ray machines, where they would take off their belts, put coins and keys in white trays to be viewed by an array of security folks, and have their bodies X-rayed as well. In other words, the security was great. No fanatics would be able to inflict death or destruction on anyone or anything here. But after all the recent brutal, ugly, violent attacks in Nice, in Brussels, in Orlando, and in other hot spots around the globe, the boy would still not feel 100 percent fine until 10:45 Friday morning, when at last the rooms were filled with many hundreds of guests, all safe and thrilled to be there.

***

Before the much-anticipated Friday morning event, though, and after their long drive from Bridgeport, the boy and Pastor Moss and his wife finally made it to dinner in the Landmark Room on the twenty-ninth floor at One UN Hotel. It was hot, and the hotel had failed to turn the air conditioning on well ahead of time. Institute trustee Joni Mara, who had flown in from Cleveland, was in the room by five thirty, frantically trying to get the air turned on as the bright sun beamed in through the glass walls overlooking hot, humid Manhattan and its skyline. When the boy walked in at seven. it still felt like a sauna. But the room was full of wonderful young people from all over the world who had worked so hard on their essays. The boy had personally helped each of them to edit what they wrote, given them tips on public speaking, collated their biosketches, and made sure that they were reimbursed for their hotel and other expenses. He greeted them belatedly and said hello to the people seated at the head table, including his family. Then Pastor and Mrs. Moss came in after freshening up, and the pastor offered some brief, inspiring words about what the essay contest symbolized for religious freedom, peace, and love.

The boy reminded the winners that they were really there because of an uncanny moment of synchronicity and the need to turn something negative into something positive. He told them:

> In fact, this is the purpose of life: have confidence in a Higher Love that will help you turn every negative into a positive, down the road and at the right time. Have confidence that the answer is already there waiting to be discovered and is flowing your

way. All of you are overcoming hatred with love, and that is the only way hate can be overcome. Rev. Martin Luther King, Jr., said, "Darkness cannot drive out darkness, only love can do that. Hate cannot drive out hate, only love can do that."

They wrapped up by eight o'clock, though many of the young people stayed around after dinner because they were enjoying getting to know each other. The boy went out to a deli on Second Avenue and 44th Street with his family to get some cold drinks and catch up. He reminded them that they would meet at eight the next morning on the dot in the hotel lobby before heading to the 46th Street UN gate as a group.

That night, boy and son shared a room on the thirty-fifth floor of the hotel with a great view of Manhattan. As they got ready for bed, the boy was still checking last-minute emails, and saw that Maria, one of their young speakers from Bogota, had written him about being charged three hundred dollars by a limo driver for a ride from JFK to the hotel. It was all the money she had, and she was obviously anxious. The boy wrote back and told her to meet him in the lobby at seven thirty the next morning and he would give her eight hundred dollars in cash, to reimburse her for her airfare and allow her to enjoy her stay in New York.

It is now 8:00 a.m. Friday morning, August 12—at last! People from the institute group have been out on Second Avenue getting breakfast at various diners and delis, and now they're beginning to assemble. Guards and their dogs are out in front of the hotel entrance, keeping their eyes on things. The boy was up early to get cash for Maria, and after giving it to her as promised he walked with her to a cab waiting outside the hotel and asked the driver how much the fare was to JFK. The driver replied that fifty-two dollars was the standard rate. So now she knew, and she would be okay when she returned on Sunday to Bogota.

They have the easel, two big Essay Contest signs, and a box full of flyers and biosketches to be handed out at the event signs. Pastor and Mrs. Moss come down, and now everyone is gathered, including a documentary film team. Drew carries the heavy box of flyers, Mitsuko takes the signs, and the boy picks up the easel. They are happy to encounter a bomb-sniffing dog and a nice security guy at the hotel entrance as they leave.

Leaving the UN Plaza Hotel

Off they go across 45th Street to 46th and then head east, past First Avenue and the big steel pillars into the UN complex, with its serious security. Mitsuko, Joni Mara, and institute staffer Gloria Williams set up the easel and sign at the base of the five cement steps leading up to the black UN security gates. They greet the guards and thank them for being there. Already, a few dozen guests are lining up in front of Mitsuko and Joni, getting their names checked off the lists before being handed their tickets, and proceeding up the steps. Now the entourage of speakers is also inside the gates, tickets in hand, and walking through the X-ray machines onto the UN Plaza and into the UN Headquarters building. The ten young presenters filled the front semicircle of seats, along with Pastor Moss, the boy, Luis Mora, and Sister Alisha of Women in Islam, who will both also speak at the event. Joanna, the violinist, is sitting behind them.

Contest Winners from across the globe!

At 9:15 a.m. they begin rehearsing. The boy makes some opening remarks, as do Pastor Moss and Sister Alisha. Then they give each of the young people a chance to perform their magnificent speeches, coaching them in a way that is both supportive and uplifting. During the rehearsal the young speakers also provide feedback to each other, and a big thumbs-up. The lively rehearsal wraps up at 10:45, just as the rooms are filling up with guests. In the end, the audience in that one room numbers 583 people, with many others conferencing in from other rooms throughout the building.

The UN hall is full and joyful

It is now 11:00 a.m. Friday morning, August 12. Everyone is here safe and sound, and the rooms reserved for the event are mostly full. The UN webcast system is up and running, and everyone is pleased that the event is being broadcast simultaneously to over eight hundred thousand people watching worldwide on their cell phones.

Pastor Moss delivers a fabulous opening speech about how we each have to be the change we wish to see in the world, drawing from Gandhi and his mentor Rev. Dr. Martin Luther Kind, Jr. Many in the audience are mesmerized and even moved to tears. The astonishing quality of all ten young presenters is impossible to exaggerate, as they perform and present their essays and poems magnificently and their creativity spreads across the globe. Luis Mora delivers some memorable closing remarks, and Joanna, wearing a bright blue dress—the UN color and the one that Chagall termed "the color of love"—plays a beautiful violin meditation at the close. She says she had such a strong "spiritual intuition" about wearing blue.

In his farewell message, the boy has a chance to tell everyone gathered there how much he appreciates the blue of the UN and of Joanna's dress because of a blue angel dream he had as a kid and managed to follow. Then he says a few words about Chagall and the UN *Peace Window* and how they are all blue angel dreamers for the future.

Rev. Dr. Otis Moss, Jr., the most distinguished of African-American pastors; the world-renowned violinist Joanna Kaczorowska, who has performed with Yo-Yo Ma, Itzhak Perlman, and the Emerson String Quartet; and the boy, at the UN

Representatives from forty nations

It is now 2:00 p.m. on Friday afternoon, August 12, and they are done! Mitsuko and the boy are headed over the George Washington Bridge via the FDR north and Harlem River Drive, avoiding the Cross Bronx. Then they will follow Route 80, where the boy's journey began, to a really peaceful Best Western Motel on Route 115 in Lewisburg, Pennsylvania, just a few miles from where he had left his dad's Mercedes so many years ago with that elegant little note to the police.

The boy is in a particularly synchronicity-filled mood and, especially after the resounding success of the essay contest, is gratefully aware that infinite Mind is at work behind the scenes. He feels like he did years ago, crossing the Golden Gate Bridge, encountering the youth on the ledge, and picking up Mom's phone call at Reed after her premonition.

Interlude

*Water is the softest thing yet it can penetrate mountains and earth.
This shows clearly the principle of softness overcoming hardness.*

—Lao Tzu

*The two most important days in your life are the day you are born and
the day you find out why.*

—Mark Twain

*You have no need to travel anywhere. Journey within yourself, into
the mine of rubies, and bathe in the splendor of your own light.*

—Rumi

To bring anything into your life, imagine that it's already there.

—Richard Bach

How to Follow a Dream—Lesson Twelve: It just takes one line to turn a negative (-) into a positive (+). On Route 80 life is always an expanding canvas, and what looks bleak can be transformed into something luminous with prayer and help from the infinite Mind. Potholes are just part of the highway. The boy was smiling because the miracles in his life just kept coming, and they can come for all of us. But we have to open our eyes. We don't need flashing lights and big revelations, we just need to awaken to our interconnectedness and oneness with the infinite Mind that dwells in each one of us and always has. Then love will overcome hate, and the consciousness of good will overcome evil. Light overcomes darkness just by its presence. It drives out the darkness. When the light goes on, the darkness in the room is gone. We need to listen deeply and joyfully and expectantly to a power and divine presence of love at the very center of our being in all its beauty. We need to permit ourselves to be guided by this infinite Mind and bless everyone we encounter with complete love.

It began with a prayer

Who are the happiest people you have ever met? Let us write down the names of ten persons who continually bubble over with happiness, and we will probably find that most are men and women who radiate love for everyone.

–John Marks Templeton

To Give and Glow: Ten Route 80 Ways of Love

Scent lingers on the hands of those who deliver flowers.

—Ancient Chinese Proverb

I f you save him, you too shall live," spoke the blue angel, real or not, and the boy followed along, having nothing better to do. Translation: to stay on the journey, you need to give and glow, which is only possible when you are aware of your inner being and oneness with the infinite Mind of pure love. The source is Spirit.

This is the universal law of the giver's glow: when we are contributing to the lives of others, abiding in the Golden Rule of "do unto others," and focusing on the well-being and security of our neighbor as well as our own, we manifest the giver's glow, so long as we do not ignore the need for balance and self-care. When we live such good lives, the infinite Mind that is also Higher Love can more easily surprise us with synchronicity, and our feeling for the interconnectedness and Oneness of Being can increase. Synchronicity whispers are more likely to occur when we follow a path of love, though in a larger sense all synchronicity is grace because we are all flawed creatures.

***

In the quest for, and invention of, meaning in life, the boy found great strength in simple acts of giving, as blue angel dreamers do. One evening in 2005, when he was on the road headed back to Cleveland from a presentation in Washington, DC, to the US Congress, he passed a shiny wheel with metal spokes by the side of the road, and it inspired a powerful intuitive insight about the nature and modulations of love. This "wheel of love" continued to resonate in his consciousness, and a year later became the basis of *Why Good Things Happen to Good People*. The "wheel of love" is an image that could only come to mind on the highway, where the routines of everyday life in the office vanish, the phone isn't ringing, no one is at the door, and there are no emails to disrupt the mind.

The psychiatrist Harry Stack Sullivan (d. 1949) of University of Chicago fame wrote, "When the happiness, security, and well-being of another person is as real to you, or more real, than your own, you love that person." We can all relate to this definition of love, whether we are contemplating friendship, parenthood, a special calling to assist a needy group, or affirming our shared humanity. We can also extend love of this sort to other species and to nature generally. The centrality of such love in our everyday lives should be obvious.

Back to the image of the hub and spokes. Love may be expressed in different ways, depending on the needs of those around us, and on our own personality and strengths. Each "way of love" constitutes a spoke on the wheel.

And we are all called to align with, and express, some spokes more than others.

Here are ten spokes, or ways of giving and loving:

> *Celebrating* is taking time to acknowledge and affirm the lives and achievements of others

> *Helping* others in ways small and large without being limited by a "payback" mentality is as good for the giver as for the recipient

> *Forgiveness* is breaking free of destructive emotions by concentrating not on our own resentments but on contributing to the lives of others, and knowing that time will reveal a more meaningful perspective

> *Carefrontation* is standing firm against the destructive behavior of individuals and society, while staying grounded in an underlying love for all people without exception

> *Mirth* is the gift of tastefully reframing a situation with loving laughter that does not diminish but rather uplifts; mirth is the lightness of love

Respect ("re-spectare" or "re-look") means looking more carefully at the opinions and lives of others, striving for civility in discourse, and practicing etiquette in speech and behavior

Attentive listening is setting aside one's own voice in order to focus on, and be fully present to, another, undistracted and unhurried

Compassion is responding wisely and actively to suffering when we see it

Loyalty is sticking with others through both the peaks and valleys of their lives, so they know that they can count on us in tough times

Creativity used for noble purposes is the tool that allows unique, personalized expression of our love for others

The Ways of Love

The Way of Celebration

Love means rejoicing in the presence of another, in that person simply being alive, and in his or her achievements. Rejoicing holds a central role in most spiritual traditions: "O give thanks unto the Lord, for He is good: for His mercy endures forever."[39]

Rejoice in the newness of life each day. Morning has broken! Rejoice in the red and gold of autumn leaves; clouds and sun, hills and streams, ice and snow; for trees in spring, and fruit blossoms, and birds; for the smell of the earth after rain; for firesides and friendly conversations; for meals eaten together in fellowship; for games; for good times in

---

39 Psalm 107:1.

the open air; for birthdays, festivals, and holidays; for musicians and painters, poets and artisans; for scholars and dreamers. Imagine how bleak life would be without rejoicing and celebration.

The Way of Helping

Roll up your sleeves and do some concrete deed to help someone or to improve the community. Suffering and compassion need not be involved. Be a helper, be a neighbor. Rake the leaves, take out the garbage, clean up the room, milk the cow, paint the fence, mow the lawn. It could be helping a neighbor shovel a little snow or lift a heavy bag, addressing envelopes for a local fundraising drive, doing some tutoring for folks who cannot read, volunteering in a hospice, hospital, or nursing home, or paying the fare for someone who otherwise can't afford to take the bus. The helping that goes on in everyday life, in the home, between friends, at work or school, or with a stranger in the cafeteria line, is not what we would call heroic.

Back when the boy was bored and his mom would say, "Why don't you just go out and help someone?" he would head across the street and give old Mr. Muller a hand raking leaves. It always felt pretty good. There wasn't anything especially deep or profound about it. These are just things we can do that connect us with others in a web of helpfulness.

The Way of Forgiveness

Life is in many ways a story of forgiveness.

Forgiving is more complex than giving. The pop psychology teachings on forgiveness trivialize the really deep betrayals and injuries that seem to be part of every life. And there are most definitely some people in this world who have done such terrible things that they are beyond mere human forgiveness. Their evil is so great that only God can forgive them. To those willing to embrace a spiritually grounded response to such hurts, the best course is to turn their rage over to God and sublimate the urge for "sweet revenge." Let go and let God, if possible.

Nothing interferes with creativity and good judgment more than bearing grudges, and few things have destroyed more otherwise good and promising lives. The secret is to concentrate on helping others, and letting time pass so that hurts recede. In some cases, it is even appropriate to eventually come around to realizing that "I" might have been somewhat responsible for events, or perhaps overreacted. The more time passes, the more one forgets the details. Help others and let grudges fade.

The Way of "Carefrontation"

"Carefrontation" means confronting those people with destructive or self-destructive behaviors and attitudes in a way that allows them to still feel cared for, significant, and hopeful that change is possible. It is about giving critical feedback without causing humiliation. It is about seeking justice against the odds. The line between what we must accept and what we should try to change is often unclear. One key expression of love is the readiness to confront evil while continuing to demonstrate grace and caring.

M. Scott Peck, author of the popular classic *The Road Less Traveled*, graduated in psychiatry from the School of Medicine of Case Western Reserve University in the 1950s. While the boy was on the medical school faculty, they were pen pals, from about 2001 until Scott's passing a few years later. Scott wrote the boy a letter on April 15, 2002, that begins, "Please forgive me for using your first name, but I more than sense that we are rather kindred spirits." In that letter, Scott commented that "unlimited love" or "unconditional" love "does not seem to make much room for 'tough love,' " or for the times when we must focus almost entirely upon loving ourselves, or for the thousands of complex decisions involved in loving well. As a psychiatrist treating people with every kind of personality disorder, Scott naturally emphasized that love must often be firm and tough in order to be clinically successful. The boy could agree that Unlimited Love must affirm all people as they are but also as they can become, for we should all be busy being born.

In the end, one must skillfully engage in "carefrontation" or live a life of avoidance. As Gandhi famously stated, "A coward is incapable of exhibiting love; it is the prerogative of the brave."

The Way of Mirth

Never rebuke the merry. The boy knew a wonderful preacher who carried two books everywhere he went: the Gospels, and a collection of tasteful jokes for all occasions. We can challenge any depiction of spiritual leaders as people who never laugh, who are always busy with pious talk and solemn prescriptions. In the Buddhist tradition, the first experience of enlightenment is often associated with an outburst of laughter, and in Judaism, the very word *Isaac* means "laugh." Why? Because Sarah, wife of Abraham, laughed when three angels appeared and predicted that she would have a son.[40] In the Gospel of Matthew, a passage admonishes "Do not look dismal."[41]

Much good is achieved by cheering people up. Clevelander Bob Hope lived to be one hundred, dying on July 27, 2003. What made him so great? His mirth and laughter brought smiles to millions, and his wholesome, tasteful humor cultivated hope in troops stationed in war zones across the world for over seven decades. He always made time for quiet moments with wounded soldiers, no matter how tired he might have been after a long flight or from keeping up a busy schedule.

---

40   Genesis 18:12.

41   6:16.

Levity is another way to express love. Although not all of us are called, like Bob Hope, to be love's jesters, it is hard to imagine loving someone you can't laugh with, at least a little. Kierkegaard wrote that love is not always "stupidly serious." Of course, the way of love rejects the bawdy, cruel humor that puts others down rather than lifting them up.

Laughter also frees us from anxiety and despair. When we laugh, the ego self seems to disappear. Our worries go out the window. We forget about the weight of life and experience a new beginning.

Humor and laughter, too, propel us beyond *chronos*, outside of chronological time, and into the future. Laughter leads us to time outside of time, where we forget about watches, and distracts us from the constant march of chronological time, with its incessant demands. In religious festivals all over the world, people dress up in masks and costumes and march through the streets in a chaos of irrationality in which the authority of *chronos* and the clock become utterly unreal. In this sense a moment of laughter is a hint of eternity, where there is no time, or at least none to worry about.

Laugh at your mistakes and embrace your imperfections. Perfection can be the enemy of laughter. Proverbs 17:22 reads "A cheerful heart is a good medicine."

True, life is not a joyride. But the fact that there is suffering in our lives and in the lives of others is no reason to silence mirth.

The Way of Respect

Respect as an affective expression of love embodies a sort of *emotional awe or reverence for the beloved*. It suggests a sense of quiet amazement at the existence of another person, a sense of wonder at his or her unique qualities, a basic acceptance of that person without seeking to refashion them into a replica of oneself. Minimally, this implies an unwillingness to manipulate or overpower them, an appreciation for the freedom of the beloved as he or she navigates the journey of life. Reverence does not seek to absorb the other into the self but recognizes and accepts the "other as other" while retaining an intense interest in them and their well-being. In this sense, love keeps its distance even as it draws near, and exhibits a certain hesitation as it holds the other inviolable.

Respect derives from the Latin *respectare*, "to look again," or "to look twice." *We need to look twice and three times at others*, seeking to understand their personal histories, their struggles, their life journeys. A great deal of human cruelty stems directly from an irreverent unwillingness to respect the lives, thoughts, and feelings of others.

The Way of Listening

Take the six letters in the word SILENT and spell from these the word LISTEN. The healer is one who listens attentively in order to understand; reassurance, consolation, comfort, and advice flow from this listening. To be human is to speak, and to be a healer is to listen. Those who work with people in crisis know that often the only thing they can offer is an attentive, listening presence. Much as we might wish for a path to helpful action, there is often nothing that we can do other than being present, listening, and hearing in an affirming way. This is not so easy, because we have to turn off our usual talkativeness and enter into a kind of holy attentiveness to the other that is completely unconditional. This is meeting people where they are, as they are, and allowing them to find comfort in our simply being there.

When we think of an infinite Mind in this universe, of "God," we immediately sense that God is a listener. Much of spirituality is about finding a true listener, a fully available and approachable one who has room for us and our thoughts and feelings. A great deal of the staying power of spirituality in people's lives comes from the simple need to be listened to by the universe, and most religious rituals and litanies are organized ways of allowing people to speak from their hearts to a listening Presence who never says, "I don't have time."

The Way of Compassion

In compassionate action we are renewed. Compassion is the ability to feel the suffering of others, at least to some degree, and to respond actively to reduce that suffering. It is different from empathy alone. The Good Samaritan[42] sees a man suffering on the roadside and "is moved by compassion." Robbers had beaten the man and left him stripped and half-dead. The Samaritan "had compassion" and he bound up the man's wounds, took him to an inn, and cared for him, even paying the bill. It is all *immediate and direct*. Compassion responds to suffering. We are "moved" by compassion to act.

A Buddhist will contend that we may not be suffering at this very moment, but things will change in this world of *dukkha* (pain, sorrow, or suffering). We may have a great job, plenty of friends, a good marriage, wonderful children, and good health. In the next moment, any or all of these things may disappear. Of course, the smiling Buddha will tell us to fully enjoy good fortune and to savor the sunny days of life, partly because suffering always lurks around the corner, even in the best of times. There is much truth to this Buddhist philosophy. Yet, the idea of this imminent suffering seems a bit overstated to me. There are times of immense joy, creative flow, and meaningful, generative productivity that seem to sidestep suffering entirely, even as just a nagging sense of possibility. At a deeper level, of course, there are always things will sadden and even crush us along the journey of life. We all carry wounds and regrets, some of our own making and some inflicted by others.

---

42   Luke 10:30-35.

The Way of Loyalty

Love is not an extinguishable project. Love's sincerity and honesty of intention is demonstrated in fidelity and permanence over time. Only an erotic love of the sort Don Juan made famous knows nothing of constancy, and one might well question whether to call his fleeting escapades true love.

Constancy means being committed in one's relationships. This provides an emotional safe haven, the security of attachment that every newborn deserves and that we never stop wanting over the course of a lifetime. Constancy also offers the possibility for a deepening of the relationship over time, even in the midst of the unforeseen. Growth unfolds with constancy. In our consumer society, more temporally limited engagements are the norm. Lesser commitment gives way to affairs. In all of this, love is lost.

Of course, everyone realizes that all relationships, whether marriages and friendships, or the connections between parents and children or siblings, may at some point end. The cause might be intractable neglect, intense and continuing conflict, or a lack of intimacy that betrays an underlying absence of common interests. Not everything in life is meant to last forever, but neither can life be very fulfilling, or even functional, when meaningful relationships lack commitment. "I love you just for these five minutes" does not make any sense.

Tom Smith, the horse trainer in the movie *Seabiscuit*, looks over at a tattered horse and says, "Don't ever throw away a whole life just because it's a little banged-up." Most of us live two lives—first, one that we learn from, and a second one that is better as a result of lessons learned. Loyalty requires patience and forbearance and tolerance. No relationship will endure without these qualities.

Love without reasonable commitment has costs. Among the hurt are those who suffer from broken marriages, damaged self-esteem, bewildering isolation, anxiety, or haunting depression. Many people seek to connect physically for the sake of sexual intimacy alone, failing to see physical touch as potentially expressive of a deeper, spiritual meaning and enduring love.

In order for love to be meaningful, it needs to endure over time. Without this temporal glue, friendship becomes impossible, mutual covenants disappear, and the social world becomes dishonored.

The Way of Creativity

Another Cleveland friend of the boy's, Bonnie, was diagnosed with multiple myeloma. On her first visit to the hospital, she was taken into the treatment room and given a small, gray blanket to put on her lap. Bonnie thought this was sad. "When I got home," she told me, "I started knitting, a pastime that I had always found calming. It didn't take long before I had a pretty, colorful lap blanket. I made a few and then it came to me—I could bring these in to the oncology department for other patients to use during their treatment."

"What started as a little project," Bonnie continued, "has become my full-time job. I make about two blankets per day and when I have about fifteen, I take them to the hospital. Each blanket has a tag that says "Free—To keep you warm during treatment." Each person can keep the blanket and take it home. The receptionist told me that within a half hour all the blankets are gone. At my request, the patients never know where their present has come from. I get a blood workup, urine analysis, and bone infusion every three months. Since I started making the blankets, my blood tests have improved. My oncologist said, 'I have no way to explain this medically. All I can say is, just keep making blankets.' Nothing in my life has given me more enjoyment or personal satisfaction except the birthing of my three sons."

Bonnie expresses love through creativity, and she takes such joy
in doing it.

"The heavens are telling the story of the glory of God; and the
firmament proclaims his handiwork."[43] This universe is not just
functional and utilitarian; rather, it overflows with every imaginable
beauty. God is a creative artist, and we enjoy God's ever-changing
canvas. There are divine fingerprints to be seen in blooming fields and
starry skies.

Love takes different forms, and none of us is a master of them all. When
it comes to expressing love, we all have different strengths, but together
we make up a solid wheel: different strokes for different spokes! Love
ain't easy and it's not for wimps. Once you start out on a Route 80
journey, the one thing you must always be true to and not betray is the
Ultimate Reality of Unlimited Love.

Rx Give and Glow

Giving and loving and contributing to the lives of others is the
prescription for meaning and at least some degree of happiness. The boy
calls this "give and glow," or the "giver's glow."

The twentieth century Hindu sage Krishnamurti had it right: "It is
no measure of health to be well adjusted to a profoundly sick society."
To be enduringly happy in the ways of materialism and the sensate
indignities that characterize much of the popular culture can be a
challenge. Judging from the epidemic of depression that defines our era,
self-indulgence and materialism may be near exhaustion and about to
collapse, although propped up by thousands of psychiatrists medicating
younger and younger patients who are hitting bottom in our cathedrals
of consumerism.

---

43 Psalm 19:1.

This is all part of the perennial philosophy that Emerson was drawing on when he wrote, "No man [or woman] can sincerely help another without helping himself." Or, as Oscar Wilde put it, echoing Plato, "To be good is to be in harmony with oneself." Thoreau wrote, "Goodness is the only investment that never fails." And Proverbs 11:25 assures us that "Those who refresh others are themselves refreshed."

On the inside cover of the boy's copy of *The Book of Common Prayer*, given to him two decades ago by the Rev. William B. Eddy of Christ Church, Tarrytown, is the boy's ever-growing list of people he has seen as models of kindness and generosity over the course of his life. All of them have died, and by all accounts, they continued to show generosity to all even in their final days, or at least prior to the onset of dementia. From time to time, he reflects on the lives of these good people and recalls that each of them took joy in being consistently generous and affirming to all, even in difficult moments when they had to solemnly "care-front" (rather than simply "confront") destructive or unjust behaviors, jealousy, betrayal, and other manifestations of the shadowy side of human nature. They did not all live easy lives, but the lives of all of them were good.

Their lives are proof that giving to others without thinking about payback is vital and fulfilling. Their wise giving constitutes genius in the spiritual and moral sense. They understood that happiness is not to be found so much in getting (although this is often a very good thing) as in giving, and they taught by example.

Have you ever noticed feeling an especially warm glow during seasons of gift giving? Jesus of Nazareth said, "It is more blessed to give than to receive."[44] This blessed feeling seems to be a common experience, however much it is outmatched by our dominant "I don't do nuthin' for nuthin' " cultural message.

---

44 Acts 20:35.

Most people already know this from experience, and now there are fMRI studies of the brain that show how planning a donation activates the mesolimbic pathway, which is associated with increased dopamine (one of four natural happiness chemicals). Helping others directly triggers activity in the caudate nucleus and anterior cingulate, portions of the brain that turn on when people experience happiness. No wonder, then, that old St. Nick (also known as "Santa Claus") is always laughing and cheerful as he gives away his gifts. No wonder that most of us actually do find a little more joy in giving gifts than in receiving them. The brain science is not terribly surprising; it just confirms the obvious.

Is it really more blessed to give than to receive? Do benevolent people experience higher levels of mental well-being? Are they healthier? Do they live longer? Increasingly, mainstream scientists are studying people who take a kindly, charitable interest in others, and the behaviors that go along with it, to find out whether there are associated health benefits.

How are we changed when we extend active love?

First, we are freed from preoccupation with the self and its problems, over-thinking, and destructive emotions. Of course, disappointments and betrayals are unavoidable in life; it is easy to get sucked down into a negative vortex of bitterness, despair, and resentment. But simple acts of loving-kindness can transform us emotionally. It is said that even if you do not feel happy, smile anyway and happiness will likely follow. The key to forgiveness is acts of love coupled with patience, because with the passing of time our perspectives mature.[45]

Second, life becomes interesting. Selfishness is boring, but when we seek the happiness, security, and well-being of another as an expression of creative love, the world becomes full and engaging. Sir John Templeton once wrote that it is impossible to be bored if you love your neighbor.

---

45   See www.stephengpost.com/the-hidden-gifts-of-helping.

Third, loving others gives us a reason to develop our gifts. Students learn more when they tutor younger peers, or when they learn in groups and are responsible for teaching one another. Most great people have fine-tuned their talents through service to their neighbors.

Fourth, we make deeper friendships. Our friends are no longer the people we just hang out with, but the ones with whom we share an exhilarating common cause and commitment. When we extend active love, we finally gain serious friends, the kind who are loyal and want to keep us on our course and true to our higher selves.

Fifth, loving others is a source of hope, because as active agents we use our strengths to make a difference in the lives of others, and we can therefore have greater confidence in shaping the future. This is an active hope, rather than the passive variety that just waits for something to happen.

Sixth, loving others is a source of joy. Happiness is to joy as optimism is to hope. Joy, like hope, is not a mere innate disposition, but a virtue honed through bringing creative goodness to the life of the beloved. Thus, we should not worry much about reciprocity, because we are already reaping the benefits inwardly. As they say, "pay it forward," although a note of gratitude is nice.

Love Heals

Sir John Templeton once quietly told the boy that "Love heals mental illness." He further thought that, since love helped heal emotions, it could also, by doing so, help heal physical illness.

Imagine being ill and having a caring physician, nurse, social worker, or pastor connect deeply with you at the level of affective empathy and compassionate love. You suddenly feel a renewed sense of significance, free at least for a short while from anxiety, fear, anger, bitterness, despair, and the other negative emotions that come with the territory of illness. Perhaps just yesterday someone said something callous and demeaning that caused those emotions. But now you are grateful just to be alive, you feel shielded from stress, and you are able to gather the strength you need to move forward. You may even be able to laugh, as you suddenly experience the sense of affirmation, tranquility, and security that comes with the experience of being loved. All because someone has bestowed upon you her full and attentive presence.

This person did not do anything "big." She did not put herself at any risk, although sometimes risks do come with the territory of being a healthcare professional. She simply behaved with warmth, kindness, patience, and understanding. Perhaps she just asked, in a tone of voice that expressed empathy and caring, "Is there anything you might want to make your stay with us a little more comfortable?" Small is beautiful. The quality of your experience—or anyone's—as a patient is mostly the accumulation of just such small interactions that leave you feeling respected and cared about. These acts heal, and they are themselves a form of medical intervention and treatment.

Interlude

The Route 80 wheel of love

To find yourself is to lose yourself in the service of others.

—Gandhi

It's a little embarrassing that after forty-five years of research and study, the best advice I can give people is to try to be a little kinder.

—Aldous Huxley

Whatever you do in your life, how rich and famous you become, only those of you will be happy who have served others.

–Dr. Albert Schweitzer

The Golden Rule (where's the boy?)

You know what the issue is with this world? Everyone wants a magical solution to their problem, and everyone refuses to believe in magic.

–Alice in Wonderland

The Route 80 Philosophy

Afoot and light-hearted, I take to the open road, healthy, free. The world before me.

—Walt Whitman

Be grateful that there is a loving infinite Mind who wants to see each of us express the spirit of creative love for which purpose we were created. They key thing is to pray or meditate to be gratefully one with your peaceful soul and its connectivity with the infinite Mind, envision loving goals from this place within, and work hard, trusting that there is a power for goodness that is higher than ourselves that will help you along the way so long as you let it. Sometimes it is enough just to remove the obstacles of bitterness and rumination that block the flow of God within us, and by getting these destructive emotions out of the way we let God do things through us.

***

It was early morning, silver-gray misty, up high over the sea, at the end of a road to the unknown west. A long-haired blond youth leaned outward over a ledge, about to let go, when out of the mist appeared the light blue image of an angel's face, and it spoke these few words softly with great love: "If you save him, you too shall live." Then she faded back into the silver-gray haze of the dawn.

The blue angel dream was filled with symbols, but they were hard to interpret. Later in life, the boy met a gifted and empathic spiritual Christian named Jodi who interprets dreams for lots of people, and she said that the gray at the beginning and end of the dream represents the looming shadow of death,[46] but that the silver is a color of redemption. The blue of the angel's face is the color of the sapphire gemstone, associated with things celestial and heavenly and representing truth. The Lord, she said, appeared on a pavement of blue sapphire when meeting with Moses and the seventy elders on the mountain.[47] So she thought that the blue in his dream was God calling the boy to come up onto the mountaintop and gain a heavenly perspective on life.

---

46   Psalm 23:4.
47   Exodus 24:10.

Gary's white truck, she said, is like a white horse with the rider called to be faithful and true and show the courage of a warrior. She pointed out that sunrise captures the hope of new life, and that the sun was rising both when the boy left his dad's car behind on Route 80 and when he ventured across the Golden Gate Bridge. The boy's journey from east to west followed the daily course of the sun circling the earth.

She believed that the dream was given by God never to be forgotten, which is why it recurred so many times. As for the meaning of "If you save him, you too shall live," she suggested that if you are inspired by God to save someone, you too are blessed with new life. By following the dream, the boy was doing exactly what he was supposed to do, she said, and she was convinced that that there was much more to come on Route 80.

The blue angel dream felt deeply spiritual and provided a path for the boy when he embraced it as a guide. Such dreams can arise in the minds of people from any spiritual tradition and be equally meaningful. The infinite Mind transcends all human cultural limits and symbols, and does not wish to be named, perhaps because, once one group of humans decides that "my name for God is better than yours," it can lead to conflict and even war. In a significant revelatory moment, standing before a burning bush, Moses asked God for a name, but God answered, "I AM WHO I AM."[48] The Chandogya Upanishad (c. 600 BCE), an ancient Hindu sacred text, stresses the phrase, "*tat tvam asi*," or "thou art that," as an expression of the nature of Brahman, or the Supreme Reality, with "that" referring to the infinite Mind that is both the highest as well as the inmost. Indeed, "Allah" is used by Arabic speakers of all the Abrahamic faiths (including Christianity and Judaism) to refer to God and is based on the word for "I AM," as is Yahweh in Hebrew, so it is not a name at all. These days, many spiritual people refer to the infinite Mind as "the Universe" or "Universal Mind," which also suggests

---

48   Exodus 3:14.

something too profound to be named. It is good to give people and dogs names, but bad to give God names.

When we acknowledge that in this original, universal, and infinite Mind we "live and move and have our being,"[49] we are unconsciously guided toward our destiny, and we are empowered to love and value other human beings in a much deeper sense, as equally gifted with some part of the Mind of God. Our minds are part of something infinite just as they are, and we can consciously cooperate with God in creative love. Every conscious mind is in union with the infinite Mind, an individualized separate mind is never separated from Mind. Genius flows from infinite Mind omniscience. Greatness is not so much a matter of exceptional talents as it is an action that flows from the unity of soul with God, so anyone can be great if they are aware of this unity and nurture it. We are each a point of infinite Mind within the total infinite Mind field. Realizing this quite young, the boy understood that, in its simple natural state, the mind crowns us with glory and honor and dignity. Of course the whole infinite Mind field is much greater than any single point within it, but our precious minds are continuous with the eternal. We are a spark of and in the divine Mind. So we have a natural tendency to pray, to meditate, to receive meaningful dreams, to enter flow states beyond time and place and find the silent oneness within. Infinite Mind is at the center of our own being, and unreluctantly responsive to us as we are responsive to it. But we have to be precise and clear in the things we aspire to and consistent with creativity and love for self and for others.

Every one of us is then a treasure in an earthen vessel while embodied on this earth. But all visible things at the quantum level are shaped and formed and even comprised by divine Mind, which sustains the universe in energy and the material form of that energy. That Mind gave infinitely sophisticated mathematical order and constants of energy to a beautifully formed universe.

---

49 Acts 17:28.

Whether looking at the internal soul or mind that lies within or looking outward at our universe and all that is, life is an awakening to the constant union with God. No limit can be placed on the individual mind in conscious union with infinite Mind. We are in God as God is in us.

Ethics and conscience have their ultimate ground in the realization that we are each a small circle within the infinite Mind that includes all people without exception. Our connectedness to God and to one another is much more powerful and real than we often know.

The great Jewish philosopher Martin Buber wrote that at our lowest state of awareness, we relate to others only to the extent that they contribute to our little selfish agendas. He called this way of living "I and It" because we treat others as mere means to our ends. As an alternative, Buber proposed "I and Thou," meaning that we are in awe of others and honor them as ends in themselves. There is still an "I," of course, but at a higher spiritual and ethical awareness. But going beyond Buber, when we help others in our oneness, we also are helping ourselves because of that oneness, so therefore the highest state is not "I and Thou" but "I and I." When "I" realize that the security and well-being of another is inextricably a part of my own security and well-being because all are equally participating in infinite Mind, then "I" have arrived.

Back on the Golden Gate Bridge, the boy was given a little dream-driven lesson into "I and I" with Harry. And when his mom called him from New York with her premonition, he grasped this connectivity even more.

***

The boy was always grateful for what he learned on Route 80—in essence these ten things:

1. Infinite Mind, which has no beginning or end, undergirds and sustains the universe with all its mathematical elegance and thermodynamic constants.

2. Infinite Mind is the prime source of all the energy and matter in the universe, underlying and supporting moment by moment all things seen and unseen, such that truly "in God we live and move and have our being."[50] Beneath the multifaceted but illusory surface of the material world, everything is basically one at the level of what mystics and many quantum physicists describe as the Ground of Being, which is also the Ground of Love.

3. However much we have been conditioned to think of mind as nothing more than physical matter—the tissues and fluid that constitute the brain—in fact a small drop of the infinite Mind resides within each of us as pure spiritual essence divorced from matter; consequently all of us are connected spiritually, so what affects one of us affects all of us, and when we save another we also save ourselves ("If you save him, you too shall live"), just as when we hurt another we hurt ourselves.

4. Loving God with all of our heart and mind is the first great commandment,[51] and once we realize that the divine dwells in every human being without exception we naturally love our neighbor as ourselves, since we are each made "in the image of God" and as such possess a sacred dignity that deserves respect and love (Namaste: "I honor the place in you that is the same in me, where the whole universe resides").

5. God wishes to extend creative love to the world through each one of us, and thus as a manifestation of our spiritual unity, each of us can be a conduit for inspired dreams, intuitions, synchronicity whispers, premonitions, intense creativity, and unlimited love; but we all fall short and this is where the idea that Jesus atoned for us all for all time comes into play.

---

50   Acts 17:28.
51   Matthew 22:37.

6. The purpose of life is to freely align with infinite Mind ("God") in love for others as for self, and for the universe including nature; to express love is to acknowledge our true unity within infinite Mind, and that our highest flourishing and joy comes from service.

7. Prayer and meditation free us from the heavy pulls of a world that is too much with us (Wordsworth), allowing us to be gratefully aware of the infinite Mind within that can be a constant source of and support for loving thoughts, words, and actions.

8. God has absolutely nothing to do with evil, which is a purely human creation that results from our ignoring infinite Mind and our soul essence of peace.

9. Follow the positive Golden Rule (the dos already encompass the don'ts) and for the most part good things will happen to good people. However, when bad things do happen, turn them into positives, because event + reaction = outcome (e + r = o), and how we choose to respond makes all the difference in expanding the canvas.

10. At times we are called to take a journey to discover our destiny— so take it and remain grateful for every wonderful person you meet along the way. There will be hardships and suffering because life is this way until the end of the journey when we each return in dying to full and incandescent joy within the love of infinite Mind, though, until you make it to the end of Route 80, always be grateful and kind because people carry so many burdens and you can help them in some way so they don't jump off the ledge.

Listen for guiding dreams. Dreams meant a great deal in early civilizations, and dream interpretation fills the Akkadian *Epic of Gilgamesh.* The ancient Greeks constructed healing temples they called *Asclepieions*, where cures could come from dreams. Many Muslims to this day place a great deal of emphasis on dreams as the way Allah communicates with us, especially when we pray for direction. But Muslim scholars recognized three kinds of dreams: true, pathogenic (due to infections and illness), and false. Sometimes, your dreams might not be true and trustable. But, if a dream recurs and is filled with the loving guidance of a blue angel, follow it. The boy would surely not have followed any old dream, but he followed this one and was always grateful for what unfolded, which was a fruitful life entirely different than what he would have known had he not ventured West and walked through the silver morning mist on the Golden Gate Bridge.

The boy did not pay much attention to people's expectations because he knew that if he did, he would stop following the whispers of infinite Mind. This is why he rose at around five each morning throughout his adult life to meditate and pray a bit, to maintain a connection with his inner self and hence with original Mind. He did this from his days in the Mission District because on Route 80 we all need quiet spaces and places to catch our breath before the hustle and the bustle begins, in the still quiet hours when we first rise and are not caught up in a total awareness of time and place. After all, before the Big Bang there was no time and no space, but there was the eternal divine Mind, and early morning was for the boy always a time for an inner rendezvous. It is hard to do that when the phone starts ringing.

As the boy looked back, he gratefully remembered the many good people he had encountered from every background and tradition, and he loved them all. Divine kindness is really at the core of all genuine spirituality and religion. But for him Christianity had a special place, and he remained thankful for Mr. Muller, Rev. Welles, Gary with his white truck, Dr. Foley, Pastor Moss, and so many more, who made his journey such a gift.

All along Route 80, the boy was keenly aware of a deep darkness in human nature that comes to the surface when we lose the spiritual path, lured away by more money, more prestige, more glamour, and more so-called success. There are those who get started on Route 80, but they get mixed up and crash, so the ambulances scream down Route 80 with sirens echoing in the night. At least remember karma: if you hurt others, you inevitably hurt yourself, and even if it looks for a while like you are getting ahead, you will die with an empty soul and a tear.

The boy was, like old Mr. Muller and Sir John, realistic about human nature disconnected from the infinite Mind; he saw the constant consequences of this separation not only in the people he met along Route 80 but also in the daily newspaper stories about unimaginable brutality, or in the constant revelations about people who seemed so good until they could no longer hide their abuses. Like Mr. Muller said, don't trust people who smile all the time: "No one is good—except God alone."[52]

But the always simple boy, living a life of service as a teacher in medical schools—because he liked to teach humanism to young healers and a pastoral approach to looking after patients and their families—was blessed to be able to stay on his journey. And he continued to look after the dignity of deeply forgetful people, who live mostly in the present, and found them spiritually deeper than meets the eye.

And he remembered from Mr. Muller's trees verses like "The Kingdom of God is within you"[53] and "You are God's temple and God's spirit dwells within you."[54] And he remembered that Jesus invited us all to do many good things, and "even greater things than these."[55]

Chagall often included the Jesus configuration of the crucifixion in his art because his Hasidic background did not prevent him from integrating a symbol of suffering for all humanity that brings Christianity together with our shared human experiences of disappointment, resilience, and joy. There are plenty of disappointments on Route 80, but there is also a faith in the light down the road.

---

52   Luke 18:19.
53   Luke 17:21.
54   I Cor. 3:16.
55   John 14:12.

A note on Christianity. Imagine the world without Jesus. Due to his immense respect for life, the gladiatorial games of death came to an end as well. In India, before Christian influence, elderly widows were burned alive on their husbands' funeral pyres, and little girls were thrown into the sea. Wives and concubines were routinely killed after an African tribal chief died. Slavery is still practiced in parts of the Middle East and Africa, but it has been abolished in the Western world primarily due to the leadership of great Christians like William Wilberforce. The boy's great-great-great grandfather John McLean was one of the two US Supreme Court justices who voted in the dissent on the Dred Scott decision, and as an evangelical Methodist from Cincinnati he coined the term "Once free always free" that applied to escaped slaves. An old man, he stood beside Lincoln at the first inaugural, caught pneumonia in the cold rain, and went home to Ohio by train to die. The portrait of Caroline Burnet McLean, John McLean's granddaughter and the boy's great-grandmother, hangs on his living room wall.

Always be grateful for the dream, and like Chagall, live it to the end. Be "all in" with the dream. He died an old man painting a blue angel in his studio outside of Paris. One day the boy will die too, but, when he dies, he will still be the boy, at last walking into the light of divine kindness as a holy, tangible substance that shines in brightness everywhere like the sun on Route 80 at noon along the Appalachians, melting the winter ice in early spring.

Being "all in" with the dream is like the gambler who sees a hand, sizes things up, and slides all their chips to the middle of the table. Being "all in" with God makes sense because otherwise there is only the ledge, emptiness staring down into the void below. "You did not choose me, but I chose you and appointed you so that you might go and bear fruit— fruit that will last—and so that whatever you ask in my name the Father will give you."[56]

---

56 John 15:16.

If you take one message from this book, it has to be this: Never give up on your dream and your soul. A soul is not just some mix of evolved human emotions and accumulated social influences. A soul is spiritual and eternal, a little bit of the infinite Mind given us to sense God and experience Oneness. So much in our culture pushes us away from spiritual focus on our inner being, and it is worth it to just leave things behind and strike out free on whatever road you like unless you have a lot of responsibilities. Have faith that God is already waiting for you down the road with wonderful surprises. Be "all in" for God and let miracles happen along Route 80 or whatever path you find.

Remember "In the beginning, God!" Infinite, creative, everywhere, loving before time and space were born. From the divine Word and Thought came the universe with the intent of creating free spiritual beings like ourselves who could, in their creative love, extend divine creativity in such a way as to bring great joy to God, to neighbor, and to themselves.

This is how we live on Route 80.

The key thing is: Take the journey and stay very grateful for it.

Interlude

In Bangalore speaking of consciousness, infinite Mind, and deeply forgetful people at the Indian Institute for Advanced Studies

Be thankful for what you have; you'll end up having more. If you concentrate on what you don't have, you will never, ever have enough.

—Oprah Winfrey

If the only prayer you said in your life was "Thank You" that would suffice.

—Meister Eckhart

The discipline of gratitude is the explicit effort to acknowledge that all I am and have is given me as a gift of love, a gift to celebrate with joy.

—Henri Nouwen

Monument to Marc Chagall

The boy at the Walt Whitman Mall

Various compassionate great grad students at Domo Sushi

Gratitude is the fairest blossom which springs from the soul.

—Henry Ward Beecher

Love All Means All (Lama): How I Live by the Deep Golden Rule & Flourish

College Scholarship Essay Contest—Seven Questions Every Kid Should Ask

The Deep Golden Rule is "Do unto Others as You Would Have Them Do unto You," which takes us deeper than just refusing to do harmful things. It means that we use our talents to contribute to the lives of others, making their security and happiness as meaningful to us as our own. When we do so with kindness, we are practicing a life of love, not just to the nearest and dearest, but also to the neediest and to all the people we encounter *without exception*. Love All Means All.

Do you feel that your ability to truly flourish—to live a life of meaning, purpose, contribution, and joy—has been greater when you have lived by this rule? How might your future well-being be related to expanding these kinds of experiences to include strangers and even enemies?

If you are a high school junior or senior, we invite you to submit a thousand-word essay highlighting in two sections: **Section One**—How and why you flourish when you live by the Deep Golden Rule; **Section Two**—Focus in on *one* of the seven core big questions listed below:

Question 1: Why Do I Feel Good When I Do Good?

Scent lingers on the hands of those who deliver flowers.

—Ancient China

Give and Glow

—Anonymous

When I do good, I feel good. When I do bad, I feel bad.

—Abraham Lincoln

Why is it that, when we contribute to lives of others by kindness and helping, we discover happiness and resilience? Of course we have to look after ourselves and not neglect our own needs, but when we move past selfishness to serve others, we find life more meaningful and interesting. We don't have to depend on others returning the favor because in the very process of giving we are liberated from the boring focus on the self and its problems, and from destructive emotions like bitterness, hate, and despair. In fact, we can never be lonely when we are busy being kind and helpful. Remember that old Ebenezer Scrooge was miserable in his selfishness, but as he discovered how to help others and be kind, he also became so very joyful. Indeed, by the end of the story he has what we call "the giver's glow" and is among the merriest of people.

Fact: In one national survey of five thousand adults, 41 percent had volunteered in 2009 about one hundred hours a year, or a couple of hours per week. How did they feel?

- **89 percent** agreed that "volunteering improved my sense of **well-being**"

- **73 percent** "lowered my **stress levels**" (serenity)

- **92 percent** "enriched sense of **purpose** in life"

- **68 percent** "made me feel **physically healthier**"

- **77 percent** "improves **emotional health**"

- **78 percent** "helps **recovery from loss and disappointment**"

- Improved **sleep**, friendships; reduced **anxiety and helplessness; 25 percent volunteer through their workplace, and 76 percent of them feel better about employer as a result**

Question 2: How Have I Healed Others by Being Kind?

"Medicine heals many wounds, but love alone heals all wounds."

—Anonymous

"Love heals. Heals and liberates. I use the word love, not meaning sentimentality, but a condition so strong that it may be that which holds the stars in their heavenly positions and that which causes the blood to flow orderly in our veins."

—Maya Angelou

Kindness, compassion, and love heal in countless ways. Children who experience parental kindness rather than adversity have much lower rates of mental and physical illness in midlife and avoid alcohol or drug abuse as teens. Patients who experience empathy from their physicians and nurses are more likely to continue on with challenging medical treatments, to share important information about their illness, and to practice good preventive health habits. In everyday life, when we encounter people who have been bullied or abused, we can have the courage to be kind and thus heal their fears. We encounter difficult people who really test our kindness, and we can heal them too with unconditional love. We might encounter a grandparent whose memory has faded, leaving them unable to care for themselves, but we can be kind to them and accepting of their deep forgetfulness—kind in tone of voice, in reading a poem that they might remember from earlier years, or in just being present and calling them by name.

Each one of us is a healer when we are kind and helpful to others, and especially to those who are suffering due to illness, loss, disappointment, humiliation, rejection, or a thousand other things. Compassion is active kindness in response to suffering, and it always heals at so many levels. When the happiness and security of another is a meaningful to us as our own, we love that person. Even if someone doesn't mean quite that much to us, it is always good to be kind and compassionate to everyone.

Fact: Kindness and empathy encourage patients to take better preventive care of themselves and adhere to treatments. Their stress levels are reduced, and their rate of wound healing is improved.

Question 3: What and Who Inspired Me to Love All Humanity Without Exception?

My humanity is bound up with yours, for we can only be human together.

–Desmond Tutu

Be kind to all creatures.

–Buddha

How did I become someone who tries to be kind to all people without exception? This includes not just the nearest and the dearest, like family members and close friends or peers, but the neediest and even total strangers. Who inspired me to treat every person with equal respect and kindness? Was it mostly my parents? My teachers? My spiritual guides or sense of a Higher Power? My friends? This doesn't mean that the nearest and dearest should be less loved, but it does mean that we should all be leaning outwards whenever possible to help even those we do not know. We can avoid all the unkind attitudes and words that dehumanize others just because they are not part of our little group. It is good to have circles of trust and friendship, but these circles should strengthen our resolve be kind to every single person we encounter.

We need true friends who encourage us to be helpful to everyone. We need role models who pass the torch of love for all humanity and lead by example. We need to fill our minds with the stories of people who inspire goodness and compassion for everyone, usually one person at a time. Who inspires you? What inspires you? The superficial differences that we think make "us" better than "them" mean nothing because we are all equally part of a shared humanity, all equally on a journey of formation and growth. Are you serving as a good role model for your peers?

Fact: We learn love for humanity from our role models and mentors, who pass the torch from one generation to the next and allow us to observe the details of their words, interactions, and interactions.

Question 4: How Will I Use My Talents to Pursue a Career That Contributes to the Lives of Others?

Work is love made visible. And if you can't work with love, but only with distaste, it is better that you should leave your work and sit at the gate of the temple and take alms of the people who work with joy.

–Kahlil Gibran

The least of things with a meaning is worth more in life than the greatest of things without it.

–Carl Jung

Every one of us has unique talents and gifts, and when we develop these so as to contribute to the lives of others our lives will be filled with meaning, resilience, creativity and purpose. When our work is an expression of creative kindness directed to those in need, everything seems to flow effortlessly. We can be doing any job at all, no matter how simple or humble, and if it is done with kindness and generous purpose it is completely fulfilling. A higher purpose to make a positive difference in the world always leads to a special form of happiness and flourishing.

Work at the highest level is possible only when the inner person of heart and soul arrives in tandem with the outer person. Without it, we can be present, yet bring only half of ourselves to our tasks. We can be exceptionally accomplished but not caring. We can act like professionals but without the empathy and compassion of a true professional. Detached from this spiritual center of love, we may come to feel a deep disillusionment and loss of motivation in work, but connected with it, we can find endless energy and creativity.

Fact: Studies show that one of the best ways to create a successful culture on the job is to engage in kindness and generous behaviors with coworkers and customers.

Question 5: How Have I Experienced, Directly or Through Others, a Spiritual Power of Love That Strengthens Me to Practice Kindness Even Toward Difficult People?

The greatest romance is with the Infinite. You have no idea how beautiful it can be. When you suddenly find God everywhere, when God comes and talks to you and guides you, the romance of divine love has begun.

—Paramahansa Yogananda

Your task is not to seek for love; but merely to seek and find all the barriers within yourself that you have built up against it.

—Rumi

God is love.

—I John 4:8

What do people mean when they report a spiritual experience of divine Love? How common is this? Is this experience associated with emotional healing and expanded benevolence? Does this experience help us to treat even the most difficult people with kindness? How might meditation and possibly prayer fit in?

Bill Wilson, cofounder of Alcoholics Anonymous, not previously a believer, claimed he saw and felt a white light that he perceived as the presence of God's love. This occurred in his hospital room at a New

York detox center on his fourth day of treatment: "It seemed to me, in the mind's eye, that I was on a mountain and a wind not of air but of spirit was blowing. And then it burst upon me that I was a free man." Bill W. never drank again after that spiritual experience of December 14, 1934, and "AA" was born.

Fact: A scientific survey of randomly selected Americans conducted in 2010 is presented by Matthew T. Lee and colleagues in *The Heart of Religion*.[57] The survey respondents were adults (eighteen years of age or older) and were selected regardless of religious background, economic strata, educational level, ethnicity, or any other factor. Thus, the survey was totally random, and designed to provide a scientifically valid portrait of the experience of God's love and its ramifications. *Almost half (45 percent) of all Americans feel God's love at least once a day and eight out of ten have this experience at least "once in a while." 9 percent claim that they experience God's love more than once a day. Only 17 percent report no experience of God's love. 83 percent indicate that they "feel God's love increasing their compassion for others."* Eight out of ten Americans claim to have experienced God's love, and they consider it to be "the greatest power in the universe."

Question 6: How Do I Understand a Loving Spiritual Presence in the Universe?

God does not play dice with the universe.

–Albert Einstein

---

57   Oxford University Press, 2013.

*There is a power for good in the universe that is greater than you are,
and you can use it.*

–Ernest Holmes

Do you see in the starry heavens, the laws and constants of physics and
math, and the universe in which we live the work of some underlying
spiritual energy and creative presence? Most people across the sweep
of human history have had an intuition that an infinite Mind has made
and given this universe to us as a place to learn to love one another.
All spiritual traditions have some concept of a divine Mind "in the
beginning," before the Big Bang, before time and space, that brought
the universe into being and now sustains it in every moment. Many
people pray, meditate, and sing songs to connect with this higher power.
Whatever your spiritual or religious tradition is, how do you understand
this supreme presence? How do you connect with it?

Fact: The young child sees the universe as "enchanted" and frequently
copes through spirituality. Lisa Miller, in her book *The Spiritual Child*,
presents her research on teens who describe themselves as spiritual.
She found that they gain benefits: 40 percent less likely to use and
abuse substances; 60 percent less likely to be depressed as teens; and 80
percent less likely to have dangerous unprotected sex. They are more
likely to have positive markers for thriving and resilience and more
likely to have high levels of academic success.

7. How Have I Encouraged People of Different Religions and Cultures to Live Peacefully by the Deep Golden Rule?

Do Unto Others as You Would Have Them do Unto You.

—Universal

The essence of all religions is one. Only their approaches are different.

—Gandhi

How can the major spiritualities and religions of the world come to abide in their various conceptualizations of love for all humanity, rather than merely for those who adhere to a particular set of beliefs? However tragic are the hateful and violent deeds done in the name of someone's small idea of God, the fact remains that such evil actions have no relevance to the question of the existence of a higher power or the validity of spirituality. A loving God must be pained to be so badly mischaracterized and then to have people hurt others based on this error. Clearly humanity must make "progress in religion." This will come mainly through the enhanced teaching, understanding and practice of unlimited Love that exists in all these traditions but has not been fully emphasized.

Religions have their unique identities and symbols, but when looked at deeply, they also have a common image of Love for all humanity and nature. For every example of rage and violence between religions there are numerous examples of mutual appreciation, acceptance, and harmony in which we can take great hope. How can we encourage these traditions to adhere consistently to the teachings of a God of Love that do in fact exist in each one of them? How can we move beyond the narrow tribal elements in religion that are used to marginalize, condemn, and attack those who happen not to share a certain set of beliefs?

Fact: All religions teach of an age of lasting peace. Hinduism speaks of the Golden Age, for example, which follows the Dark Age. Even when religious hatred dominates the papers, they tell us that there are still many points of light and love that are just coming into being.

Acknowledgments

God and Love on Rt. 80 is not any ordinary book, and so only a very special individual could have worked with me on it editorially. Ann Bradley read through the manuscript and, with her superb training in psychology of religion and world religion, as well as her fine editorial skills, was able to improve the writing and presentation. Her studies at Harvard Divinity School and at Union Theological Seminary in New York allow us to be real conversation partners, and she easily accompanied me on this surprising spiritual and intellectual journey with authenticity and critical depth.

Brenda Knight of Mango Publications was well prepared to appreciate the themes of infinite Mind in the universe and in ourselves, connectivity in divine love, and the power of synchronicity on a spiritual journey. Her years at Harper San Francisco allowed her to discover a number of important spiritual writers, from Pablo Coelho to Mark Nepo. Only someone as creative and bold as Brenda could possibly have identified *God and Love on Rt. 80* as a book that could benefit a lot of readers trying to figure out who they are in the universe. Brenda made the wonderful suggestion of including photographs and spiritual sayings after each episode. Her team at Mango is among the best, including Robin Miller and Roberto Núñez.

Very few literary agents could possibly have worked with me to get it to press. Giles Anderson started the Anderson Literary Agency in 2000, and sent me an email indicating interest in my work around the benefits of giving, what I called "the giver's glow." I was grateful when, fifteen years later, he responded to my query about his availability to help with placing *God and Love on Rt. 80*. His suggestions around presentation were invaluable, and he took a personal interest in me as an author.

I also want to acknowledge Sir John Marks Templeton, who encouraged me in writing about infinite Mind and Unlimited Love as the core concepts in world spirituality. Before he passed away in 2008, he asked me to do all I could to carry these ideas forward, not just with science but also with a journey narrative. He was the most open-minded man I ever met, and to read this book open-mindedness is a must.

I acknowledge the University of Chicago Divinity School, where I studied psychology and world religions as well as comparative religious ethics with some of the greatest spiritual and psychological minds of the 20th century.

I have always understood spirituality at its best as a pathway to well-being and health, and have at times trained in clinical pastoral care. I have had the honor of being a professor for three decades at two of the nation's leading schools of medicine. This allowed me to integrate my spiritual journey with the art of healing in ways that attuned me to the needs of patients, clinicians, and perhaps above all, medical students. I have also been able to collaborate with some great scientists. But my guess is that all my friends and colleagues in healthcare will be a little surprised that now, a little later in my career, I would write a book about an amazing spiritual journey and pathway of discovery. This, however, has always motivated me, as I pray and focus my mind on the needs of others early in the morning each day before going to work.

God and Love on Rt. 80 began in 2001 as four brief outline vignettes that I sent out in a cursory form on the Institute for Research on Unlimited Love (www.unlimitedloveinstitute.org) email newsletter just to see what the response would be. People were thrilled and wanted more. Now, quite a few years later the time came to write this book.

I want to thank St. Paul's School in Concord, New Hampshire. As a boy, St. Paul's was a place where I could wander the beautiful wooded paths and read spiritual classics, take courses in ancient history and sacred studies, and have the opportunity to reflect on a recurring blue angel dream that set my life on a certain pathway toward a destiny that I knew nothing of. I discovered there that infinite Mind wants to break through our little human worldly consciousness to awaken us to a larger universal field of Mind.in which we are all connected with God and one another in love. I have nothing but the deepest appreciation for wonderful teachers, like Rev. Rodney Welles and many others. It was, as I knew it, an exceptionally kind, pure, and nurturing place. I want to thank the infinite Mind of Pure Unlimited Love for somehow getting me up there at the right time of my life. That too was synchronicity.

I want of course to express the deepest gratitude for the Board of Trustees of the Institute for Research on Unlimited Love, for which I have served as founding President since 2001. Named personally by Sir John, the Institute was founded in University Circle of Cleveland, Ohio. Finally, many wonderfully kind "give and glow" Clevelanders made it possible, and they have been fabulously supportive of the vision.

And at the John Templeton Foundation, I want to thank a number of people who have moved on over the years. Arthur Schwartz, Charles L. Harper, Jr., Christopher Stawski, Barnaby Marsh, Pamela Thompson, and Judith Marchand come to mind immediately. Dr. John Templeton, Jr., MD, "Dr. T," was also an enduring inspiration before his passing away in 2015 and has remained so. No doubt there are aspects of *God and Love on Rt. 80* that these trusted friends would find surprising.

Finally, I want to acknowledge my family. Hopefully for them, *God and Love on Rt. 80* will be an enjoyable journey too.

Stephen G. Post PhD (The Divinity School of the University of Chicago 1983)

About the Author

Stephen G. Post, Ph.D. is the best-selling author of *Why Good Things Happen to Good People: How to Live a Longer, Happier, Healthier Life by the Simple Act of Giving*, published by Random House. He has been quoted in more than four thousand international newspapers and magazines, including *The New York Times*, *Parade Magazine*, *"O" Magazine*, and *Psychology Today*. He has been interviewed on several hundred radio and TV programs including *The Daily Show*.

The recipient of a National Endowment for the Humanities "top public speaker award," award, Post uses a highly engaging style to inspire audiences with the best of medical and philosophical knowledge about the transformative benefits of kindness, volunteering, spirituality, forgiveness, gratitude, and purpose. Martin E.P. Seligman, in his book *Flourish*, described Post at as among "the stars of positive psychology." In 2001 he founded the Institute for Research on Unlimited Love in 2001, named and supported by philanthropist Sir John Templeton, who personally selected Post as President (www.unlimitedloveinstitute.com). The Institute researches and distributes knowledge on kindness, giving, and spirituality. Post received the 2017 Paper of the Year Award from the editors of *The American Journal of Health Promotion* for his paper "Rx: It's Good to be Good (G2BG)." He addressed the US Congress on volunteerism and public health and received the Congressional Certificate of Special Recognition for Outstanding Achievement. Post served as a co-chair of the United Nations Population Fund conference on spirituality and global transformation.

Post has served as a full professor at the Case Western Reserve University School of Medicine and the Renaissance School of Medicine at Stony Brook University, where he directs the Center for Medical

Humanities, Compassionate Care, and Bioethics. In 2012, Post was awarded the Pioneer Medal for Outstanding Leadership in HealthCare from the HealthCare Chaplaincy Network. He received the Kama Book Award in Medical Humanities from World Literacy Canada in 2008. His book *The Moral Challenge of Alzheimer's Disease* was designated a "medical classic of the twentieth century" by the *British Medical Journal* in 2009. Post is an elected member of the College of Physicians of Philadelphia, the New York Academy of Medicine, and the Royal Society of Medicine, London.

God and Love on Route 80 is a highly entertaining spiritual story about the author's quest for positive meaning and purpose in life. It is sure to uplift the reader with the message that what we dream about and envision for the good of others as well as for ourselves can really come about.

PO Box 1516 Stony Brook, New York 11790

Tel. 216-926-9244 (cell)

Email: Post@StephenGPost.com